GARIA HAT
ROAD

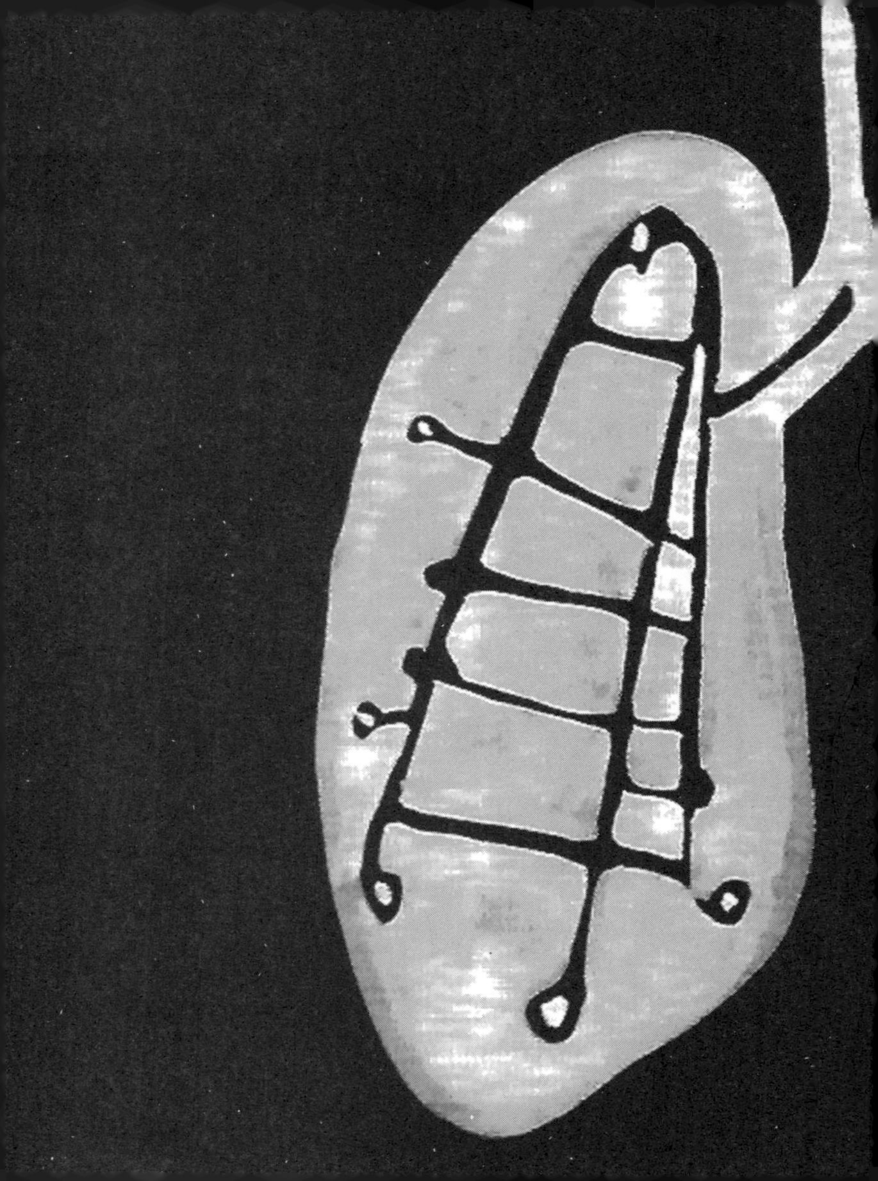

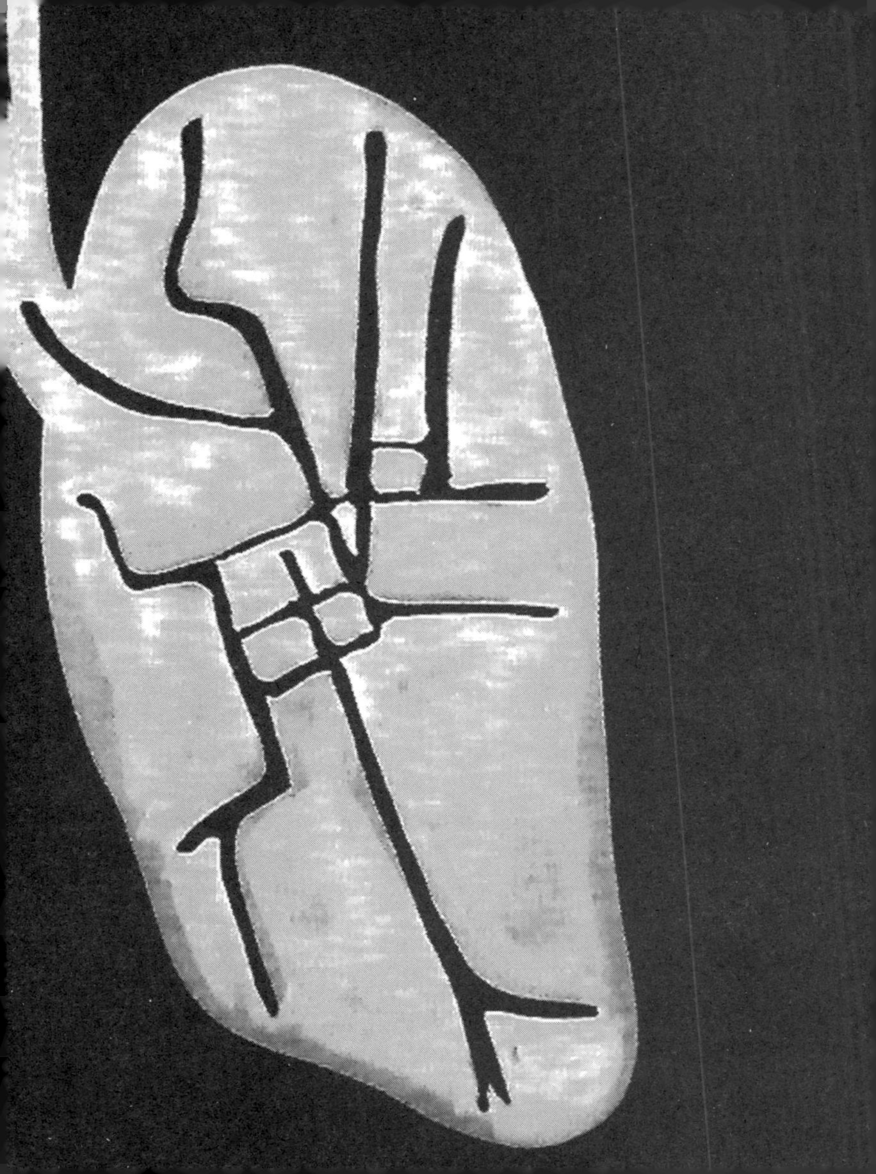

YODA PRESS

RMIT UNIVERSITY PRESS

YODA PRESS
G 93, Connaught Circus
New Delhi 110 001

RMIT UNIVERSITY PRESS
an imprint of RMIT Publishing
PO Box 12058, A'Beckett Street,
Melbourne, Victoria 8006

Co-published by YODA PRESS India and RMIT UNIVERSITY PRESS Australia
First published 2005



ISBN 81-902272-4-6

This edition for sale only in India, Pakistan, Bangladesh, Myanmar, Bhutan, Nepal and Sri Lanka.

Designed by Neal Haslem Design
English set in 8.5/12pt Trade Gothic
Bangla typesetting: Roma Chakrabarty
Bangla translation: chapters 0 and 1-Anasuya Basu; chapter 5-S.R. Rajen
Printed in India by S.N. Printers

Published by Parul Nayyar and Arpita Das, YODA PRESS
G 93, Connaught Circus, New Delhi 110 001
India
Telephone 91-11-23324096, 30960306
Email: yoda@yodapress.com
www.yodapress.com

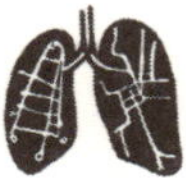

# TRAMJATRA

imagining Melbourne and Kolkata by tramways

মেলবার্ন এবং কলকাতায় ট্রাম কল্পনা

# ট্রামযাত্রা

Edited by Mick Douglas

# CONTENTS

# CONTENTS

## NETWORKING



## SHEDDING

0

# forward

In Kolkata you jostle for a position, boldly stretch out to the handrail and take a leap onto the doorless running-board to squeeze on for the ride. In Melbourne the hydraulic-controlled doors open when the vehicle is stationary and you take your turn to step into an air-conditioned cabin. Electric motors whir and hum. There's movement. A tram journey begins, departing from two tramways cities: Kolkata, formerly known as Calcutta, in India, and Melbourne in Australia.

The conductor gestures to you to take the vacant seat. I prefer to remain on my feet, from where I can move around and get a feeling for the passage. At one side is the word 'tram', of English origin. To another side is the Bengali word 'jatra'. Joining the two has us underway on a *tramjatra*, a 'journey by tram', weaving connections between two cities. A group of artists, activists, tramways workers and enthusiasts have departed Melbourne and Kolkata to be aboard a *tramjatra* since 1996, attracting new passengers along the way. The book in hand is a conveyance for further lines of travel marked by tramways.

Tracks are deeply inscribed in these cities. Parallel lines curve, rise and fall together, at times seeming to join or to veer apart. Tracks can place us on the routes of cultural tradition and have us reinscribe rituals and myths. Those lines can also carry us by blind habit and deliver us to stereotypes and worn-out positions. But their smooth surface is also always being reinscribed in new ways, disrupted and derailed, hybridised and reinvented. Contradictions present themselves. Hand-painted billboards viewed from the airport taxi announce 'Welcome to Calcutta, City of Joy' as I sense the familiar sweet smell and stinging eyes brought by diesel and petrol exhaust gases. The voice of an educated woman in the first-class tramcar tells how tiresome it is to witness that common path of the

# সূচনা

কলকাতায় ধাক্কাধাক্কি করে, জায়গা করে নিতে হয়। ঝুঁকে পড়ে হাতরেলটা ধরতে হয় এবং কোনমতে লাফ মেরে দরজা-বিহীন যানে উঠে, ঘেঁষাঘেঁষি করে শুরু করতে হয় যাত্রা। মেলবোর্ণে যানটি থামলে আপনা থেকেই যন্ত্রচালিত দরজা খুলে যায়, যাত্রীরা একের পর এক আবহাওয়া নিয়ন্ত্রিত কামরাতে পা রাখে। বিদ্যুৎ দ্বারা নিয়ন্ত্রিত যন্ত্রগুলি শব্দ করে। চলা শুরু হয়। ট্রাম যাত্রা শুরু হয় দুই ট্রাম পথ সম্পন্ন শহর থেকে — ভারতবর্ষের কলকাতায় আর অস্ট্রেলিয়ার মেলবোর্ণে।

কন্ডাক্টর ইঙ্গিতে ফাঁকা সীট্‌টা দেখিয়ে দেয়। আমি অবশ্য দাঁড়াতেই পছন্দ করি যাতে কিছুটা চলাফেরা করার স্বাধীনতা পাই। একদিকে 'ট্রাম' শব্দটি যার উৎস ইংরাজী আর অন্যদিক অকৃত্রিম বাংলা ভাষা থেকে উৎপন্ন 'যাত্রা' শব্দটি - দুইয়ে মিলে 'ট্রামযাত্রা' যেন এই দুটি ভিন্ন, বিচ্ছিন্ন শহরের মেলবন্ধন ঘটায়। ১৯৯৬ সাল থেকে, একদল শিল্পী, বিপ্লবী, ট্রামলাইনের কর্মী এবং উদ্যোগী, মেলবোর্ণ এবং কলকাতা ছেড়ে বেরিয়েছে এক ট্রামযাত্রায় এবং চলার পথে নতুন যাত্রীদেরও আকর্ষণ করছে। এই বইটি সেই যাত্রারই আরেক পথ।

ট্রামপথগুলি এই শহরগুলির বুকে গভীরভাবে গাঁথা। সমান্তরাল রেখাগুলি কখনও বা বাঁক নিচ্ছে, একই সাথে উঠছে, নামছে, কখনও বা মনে হয় এই মিলছে তো ওই দূরে সরে যাচ্ছে। এই পথগুলি আমাদেরকে সাংস্কৃতিক ঐতিহ্যের গতিপথে নিয়ে যেতে সক্ষম এবং পুরোনো রীতি ও বিশ্বাস আমাদের মনে পূর্ণস্থাপন করতে পারে। আবার এই ট্রামপথগুলোই অন্ধবিশ্বাসের দ্বারা আমাদের একঘেঁয়ে , ক্ষয়ে যাওয়া মানসিকতায় ফিরিয়ে দিতে পারে। অথচ এই পথগুলির আপাতঃমসৃণতার ওপর চলে অনন্ত খোদাই — উপড়ানো আর ধ্বংসই হয় তাদের

*firingi* telling her and the world yet another romanticised hardship story of her city. Back on the streets of Melbourne and we overhear the red-uniformed, volunteer City Ambassador beaming about her hometown's recent status as 'the world's most liveable city' whilst a homeless vendor spruiks for buyers of the latest copy of a street magazine: 'Get *The Big Issue* here!'

We move, and are moved, in so many different ways. Cars on the street display their State number plates that are adorned with the political party slogan of the State Government of the day, or yesterday, as the case may be: 'Victoria: *on the move*', or, 'Victoria: *the place to be*'. I overhear the conversation from the young student couple seated ahead: 'But we are *moving beings*!' We live out our pleasures and struggles amongst personal, political and philosophical differences. And so it is that State Governments in both West Bengal (India) and Victoria (Australia) have experienced the gaining and losing of power riding their own tramways policies, just as they have strategically deployed the large public presence of the tram for the purpose of bringing the public alongside with their own political imperatives. 'Tram zindabad!' cry Calcutta Tramways Company workers in line with three decades of rule by the CPI(M), the Communist Party of India (Marxist).

Tram travel is, after all, staged on the street. Tram after tram choreograph a beat to the movement of the metropolis whilst tramways infrastructure weaves through the public imagination. An endless variety of dreams are caught amongst an urban sky that is shaped into segments by the netting of tram wires. The ground underfoot vibrates in varying tones produced by heavy movement on well-travelled tracks. A grimy young man offers his seat to a hard-nosed woman as the screech of metal on metal resounds,

পূর্ণনির্মাণের পটভূমি। সম্মুখীন হয় দ্বিমত, দ্বৈধতা। এয়ারপোর্ট থেকে ভাড়া করা ট্যাক্সি থেকে হাতে আঁকা বিলবোর্ডের "আনন্দের শহর কলকাতায় স্বাগতম" ঘোষণাটি আমায় সেই অতি পরিচিত মিষ্টি গন্ধটি এবং ডিজেল আর পেট্রলের সেই চোখ-জ্বালানো ধোওয়া উপলব্ধি করায়। এক শিক্ষিত মহিলার গলা ভেসে আসে ট্রামগাড়ির প্রথম শ্রেণীর কামরা থেকে ঃ "এ আরেক বিদেশীর আমাদের শহরের সংঘর্ষপীড়িত জীবনের এক রোমান্টিক চিত্রকরণের প্রচেষ্টা।"

এদিকে মেলবোর্ণের রাস্তায় লাল ইউনিফর্ম পরা স্বেচ্ছাসেবী শহর অ্যামবাসাডর, নিজ শহরের নতুন প্রাপ্ত উপাধি 'বিশ্বের সব থেকে বাসযোগ্য শহর' নিয়ে গর্ব করে। আরেকদিকে গৃহহীন ফেরিওয়ালা রাস্তায় 'দ্য বিগ্ ইস্যু' পত্রিকার গ্রাহক খোঁজে।

আমরা এগিয়ে চলি আর বিহ্বল হই কতভাবে। রাস্তায় গাড়ীগুলির নম্বরপ্লেটে রাজনৈতিক দলের স্লোগান লেখা - 'ভিক্টোরিয়া এগিয়ে যাচ্ছে' কিংবা 'ভিক্টোরিয়া সেরা জায়গা'। ট্রামে, সামনের সীটে বসা ছাত্রযুগলের কথা ভেসে আসে, "আমরা তো চলমান।" জীবনের সংঘর্ষে পরিতৃপ্তি খুঁজে পাই আমাদের ব্যক্তিগত রাজনৈতিক ও দার্শনিক মতভেদে। এবং পশ্চিমবঙ্গ ও ভিক্টোরিয়ার সরকারগুলিও নিজেদের ক্ষমতার লড়াইয়ে সামিল করেছে ট্রামের এই জনমুখী চরিত্রকে। 'ট্রাম জিন্দাবাদ' স্লোগান তোলে কলকাতা ট্রাম কোম্পানীর কর্মীরা, তিনযুগের সি পি আই এমের বামপন্থী শাসনের সুরে।

ট্রামযাত্রা রাস্তায় মঞ্চে অভিনীত হয়। ট্রাম শহরের তালে তালে দোলে এবং ট্রাম লাইনগুলি শহরের ভাবনার মায়াজাল মেনে এক সমাপ্তিবিহীন স্বপ্ন রচিত হয় আকাশে। পায়ের তলার মাটিতে ধ্বনিত হয় নানা স্বর বহুচলিত

and you smell your fellow travellers in close proximity, for better or worse. Being gathered in a tram is a dynamic experience of a community that is constantly created and recreated along the many different lines that pull us together or divide us apart. Hear the familiar *ding-ding*? The tram purposefully gathers us together to move. If globalisation of the contemporary world really does increase possibilities for making new connections, who chooses to move with whom?

A wave of closure to tramways systems swept throughout the world in the 1960s fuelled by the booming oil and automotive industries. The private automobile gained international dominance as the most influential mode of transport shaping urban development. Things are slightly different now, as a renewed development of tramways, originating in the late nineteenth century, has been occurring throughout the world since the late twentieth century, often now called 'light-rail'. What drives this? The wheel of the tram turns, and returns, travelling with a different logic to a century of linear-oriented urban progress driven 'forward' by industrialised 'development' and 'modernisation' with its associates of 'built-in-obsolescence', 'the individual' and 'upward social mobility'. Was the tram ahead of its time?

The back-and-forth of the tram makes a different kind of time. Rather than being driven by the overly simplistic modern march of time, tramways afford us a sense of the historically specific moment that resonates with memory and imagination. Tramways have been integral to the emergence of these two colonial cities. Yet tramways can also be seen to play a role in threading complex networks of relationships that exceed the dominant power relationship of the colonial. The tram is a poor carrier of the

ট্রামলাইনের ভারবহ যাতায়াতে। লোহার ওপর লোহার শব্দে এক নিরানন্দ যুবক নিজের জায়গা ছেড়ে দেয় এক মধ্যবয়স্ক মহিলাকে, আর সহযাত্রীর নিকট দেহঘ্রাণে যাত্রা হয়। একটি ট্রামে জমায়েত এক গতির অভিজ্ঞতা ভাঙে আবার গড়ে নানা ধরণের টানাপোড়ানে যা আমাদের কাছে টানে আবার সময় বিশেষে বিভক্ত করে। সেই চেনা 'ডিঙ ডিঙ' শব্দ শোনা যায়? ট্রাম আমাদের জড়ো করে এক সঙ্গে এগিয়ে নিয়ে যাওয়ার পথে। যদি আজকের পৃথিবীর বিশ্বায়ণ নতুন যোগাযোগের সুযোগ করে দেয়, কে কিসে চলতে পছন্দ করবে?

১৯৬০র দশকে তেল এবং বাহনের বাড়ন্ত শিল্পের ফলে ট্রাম পথ বন্ধের এক জোয়ার এসেছিল। সারা বিশ্বে নিজস্ব গাড়ি এক আন্তর্জাতিক প্রাধান্য পেল শহুরে বিকাশের চিহ্ন হিসাবে। এখন পরিস্থিতি কিছুটা অন্যরকম। উনিশ দশকের ট্রাম পথের এক নতুন বিকাশ ঘটল সারা বিশ্বে বিশ শতাব্দীর শেষের দিকে, তার নাম দেওয়া হল 'হাল্কা রেল'। এটি কিসে চলে সে এক যুগের শহরে উন্নতিরেখায় বা চালিতে হয়েছে শৈল্পিক উন্নতিকরণ ও নবীকরণের দ্বারা এবং তাদের আনুসাঙ্গিক নিজস্ব উপযোগীহীনতায়, নিজস্ব স্বাতন্ত্র এবং সামাজিক উন্নতিতে। ট্রাম কি তার সময়ের আগে এসে গেছে?

ট্রামের এগোনো ও পিছোনো এক ভিন্ন সময় তৈরি করে। এক সহজ সরল নতুন সময়ের দিকে এগিয়ে যাওয়ার থেকে ট্রামপথ এক ঐতিহাসিক মানের উপলব্ধি তৈরী করে যা স্মরণশক্তিতে ও ভাবনায় ধ্বনিত হয়। ট্রামপথ এই দুই ঔপনবেশিক শহরের গড়ে ওঠার মূল ছিল। তবু ট্রামপথকে এক গুরুত্বপূর্ণ ভূমিকায় দেখা যায় যা সম্পর্কের গভীরে বিভাজনে বা ঔপনবেশিকতার শক্তি সম্পর্কের প্রাধান্যের চেয়ে অনেকবেশি তাৎপর্যপূর্ণ। ট্রাম কখনও এক সাদাসিধে তত্ত্বে চলে না। সে

logic of the straightforward, for the tram criss-crosses all over the grain of one-way monologue and mono-direction to weave multiple layered interconnections within the urban condition. The tram transports dialogue.

Parallel lines cut across each other, return upon themselves, and deliver us to points similar to and different from where we start over again, and again. Settle in to a tram ride as it makes time to bypass the hasty speed of short-term trips in favour of an adventure through questions of mobility and connection. The journey ahead moves through cultural, technological and aesthetic juxtapositions. Paths laid by the book's contributors lead us through the two cities to encounter differing cultural values, skills, knowledges and orientations to the contemporary world. A familiar face fleetingly appears in the window of a tram of strangers moving in an alternative direction. Opportunities for movement spring from encountering such arrangements of difference. Rather than erasing differences, moving back and forth, working with difference, has us move forward in ways that make new differences.

This book opens out from a loosely framed question: what happens when we utilise the way of the tram to imagine two cities and relations between them? Four sections lie ahead. *DEPARTING* visits the impulses and ideas from which a *tramjatra* has gained initial momentum, and so offers preliminary thoughts to accompany your travel. *TRACKING* takes us amongst tram conductors, artists, social activists and designers in the tracks of *tramjatra* events held in 2001. Further connections to people and ideas are encountered in the *NETWORKING* section, where emerging writers and renowned scholars lead us through Melbourne and Kolkata considering the

একমুখো বক্তব্য বা চলাকে কাটাকুটি করে শহরের পরিস্থিতিতে বহুমুখী যোগাযোগ তৈরি করে। ট্রাম কথাবার্তা বহন করে।

সমান্তরাল রেখাগুলি নিজেদের কাটাকুটি করে, আবার নিজেদের ওপরই ফেরত আসে এবং আমাদের বারংবার পৌঁছে দেয় এক বা ভিন্ন জায়গাতে। একটি ট্রামে উঠে বসলে সে যাত্রা ক্ষুদ্র যাত্রার দ্রুতগতিকে পাশে রেখে এক চলমানতা এবং যোগাযোগের রোমাঞ্চ তৈরি করে। সম্মুখের যাত্রা এক সাংস্কৃতিক, যান্ত্রিক এবং সৌন্দর্যের মিলনস্থল হয়। এই বইএর লেখকরা আমাদের নিয়ে চলেছে সেই পথে যা এনে দেয় নতুন বিভেদ।

এই বইটি শুরু হয় এক আলগা ধাঁচের প্রশ্নে ঃ কি হয় যদি আমরা ট্রামের যাত্রার ভাবনায় এই দুটি শহর ভাবি এবং তাদের সম্পর্ক গড়ে তুলি? চারটি ভাগ আছে বইটিতে। ডিপার্টিং একটি ট্রামযাত্রার মূল ভাবনা দিয়ে শুরু যা আপনার যাত্রার প্রারম্ভিক ভাবনা হতে পারে। ট্র্যাকিং আমাদের ট্রাম কন্ডাক্টর, শিল্পী, সামাজিক কর্মী এবং ডিজাইনারদের মধ্যে নিয়ে যায় যারা ২০০১ সালের ট্রামযাত্রার যাত্রাপথের ঘটনাসমূহের সাক্ষী। আরো নতুন মানুষ এবং ভাবনার সঙ্গে যোগাযোগ হয় নেটওয়ার্কিং সেকশানে। এখানে নবীন এবং প্রসিদ্ধ প্রবীন লেখক ও বুদ্ধিজীবিরা আমাদের মেলবোর্ণ ও কলকাতার মধ্যে দিয়ে নিয়ে যায়, জনবাহন, শহুরে চলমানতা, রাজনীতি, গতি ও সংস্কৃতি, জলশিল্পকল্যাণ, শিক্ষা, উন্নতি, বিশ্বায়ণ, কবিতা ট্রামযাত্রা এবং শহুরে সংস্কৃতিতে ভাবনা ও স্মরণের ভূমিকা আলোচনা করে। এই লেখাগুলির সঙ্গে বৈদগ্ধ ভাবনাগুলির পাশাপাশি আছে জনসমূহের বক্তব্য।

সেক্‌শনটি শুরু হয় একটি লেখা দিয়ে যা এই ট্রামযাত্রার যাত্রীসমূহের অভিজ্ঞতা বহন করে। শেষের লেখাটি আমাদের নানা সুযোগ ও সম্ভাবনার

nature of public transport and issues of urban mobility and politics, community and culture, public art, education and learning, development and globalisation, poetics and tramways, and the role of imagination and memory in civic culture. The lines of thought found in the more scholarly chapters of this section are poised between the clatter of multiple voices evident in the chapters at either end. The section opens with a chapter that collects diverse commentaries by 'passengers' who speak of how they have been transported by their encounter with *tramjatra*, whether with dismay, difficulty or delight. The last chapter at the furthest end of the section veers toward possibilities, taking us through the speculative ideas of artists and designers that reveal some of the extraordinary potential value of tramways – a domain of urban culture little travelled. And just as all tramways systems have a place to gather, rest and share resources, the *SHEDDING* section is where you will find curious and useful evidence of tramways, *tramjatra* and this book's contents.

I got started by 'tracking' back and forth. Bimal cut '*tramjatra*' in sticky vinyl letters of Bengali script. Friendships formed. We moved letters toward words and into phrases that we painted in lines behind the heads of passengers seated onboard their trams. Eight years later my step from the Esplanade tram is met by one of those phrases keenly recited back to me by a young man. 'His city is a collection of the routes he has travelled.' *Bhalo*. You make up your own mind. Your tram is here, your ticket is issued.

Mick Douglas
Melbourne, November 2004

কথা বলে যা শিল্পী ও ডিজাইনারদের ভাবনাপ্রসূত এবং যা ট্রামযাত্রার কিছু অসাধারণ সম্ভাবনার ইঙ্গিত করে।

আর যেমন সব ট্রামের একটি শেড থাকে, একটি জায়গায় জড়ো হবার, জিরোবার এবং জিনিষ ভাগ করে নেওয়ার তেমনি শেডিং সেকশানে পাবেন কিছু দুর্মূল্য তথ্য, ট্রাম, ট্রামযাত্রা এবং এই বই-এর সম্পর্কে।

আমি শুরু করেছিলাম সামনে ও পিছনে ট্র্যাকিং করে। বিমল ট্রামযাত্রা শব্দটি চটচটে ভিন্যাইলের বাংলা অক্ষরে সাঁটল। বন্ধুত্ব হল। আমরা অক্ষর কেটে শব্দ তৈরী করলাম এবং শব্দ থেকে কথা যা আমরা ট্রামের যাত্রার মাথার পেছনে রেখাতে আঁকলাম। আট বছর পরে এসপ্ল্যানেডের ট্রামে আমার সঙ্গে দেখা হল এক যুবকের যে আমারই লেখা আমাকে শোনালোঃ ওর শহর হচ্ছে ওর যাত্রার পথসমূহ। ভালো।

তুমি তোমার মন ঠিক কর। তোমার দিক নির্ণয় কর। তোমার ট্রাম এসে গেছে। তোমার টিকিট কাটা হয়েছে।

মিক্ ডগ্‌লাস
মেলবোর্ণ, নভেম্বর ২০০৪

DEPARTING

TRACKING

NETWORKING

SHEDDING

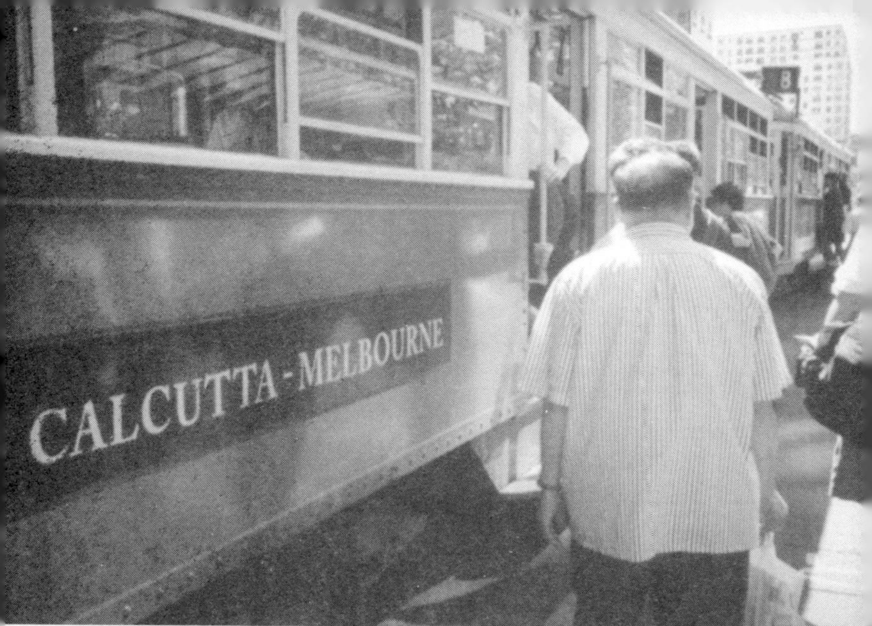
CALCUTTA - MELBOURNE

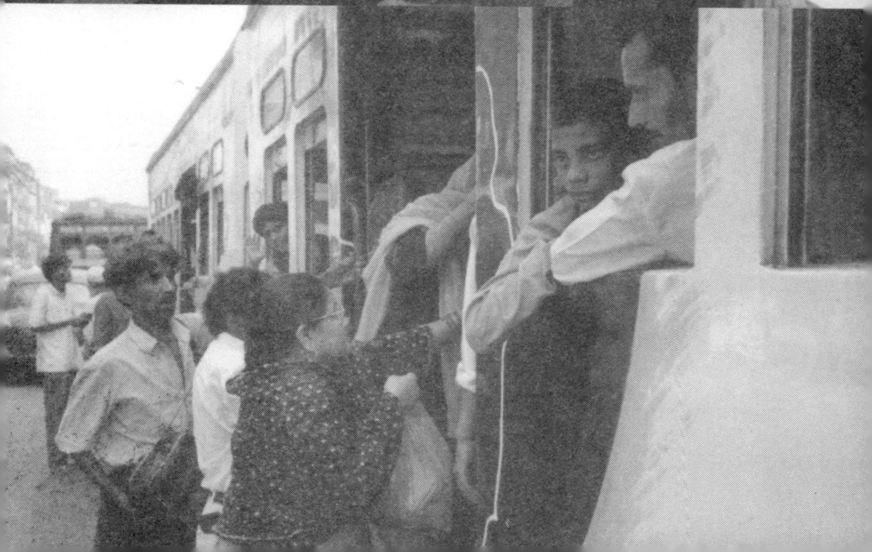

Copy to: Mr. Mees

भारतीय रासायनिक जीवविज्ञान संस्थान
INDIAN INSTITUTE OF CHEMICAL BIOLOGY
4, राजा एस. सी. मल्लिक रोड, यादवपुर, कलकत्ता-700 032
4, RAJA S. C. MULLICK ROAD, JADAVPUR, CALCUTTA-700 032
ভারতীয় রাসায়নিক জীববিজ্ঞান সংস্থান
৪, রাজা এস, সি, মল্লিক রোড, কলিকাতা-৭০০ ০৩২

IICB

दिनांक
Date 17th Jan 94

प्रेषक
From Debasish Bhattacharyya
Dvn. Protein Engineering.

निदेशक
The Director

TO: Mr. Paul Mees.

Australia

Dear Sir,

Hoping that you will be sympathetic to the citizens of Calcutta in terms of the citi's mass transit problem, I draw your kind attention to the serious and depressing condition of Calcutta Tramways Co (CTC). Prof. John Whitelegg of the University of Lancaster, U.K. has suggested me to contact you for any possible help. Copy of his letter is enclised herewith.

Calcutta tramways is at the verge of collapse on ground of "unbearable subsidy" by the State Government. We believe the arguments placed by the authority are totally unacceptable. The move has been highly opposed by all scientific, economic and social-welfare bodies. To save Calcuttans from a deadly situation, there is no way but to revive CTC.

The very acute side effects created by unlimited car use in Calcutta have been described in the newspaper reportings. This is only a fraction of the ill-effects; many other stories have not been highlighted. Since abolition of CTC is a state sponsored drive, there is little hope of fare judgement against this suicidal decision. So we wonder whether any global human right agency or Greenpeace activists could take up the matter. Our fullest effort to save the tramways seems to be insufficient.

With best regards, thanking you

Sincerely yours,
Debasish Bhattacharyya
Debasish Bhattacharyya
scientist-c
Dr. DEBASISH BHATTACHARYYA
Scientist
Indian Institute of Chemical Biology
Jadavpore, Calcutta-32.

correspondence at:

Kalighat, Calcutta-700026
INDIA.

फोन ऑफिस : 46-5421 ( 8 लाइनें ) टेलिग्राम : 'लिविंगसेल' टेलेक्स : ...
Telegram: 'LIVINGCELL' Telex: ... Back Code IICB

**ROBERTO D'ANDREA**
**& MICHAEL DOUGLAS**

Room 504 Bourke House
145 Russell St
Melbourne 3000
AUSTRALIA
Ph / Fax: +61 3 9654 7820
Email: mdouglas@rmit.edu.au

20 March 1996

**Dr Debasish Bhattacharyya**
P.O. Kalighat Calcutta 700026
India

Dear Dr Bhattacharyya,

We write to you with a shared interest in maintaining and improving tramways as an ecologically and socially appropriate form of urban transport. Ms Niva Finch of the Public Transport Users Association in Melbourne has made available to us your correspondence with PTUA, which we have enthusiastically enjoyed, and hence have become aware of your role in promoting the Calcutta tramways against much political pressure. Please find enclosed a variety of items and letters which will give you some insight into the background of Melbourne's tramways and our recent activities.

Roberto D'Andrea is a conductor / driver employed on the Melbourne tramways for the past eight years who has been active in the tramways union and in cultural projects around the tramways.

Michael Douglas is a designer / artist, and lecturer in design at the Royal Melbourne Institute of Technology. I have been pursuing an interest in researching the social life around the Melbourne tramways in recent years. This has most recently involved facilitating workshops with tramways workers and public transport users to generate images and stories of life around Melbourne's tramways. This work was presented in the exhibition *Tracking*. (Please find an exhibition catalogue enclosed.)

Roberto & I have worked together with this shared interest over the past few years. I recently met a Delhi based designer Jogi Panghaal who shares an interest in the tramways, and whose friend and colleague Mahadeb Si is preparing to make a documentary film about Calcutta tramways. We are expecting to receive a video copy of the preliminary film work via post in the next week, with a view to collaborating in the development of international tramways knowledge.

Given Roberto's existing connection with Balagachia and our discovery of shared interests with Panghaal and Si, we are considering how we might pursue undertaking an exchange which supports our mutual interests in promoting Melbourne's and Calcutta's tramways. The Public Transport Corporation (PTC), the government body who manages the Melbourne Tramways, has recently entered into a Tramways Friendship Agreement with the tramways management of two European cities. Enclosed are copies of letters of our attempts to encourage PTC to consider entering into such a supportive agreement with Calcutta. Whilst their reluctance to enter such a formal agreement is politically understandable (however regretful), we believe we have support in principle for establishing a cultural exchange project between our two tramways systems.

We are considering making arrangements to bring an expanded version of the *Tracking* exhibition to Calcutta in January of 1997, and undertaking consultation with Calcuttan tramways workers and users to generate an exhibition about the social value attributed to Calcutta's tramways. This exhibition could be exhibited in Calcutta and then Melbourne, with the potential of the exhibition travelling to other tramways cities around the world. We imagine that this may assist in promoting awareness of the Calcuttan tramways issue. We expect that an Australian government arts funding agency may lend its support to our undertaking such a project.

We would appreciate obtaining your opinion on the interest and support our ideas for a Melbourne / Calcutta tramways cultural exchange project may obtain from Calcutta's tramways community.

Our best wishes and support for your campaigning,

Michael Douglas

Roberto D'Andrea

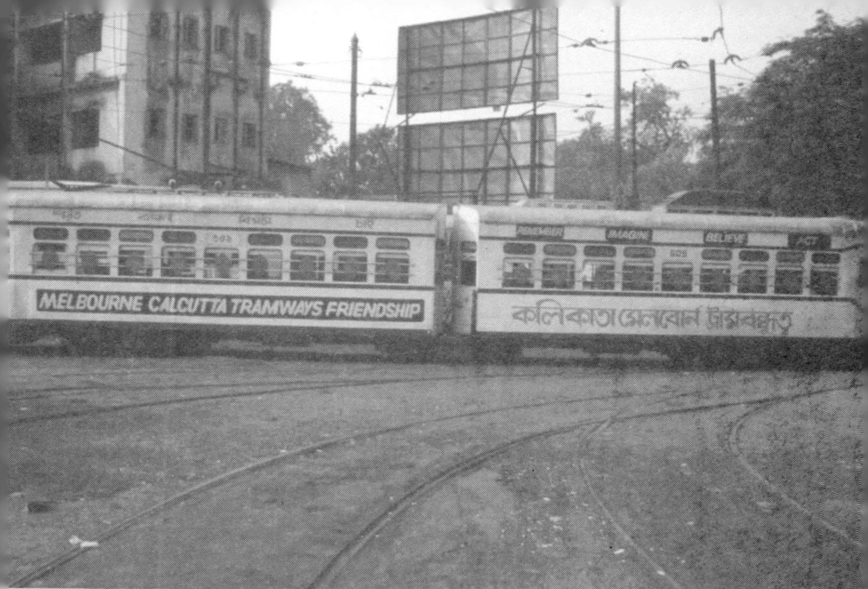
MELBOURNE CALCUTTA TRAMWAYS FRIENDSHIP
IMAGINE
BELIEVE
ACT

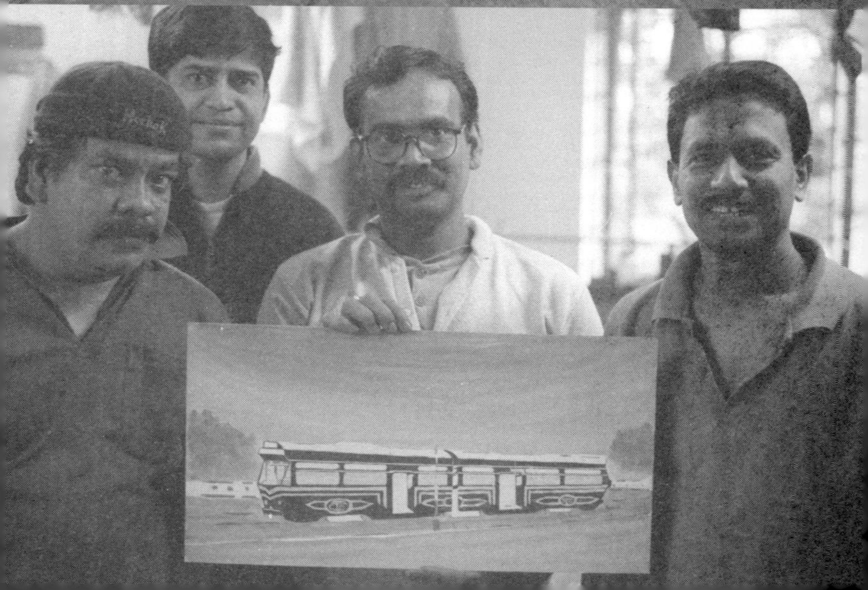

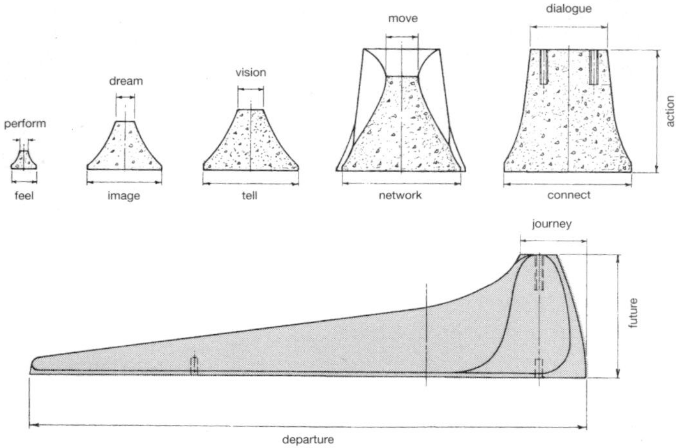
perform
feel
dream
image
vision
tell
move
network
dialogue
connect
action
journey
future
departure

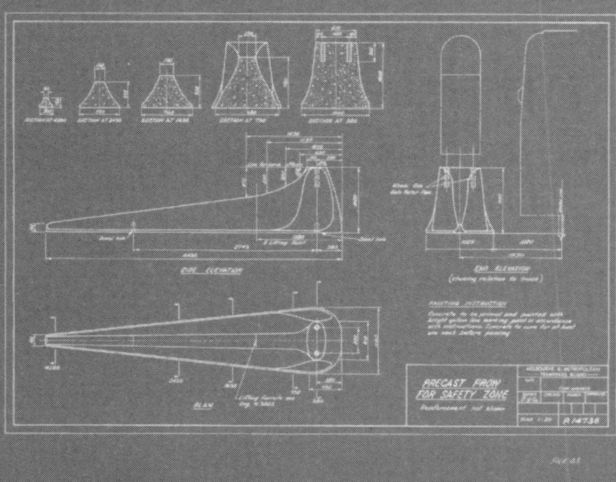
SIDE ELEVATION
END ELEVATION
PLAN
PRECAST PROW
FOR SAFETY ZONE

1

## which tram?

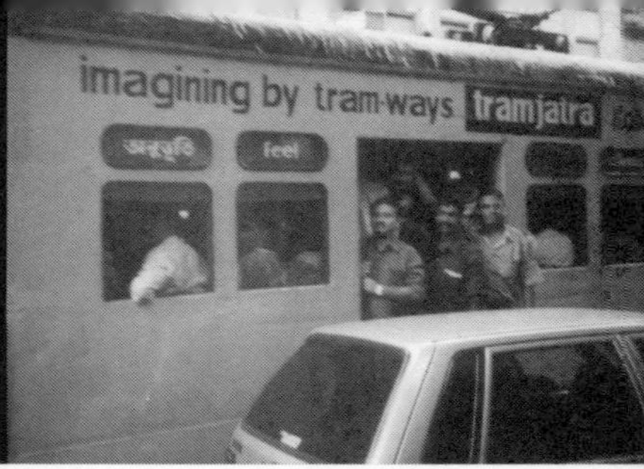


Debasish was writing letters seeking international support to argue for retaining tramways in Kolkata. Mahadeb was making a film on Kolkata featuring the tram as central character. Jayanta was feeding the Kolkata press with stories of environment and transportation. Roberto was working as a Melbourne tram conductor who had been magnetically drawn to the Kolkata tramways when on holiday in India. Mick was working on an arts project exploring Melbourne tramways and came across a letter from Debasish.

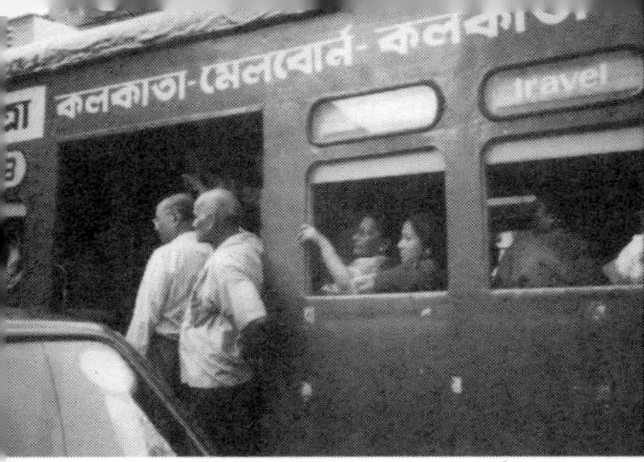


1

# কোন ট্রাম ?

দেবাশিষ কলকাতার ট্রামপথ বাঁচাবার জন্য চিঠি লিখে বিশ্ব সহযোগিতা যোগাড় করছিল। মহাদেব ট্রামকে মুখ্য ভূমিকায় নিয়ে কলকাতার ওপর একটি চলচিত্র তৈরি করেছিল। জয়ন্ত কলকাতার সাংবাদিকদের পরিবেশ ও যানবাহন সম্পর্কে খবর যোগাচ্ছিল। রবার্তো, একজন মেলবোর্ণের ট্রাম কন্ডাক্টর, ভারতবর্ষে ছুটি কাটাতে এসে কলকাতার ট্রামপথের প্রতি আকৃষ্ট হয়ে পড়েছিল। মিক্ মেলবার্ণের ট্রামপথের ওপর একটি কর্ম পরিকল্পনার সঙ্গে নিযুক্ত ছিল এবং দেবাশিষের চিঠির সংস্পর্শে এসেছিল।

*<DB>*

In the past ten years or so Kolkata tramways was in deep crisis. Our policy makers and the politicians almost erased the tramway from our city. People from different forums in Kolkata protested and got support from the overseas people. The *tramjatra* project is part of that support. When foreigners visit Kolkata for the purpose of Kolkata tramways, their work activities are reported many times afterwards in the media and discussed in writings and seminars. Accumulation of this type of information has a lasting effect beneficial to the Kolkata tramways. From the *tramjatra* project I learnt that we are not alone. I feel reassured that when you are fighting for a good cause you will find people in solidarity anywhere in the world.

Tramways around the world are not liked by the automobile lobbies. The strength of the automobile lobby is there – people influencing the politicians and policy makers of the city creating some imbalance in their judgement. Tramways in a city offer what I view as a much better way of living. You can live as we are here or we can improve our living quality.

The difference between the human race and an animal is that we can understand art. So while improving an art, I see a reflection of a tramways which is 'an artwork in a city' improving our quality of lifestyle in a much better sense. *Tramjatra* asks people to be more conscious about their environment, their quality of life, their living, the safety of the city, the beauty of the city itself, the signature of the city. What have we inherited and what is the future? This we can ask ourselves, our society and our policy makers.

*Debasish Bhattacharyya*

<ডিবি>

গত দশ বছর ধরে কলকাতার ট্রামপথ এক গভীর বিপর্যয়ের মধ্যে দিয়ে যাচ্ছে। আমাদের কূটনীতিক ও রাজনীতিবিদরা আমাদের শহর থেকে ট্রামপথ প্রায় উঠিয়ে দেবার যোগাড় করেছিল। কলকাতার জনগণ এর বিরুদ্ধে বিভিন্ন মঞ্চ থেকে প্রতিবাদ জানায় এবং বিদেশ থেকে সমর্থন পায়। 'ট্রামযাত্রা' নামক কর্মপরিকল্পনা সেই সমর্থনেরই প্রতিফল। যখন বিদেশীরা কলকাতার ট্রামপথ বাঁচাবার জন্য শহরে আসে তাদের কাজকর্ম সম্বন্ধে সংবাদ মাধ্যমে প্রচুর লেখালেখি হয়, সেমিনার বসে। এই সকল খবর ও তথ্যাদির এক হিতকারক ফল হয় কলকাতার ট্রামপথের ওপর। এই 'ট্রামযাত্রা' কর্মপরিকল্পনায় নিযুক্ত থেকে আমি জেনেছি যে এই লড়াইয়ে আমরা একলা নই। আমি নিশ্চিন্ত হই এই ভেবে যে একটি সৎ ও ভালো উদ্দেশ্যের জন্য লড়লে বিশ্বের যে কোনো জায়গা থেকে সহযোগিতা ও সমর্থন পাওয়া যায়।

মোটর গাড়ি শিল্পের সমর্থকরা ট্রামপথের বিরোধী। এরা খুব শক্তিশালী দল — শহরের কূটনীতিক ও রাজনীতিবিদ-দের এরা প্রভাবিত করে। ট্রামপথ একটি শহরে এনে দেয় এক স্বাস্থ্যকর জীবনযাপন। হয় আমরা এখন যেমন জীবন যাপন করছি সেই রকমই থাকুক নয় আমরা এর থেকে ভালো এবং উন্নতমানের জীবনযাত্রার চেষ্টা করতে পারি।

মানুষ ও জন্তুর মধ্যে ফারাক হচ্ছে যে মানুষ চারুকলা বোঝে। তাই চারুকলার উন্নতি করতে গিয়ে আমি ট্রামপথের প্রতিচ্ছবি দেখি যা এক শহরের শিল্পকলা এবং যা আমাদের এক উন্নততর জীবনযাপনের পথ দেখায়। ট্রামযাত্রা লোকেদের নিজেদের পরিবেশ, জীবনযাত্রার মান, শহরের নিরাপত্তা, সৌন্দর্য্য এবং তার পরিচিতি সম্বন্ধে সজাগ হতে আহ্বান জানায়। আমরা কি উত্তরাধিকার সূত্রে পেয়েছি এবং আমাদের ভবিষ্যৎই বা কি? এই প্রশ্ন আমরা নিজেদের সমাজের এবং কূটনীতিকদের সামনে রাখতে পারি।

*দেবাশিষ ভট্টাচার্য্য*

*<RD>*

My Calcutta dreaming begins in 1994 with the sound of the tram gong. Central Cal ding-dinging with that familiar tram tune – same as Melbourne!! I introduce myself with a bit of tram theatre and am hijacked by Belgatchia trammies. First tram ride in a wooden bodied rattler, the controller for driving just like the 'W' class tram, and connies serving and directing the locals – just like we did in Melbourne. At the depot, excitement and intrigue as trammie meets trammies. I'm drawing maps of Australia in the dust of the depot floor. A tour: the starters' office, connies' pay in tables, rosters, Communist Union rep, pitmen, jamadahs, inspectors, drivers and the bare-chested canteen bloke serving sweet chai in little clay pots.

Kolkata's trams were vulnerable. Buses had already replaced some trams. The line to Howrah had closed. Maybe we could help each other out? Melbourne connies in Kolkata? It would help our chances of surviving back home and Kolkata could surely do with some help from a tram mate from across the Indian Ocean.

Two rare surviving tram cities and their eccentric tram-loving citizenry have come together. A shared British colonial heritage left us with things in common: secularism, architecture, language, cricket ... and trams. We've explored our similarities, differences and each other's tram tradition while highlighting issues facing our contemporary tramways.

To hold the daily movement of the trams through the city is an art form. If you just keep putting your hand up things can change for the better. I'd love Kolkata's tramways to be strong, moving masses of people, reducing heavy congestion and air pollution. I'd love our connies back on board the trams of Melbourne sharing 'the human touch'.

*Roberto D'Andrea*

<আরডি>

আমার কলকাতার স্বপ্ন ১৯৯৪ সাল থেকে শুরু হয় ট্রামের সঙ্গে। মধ্য কলকাতার সেই বহু পরিচিত ডিং ডিং শব্দ যা মেল্‌বোর্ণে শোনা যেত। আমি নিজেকে ট্রাম থিয়েটারের মধ্যে দিয়ে উপস্থাপনা করি এবং বেলগাছিয়ার ট্রামকর্মীদের দ্বারা উপহৃত হই। প্রথম ট্রামযাত্রা একটি কাঠের যানে, 'W' শ্রেনীর ট্রামের চালকের মত চালিয়ে নিয়ে গেল। 'কন্‌ট্রোলার' এবং 'কর্মী'রা স্থানীয় লোকেদের দিক দেখাতে এবং পরিবেশন করতে ব্যস্ত — ঠিক যেমন মেলবোর্ণে হয়। ডিপোতে অনেক উত্তেজনা এবং হয়রানি — এক শহরের ট্রামকর্মী আর এক শহরের ট্রামকর্মীর সঙ্গে মেলে। আমি ডিপোর মেঝেতে অস্ট্রেলিয়ার ম্যাপ আঁকি। একটি যাত্রা শুরু হয় চালকের অফিস, কর্মীদের মাইনে, পর্যায় তালিকা, কম্যুনিষ্ট ইউনিয়ানের কর্মীরা, জমাদার ইনস্পেকটর, চালক এবং খালি গায়ে ক্যান্টিন কর্মীরা মাটির ভাঁড়ে চা পরিবেশন করে।

কলকাতার ট্রামগুলি আঘাত প্রবণ। বাস কিছু ট্রামের জায়গা নিয়ে নিয়েছে। হাওড়ার ট্রামলাইন উঠিয়ে দিয়েছে। আমরা হয়তো একে অপরকে সাহায্য করতে পারি। মেলবোর্ণের কর্মীরা কলকাতায়? এতে হয়তো আমাদেরও সাহায্য হবে এবং কলকাতা নিশ্চয় উপকৃত হবে ভারত মহাসাগরের ওপারের এক ট্রামবন্ধুর দ্বারা।

দুই বিরল জীবিত ট্রাম শহর এবং তাদের বাসিন্দারা একত্রিত হয়েছে। এক বিলাতি ঔপনবেশিক উত্তরাধিকারসূত্র আমাদের এক সঙ্গে গেঁথেছে যেমন ধর্মীয় নিরপেক্ষতা, স্থাপত্য বিদ্যা, ভাষা, ক্রিকেট ...... এবং ট্রাম। আমরা আমাদের ট্রাম পথের বিতর্কগুলি আলোচনা করতে গিয়ে নিজেদের সাদৃশ্য, ভেদাভেদ এবং একে অপরের ট্রাম ঐতিহ্য মিলিয়েছি।

শহরে ট্রামের দৈনিক যাতায়াত ধরে রাখা একটি শিল্প। তুমি যদি পদে পদে প্রতিবাদ কর তাহলে উন্নতির পথে যাবে। আমি কলকাতার ট্রামপথকে দেখতে চাই এক শক্তিশালী জনসমূহের যান হিসাবে যা ভীড় ও পরিবেশদূষণ কমায়। আমি চাই কর্মীরা মেলবোর্ণের ট্রামে ফেরৎ আসুক, তাদের মানসিক উপলব্ধি ভাগ করুক।

*রবার্তো ডি অন্দ্রীয়*

*<JB>*

I am in this project for the sake of Kolkata tramways. People in Kolkata like Debasish and me have been fighting for the cause of Kolkata trams. A World Bank study stated almost ten years back that more than 10,000 people in Kolkata die annually due to air pollution. The situation has not improved with the continuing dominance of petrol and diesel-run vehicles. When Roberto and Michael came, we felt this may be a good platform where we can work together because we have a lot to share. We in Kolkata had started seeing the Kolkata trams in a completely downgraded way, as a thing of the past. This *tramjatra* project has brought the whole issue of tramways to the headlines. Kolkatans started to learn the importance of having tramways.

Many of my friends in the media started believing that fighting for the tram is fighting for a losing cause. How do you convince people who have apparently formed such an opinion? Through this project these people started saying: no, hang on, maybe you are fighting for a good cause. Knowing how to work in a struggling condition, that is a part of activism I learnt from this project.

Tramways are different from other transports. They are part of the social fabric and socio-economic condition and can reduce environmental pollution. Culture and art have an important role to play in the continual survival of trams. In one of Rabindranath Tagore's poems he wrote that 'tramer pore tram darieye ache', which really means that in Kolkata you find tram after tram after tram after tram. I hope for the day when that will become a reality in Kolkata.

*Jayanta Basu*

<জেবি>

আমি এই কর্মপরিকল্পনার সঙ্গে যুক্ত হয়েছি কলকাতার ট্রামপথের জন্যে। দেবাশিষ, আমি এবং কলকাতার আরও অনেক মানুষ অনেক লড়াই করেছে কলকাতার ট্রাম বাঁচানোর জন্যে। দশবছর আগে ওয়ার্লড ব্যাঙ্কের এক সমীক্ষায় দেখা গেছে কলকাতায় দশ হাজার লোক বায়ুদূষণের কারণে মারা যায়। পেট্রল এবং ডিজেল চালিত গাড়িগুলির দাপটে সে অবস্থার কোন উন্নতি হয়নি। যখন রবার্তো আর মাইকেল এলো আমরা ভাবলাম ট্রামপথ বাঁচাবার জন্য একটি মজবুত মঞ্চ তৈরি হল কারণ আমদের পরস্পরের কাছ থেকে অনেক কিছু দেখার ছিল। আমরা কলকাতায় কলকাতার ট্রামকে তুচ্ছ করেছিলাম, তার কবর খুঁড়ছিলাম। এই 'ট্রামযাত্রা' কর্মপরিকল্পনা ট্রামপথের বিষয়টিকে সম্মুখে এনেছে। কলকাতার লোকেরা ট্রামপথের গুরুত্ব শিখতে শুরু করেছে।

সংবাদ মাধ্যমের অনেক বন্ধুরা ট্রামের লড়াইয়ের বিশ্বাস হারিয়ে ছিল। এ সকল মানুষদের বিশ্বাস কি করে ফেরানো যায়? কিন্তু এই কর্মপরিকল্পনার মধ্যে দিয়েই লোকেরা ভাবতে লাগল ঃ না হয়তো তুমি একটি ভালো কারণের জন্যই লড়ছো। সংগ্রাম করে কি করে কাজ করা যায় — এই কর্ম পরিকল্পনা থেকে সেটাই আমি শিখেছি।

অন্য যানবাহনের থেকে ট্রাম পথ আলাদা। ট্রাম আমাদের সামাজিক ও অর্থনৈতিক পরিবেশের অংশ এবং পরিবেশ দূষণ রোধের এক বড় হাতিয়ার। ট্রামের বাঁচার লড়াইয়ে চারুশিল্পের এক মুখ্য ভূমিকা আছে। রবীন্দ্রনাথ ঠাকুর লিখেছিলেনঃ ট্রামের পরে ট্রাম দাঁড়িয়ে আছে। সেই দিনের অপেক্ষাতে রইলাম যেদিন এ দৃশ্য সত্যিই দেখা যাবে।

*জয়ন্ত বসু*

*<MD>*

When the Melbourne trams started plying the streets again after a four-week service strike in 1990, it dawned on me that this city was not itself without its tramways flowing. I was interested in making a kind of public art that could be integrated into the life of the city and its people, and so I started working with tramways. I wondered about the possibility of a digital museum of civic memory and imagination on tram tracks – a 'tracking vehicle'. An arts project began to explore 'tracking', workshops were held on board trams to hear of people's experiences of the city through tramways and I was told: 'You need to meet Roberto – he'll be into this.' Could we understand the urban condition through tramways? What might be learnt from the logic of this non-linear system of movement at a time when the folly of various sorts of rationalisms dominate? Connections with *Calcutta* started cropping up. Curiosity got me.

Working with Kolkata and Melbourne is an opportunity to question, to be challenged and to learn with others. Could tramways be a medium through which to work with the challenges of social and environmental issues and increase global awareness of these issues?

People know amazing things and have surprising ways. People seem to need to make connections to live and make some sense of their world. Melbourne and Kolkata have compelling connections – yet so much holds these two realities far apart. Working back and forth with the simple tool of dialogue is a start. And working with the openness of art can bring disparate people and ideas together in dialogue. By working together we might learn to imagine how things could be otherwise.

*Mick Douglas*

<এমডি>

১৯৯০ সালে যখন তিন সপ্তাহ হরতালের পর মেলবোর্ণের পথে আবার ট্রাম চলতে শুরু করল তখন আমার মনে হল ট্রামপথ ছাড়া যেন এই শহরকে চেনা যায় না। আমি এক জনমুখী শিল্প গড়তে চেয়েছিলাম যা এই শহর এবং তার লোকেদের জীবনের এক অঙ্গ হয়ে থাকবে। তাই আমি ট্রামপথের জন্যে কাজ করতে শুরু করলাম। আমি নাগরিক স্মরণশক্তি ও ট্রামপথের ওপর পরিকল্পনা — এই নিয়ে এক ডিজিটাল প্রদর্শনশালার কথা ভাবছিলাম — একটি 'ট্র্যাকিং ভেহিকল্'। এক চারু শিল্প পরিকল্পনা ট্র্যাকিং নিয়ে শুরু হল। ট্রামে কর্মশালা হল, লোকেদের শহুরে অভিজ্ঞতা শোনা গেল এবং আমাকে বলা হল ঃ 'তোমার সঙ্গে রবার্তোর আলাপ হওয়া দরকার।' আমরা কি ট্রামপথের মধ্যে দিয়ে শহুরে অভিজ্ঞতা বোঝবার চেষ্টা করব? যেখানে নানাধরণের যুক্তিবিদ্যা প্রাধান্য পায় সেখানে আমরা চলনের যুক্তির মধ্যে দিয়ে কিই বা শিখতে পারি?

কলকাতার সঙ্গে যোগাযোগ শুরু হল। আমি কৌতূহলী হয়ে উঠলাম।

কলকাতা ও মেলবোর্ণের সঙ্গে কাজ করা মানে প্রশ্ন করা, শেখা এবং প্রতিদ্বন্দ্বিতা করার এক সুযোগ। ট্রামপথ কি তাহলে সামাজিক ও পরিবেশ সংক্রান্ত বিষয়গুলি সম্পর্কে সচেতনতা বাড়াতে সাহায্য করবে?

লোকেদের জ্ঞান অভূতপূর্ব। তারা বাঁচার জন্য যোগাযোগের তাগিদটা বোঝে। মেলবোর্ণে ও কলকাতার মধ্যে সাদৃশ্যও আছে আবার আছে অনেক বিভেদ। কথাবার্তার মাধ্যমে কাজ শুরু হয় এবং চারুশিল্প সব সময়ই বিপরীতগামী লোক এবং ভাবনাদের কাছে এনে দেয়। একসঙ্গে কাজ করে আমরা অন্য ভাবে ভাবতে শিখি।
*মিক্ ডগ্লাস*

*<MS>*

This *tramjatra* thing came up and I just jumped into it. The Australians' idea has two motivations as I understand. One is the tramway as an art subject, like a tram-space. The other is tram as a pollution-free, environmentally friendly mode of transport. In Kolkata very few people are really conscious about both aspects. I am a filmmaker. I have a very strong association with the tram. When I first started going regularly from Serampore to college in Kolkata, the Howrah bridge tram was still there, so I would take a tram from Howrah to Esplanade and back. The tram was the first thing that drew my attention in Kolkata. I just loved it, like a friend. I wanted to make a film of it. This is one of my dreams.

I have been making a film on the tram in Kolkata for the past six years. Every film has to create a new space. I work with tram and city through images captured on film. As a citizen of Kolkata, I have a responsibility towards my city and tram. *Tramjatra* creates this consciousness for Kolkatans – makes us stop and think, ok like, tram is there, should be there. West Bengal government never prioritised tram as a principal mode of transport. Maybe *tramjatra* will make them think again.

*Tramjatra* allowed Melbourne people to experience Kolkata beyond picture postcards. We too experienced Melbourne in a real world. I wish Kolkata could have similar tramways. The strength of *tramjatra* lies in its collective effort. Tram tracks stitch together our cities, and the tram is there, connecting Kolkata and Melbourne.

*Mahadeb Shi*

<এমএস>

এই ট্রাম এল এবং আমি তাতে চড়ে বসলাম। আমি মনে করি অস্ট্রেলিয়ানদের ভাবনার দুটি দিক আছে। প্রথম হল ট্রামযাত্রা একটি চারুশিল্প। দ্বিতীয় হল ট্রাম একটি দূষণযুক্ত পরিবেশ অনুকূল যান। কলকাতায় খুব অল্প লোকই এই দুই বিষয়ে অবগত।

আমি চলচ্চিত্র বানাই। আমি ট্রামের সঙ্গে ঘনিষ্ঠভাবে যুক্ত। আমি যখন সেরামপুর থেকে কলেজে রোজ যাতায়াত করতাম তখন হাওড়া ব্রীজের ট্রামটি ছিল এবং আমি হাওড়া থেকে ট্রাম ধরে এসপ্ল্যানড যেতাম এবং আসতাম। কলকাতায় ট্রামই আমায় আকর্ষণ করত। আমি ট্রামকে বন্ধুর মত ভালবাসতাম। আমি ট্রামের ওপর একটি চলচ্চিত্র করতে চাই। সেটাই আমার স্বপ্ন।

আমি গত ছয়বছর ধরে ট্রামের ওপর একটি চলচ্চিত্র তৈরি করছি। প্রত্যেক ছবি তার জায়গা করে নেয়। আমি ফিল্মে ছবি ধরে ট্রাম এবং শহরের সঙ্গে কাজ করি। কলকাতার বাসিন্দা হওয়ার সুবাদে আমার শহর এবং ট্রামের প্রতি আমার একটি দায়িত্ব আছে। 'ট্রামযাত্রা' কলকাতাবাসীদের মধ্যে সেই সচেতনতা এনে দেয় — আমাদের ভাবায়। পশ্চিমবঙ্গ সরকার কখনও ট্রামকে প্রাধান্য দেয় নি। 'ট্রামযাত্রা' হয়তো তাদের ভাবাবে।

ট্রামযাত্রা মেলবোর্ণের লোকেদের কলকাতার অভিজ্ঞতা এনে দিল। আমরাও মেলবোর্ণের অভিজ্ঞতা পেলাম। আমার স্বপ্ন কলকাতা মেলবোর্ণের মত ট্রামপথ হোক। ট্রামযাত্রা এক প্রচেষ্টা সমূহ। ট্রামপথ দুই শহরকে একসঙ্গে বোনে — কলকাতা এবং মেলবোর্ণ।

*মহাদেব শ্রী*

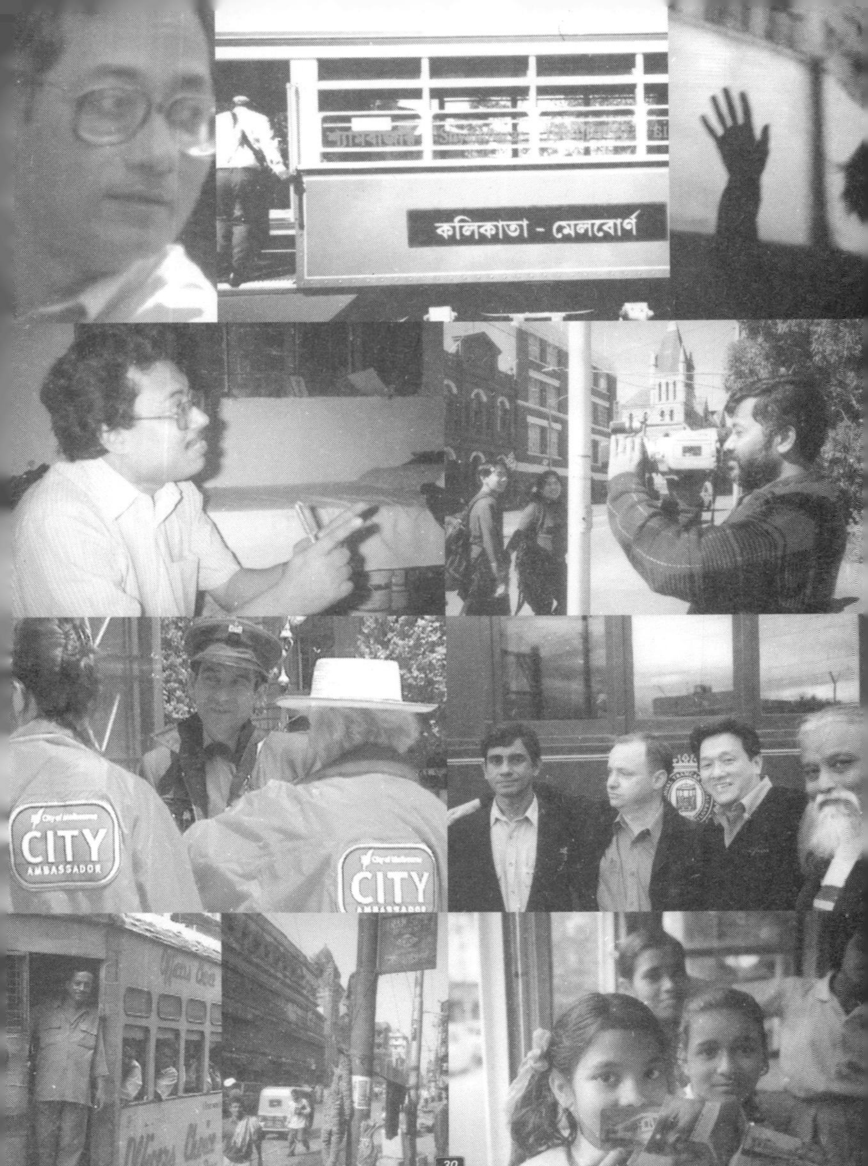
কলিকাতা - মেলবোর্ণ
CITY
AMBASSADOR
CITY

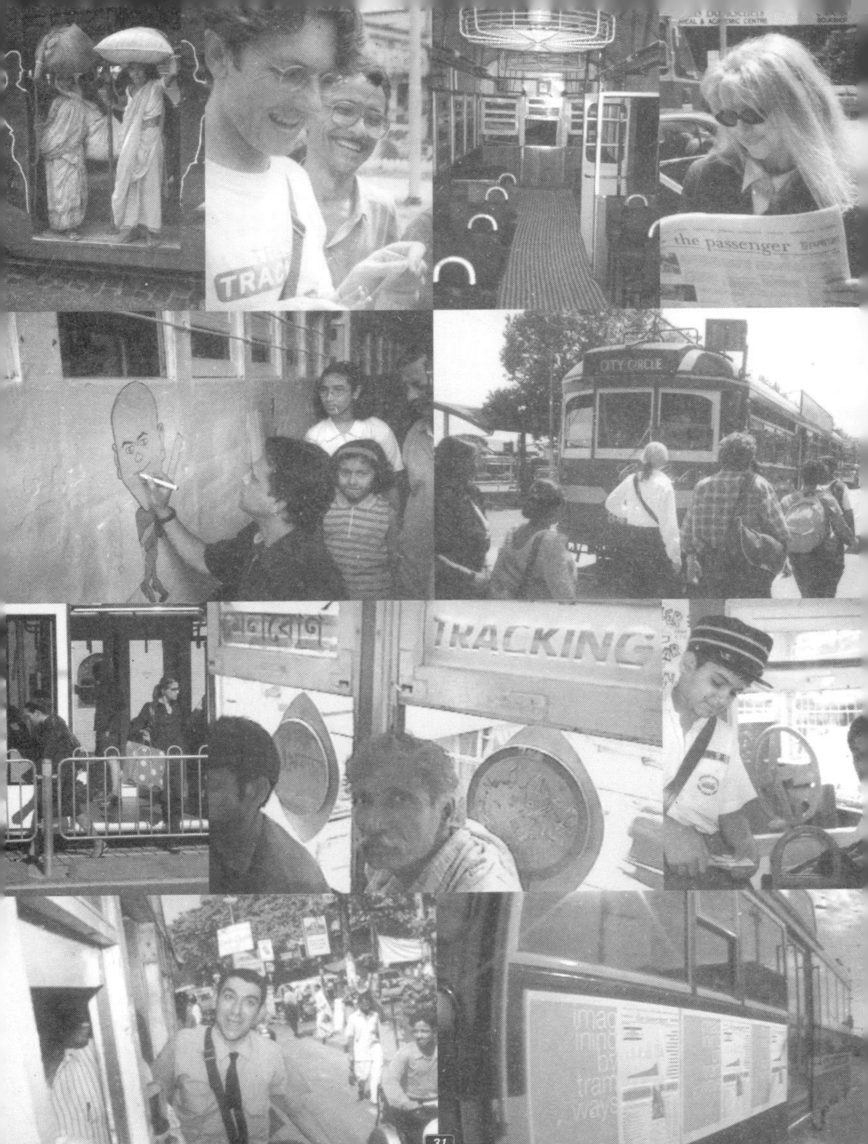
the passenger
CITY CIRCLE
TRACKING

Melbourne and Kolkata are two cities with tracks of a shared past. Both cities were once the capitals of their respective new nations and regarded by the British in the late nineteenth century as jewels in their imperial crown. Both cities have prided themselves on being national centres for the arts, and both are the only cities in their nations to have continuously retained tramways. The first fleet of convicts to arrive in Melbourne's Port Phillip Bay was indeed delivered by the British cargo ship HMS *Calcutta* – an indicator of the linkage that Kolkata, Melbourne and Britain have shared through global movement. *Tramjatra* reiterates old links between Melbourne and Kolkata in new ways through the medium of tramways.

ট্রামযাত্রা

**ZONE OF TRAVEL:**
What if tramjatra were to reveal new encounters and understandings between two cities with tracks of a shared past?

POINT OF DEPARTURE:
Melbourne / Kolkata

00001

যাত্রা শুরু
মেলবোর্ন/কলকাতা

**যাত্রার ক্ষেত্র:**
ধরা যাক যদি এই ট্রামযাত্রার সফরে সমান্তরাল অতীতের পথ থেকে আবিষ্কার হয় নতুন অভিজ্ঞতা, নতুনভাবে পরস্পরকে জানা?

tramjatra

This *journey by tram* travels over the tracks that are embedded in our histories, for tramways are woven into our experiences and stories of these cities. Tramways move us collectively as an electric mode of transport with low negative emissions into the urban airstream and with the durability of vehicles moving along fixed tracks. Trams also move us with more than just rationalist decision-making in mind: they are people movers that are laced into popular feelings of civic pride. Travelling back and forth, day in and day out, tramways have us inhabit small extraordinary experiences of value whilst participating in the larger choreography of a city's ordinary metabolism. *Tramjatra* employs artful strategies to prompt new lines of engagement within the public realm so that we might imagine the past and future of these cities and their people, travelling by tram in real and imaginary ways.

ট্রামযাত্রা

ZONE OF TRAVEL:
What if tramjatra were to provide new ways of imagining transport, environment & art in the urban public realm?

POINT OF DEPARTURE:
tramways / artful ways

00002

যাত্রা শুরু
ট্রামপথ/সৃষ্টির পথ

যাত্রার ক্ষেত্র:
ধরা যাক যদি এই ট্রামযাত্রার সফরে জেগে ওঠে জনজীবনের দুনিয়ায় পরিবহণ, পরিবেশ ও শিল্পচিন্তায় নতুন কল্পনা?

tramjatra

*Tramjatra* is built on a friendship between tramways founded at a time when Kolkata's tramways faced the threat of closure and Melbourne's tramways were undergoing privatisation and the decommissioning of tram conductors in favour of the introduction of an automated ticketing system. The friendship has grown much since 1996 when Melbourne conductor Roberto D'Andrea worked on Kolkata's trams complete in a Melbourne tram conductor's uniform, distributing free Melbourne tram tickets to a curious Kolkatan public. A number of installation exhibitions on service trams in Kolkata and Melbourne in the late 1990s generated much media attention and activated public debate about tramways in both countries. An increasing variety and number of participants and passengers have been drawn into engaging with *tramjatra*, activated by numerous series of fictional tram tickets.

ট্রামযাত্রা

**ZONE OF TRAVEL:**
What if tramjatra were to enable its participants and passengers to act upon their creative and critical potential?

**POINT OF DEPARTURE:**
tickets / action

00003

যাত্রা শুরু
টিকিট/কাজের কাজ

যাত্রার ক্ষেত্র:
ধরা যাক যদি এই ট্রামযাত্রার সকলে অংশগ্রহণকারী ও সওয়ারী সবাই পেত নিজেদের সৃষ্টি ও বিচারের পূর্ণ প্রয়োগের ক্ষমতা?

tramjatra

The experience of tram travel has us reiterate the same tracks in acts that are both a repetition of what comes before and a new inscription that creates new differences. Just as the tram gathers together an intermixing of individuals from different social sectors, *tramjatra* gathers together a diverse collection of people and their ideas to facilitate a collaborative space for dialogue. A diverse collection of core participants has been gathered together by the project to create an interdisciplinary and inter-cultural community of interest that includes tramways workers and management, creative practitioners (sculptors, filmmakers, painters, folk artists, designers and architects), social activists, scientists, engineers and business people. This *tramjatra* community gathered together for one month in Kolkata and then again in Melbourne in 2001 to produce temporary public events throughout both cities. These included sculpture and painting installations, tram exhibitions and film screenings, public forums and readings, a daily column in a daily newspaper, technical reviews of tramways and of course tram conducting and street performance. With a willingness to engage in the unique opportunities for dialogue, *tramjatra* hopes to extend us all beyond our current practices and understandings to open up the potential for ways that might produce a difference, both social and artistic.

ট্রামযাত্রা

**ZONE OF TRAVEL:**
**What if tramjatra were to generate momentum from the transforming potential of dialogue?**

**POINT OF DEPARTURE:**
**repetition / difference**

00004

যাত্রা শুরু
ফিরে ফিরে আসা / তফাতে যাওয়া

যাত্রার ক্ষেত্র:
ধরা যাক যদি এই ট্রামযাত্রার সফরে গতি এনে দেয় পারস্পরিক দেয়া-নেয়ার রূপান্তরী সম্ভাবনা?

tramjatra

Tramways significantly contribute to the sense of identity of both Melbourne and Kolkata. The tram itself is often employed as an icon of these cities. This mode of mobility offers particular spatial experiences and types of social encounter as it establishes deep rhythms in the city amongst a diversity of transportation forms and architectural types. Whilst Kolkata is stereotypically depicted in international arenas as a heavily polluted and poverty-stricken city lacking cohesive planning, Melbourne, with its rationalist inner-urban grid structure, has been tagged a 'most livable' city. Both cities are subject to political and commercial pressures that prevent tramways making their full potential contribution toward civic wellbeing. Mobilising *tramjatra* is the ongoing exploration of the environmentally sustaining and culturally enriching potential tramways hold for their cities. Currently there is a lack of language and concepts that may be used to engage with and discuss the cultural and environmental advantages of tramways. *Tramjatra* utilises the communicative potential of art to incite a diversity of social actors to imagine how tramways and their cities might be otherwise.

ট্রামযাত্রা

**ZONE OF TRAVEL:**
**What if tramjatra were to explore the environmental and cultural potential of tramways?**

**POINT OF DEPARTURE:**
**sustainability / diversity**

00005

যাত্রা শুরু
ধারণক্ষমতা/বৈচিত্র

যাত্রার ক্ষেত্র:
ধরা যাক যদি এই ট্রামযাত্রার সফরে প্রকাশ পায় ট্রামপথের পরিবেশরক্ষী, সংস্কৃতি-সমৃদ্ধকারী সম্ভাবনা?

tramjatra

A dialogue between Melbourne and Kolkata is one between two sisters born from the same imperial British parents within the shadow of a colonial past. The imperial parent appears absent in the conversation between sisters, but we know it is deeply inscribed. Through an exploration that draws together many threads from the fabric of each city, *tramjatra* might remain buoyant as a project difficult to reduce to traditionally defined outcomes, but resonant in its provocations to the imagination. Can we rethink how we move and are moved? This international tram journey just might make a small inscription into the consciousness of the social fabric of these cities. It might inscribe a historical moment of searching for post-colonial becoming, environmental care and international social equity.

ট্রামযাত্রা

**ZONE OF TRAVEL:**
What if tramjatra were to re-value threads of social fabric and challenge the possibilities of popular imagination?

**POINT OF DEPARTURE:**
memory / imagination

00006

যাত্রা শুরু
স্মৃতি/কল্পনা

**যাত্রার ক্ষেত্র:**
ধরা যাক যদি এই ট্রামযাত্রার সফরে আবার যাচাই হয় যত সমাজ-বাঁধা সুতো, জনতার কল্পনায় আসে সম্ভাবনার জোয়ার?

tramjatra

DEPARTING

# TRACKING

NETWORKING

SHEDDING

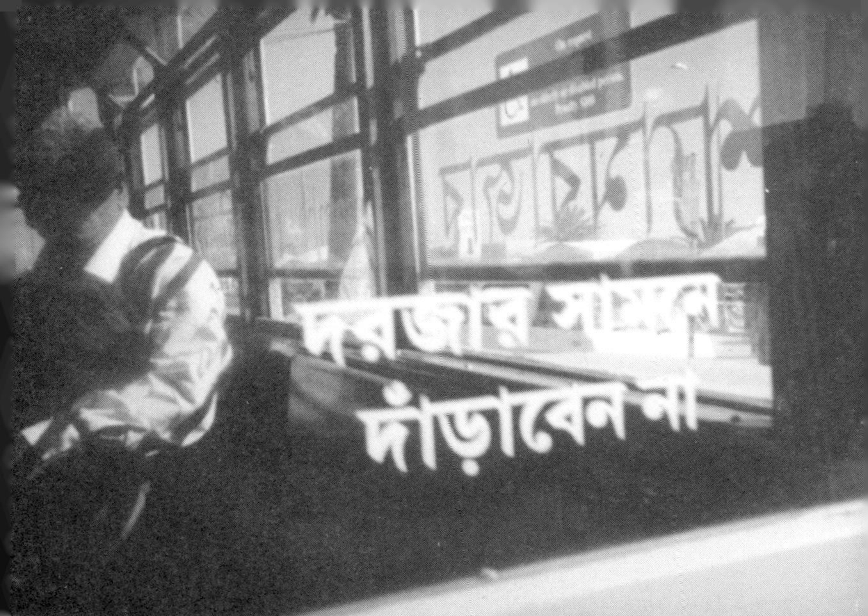
দরজার সামনে
দাঁড়াবেন না

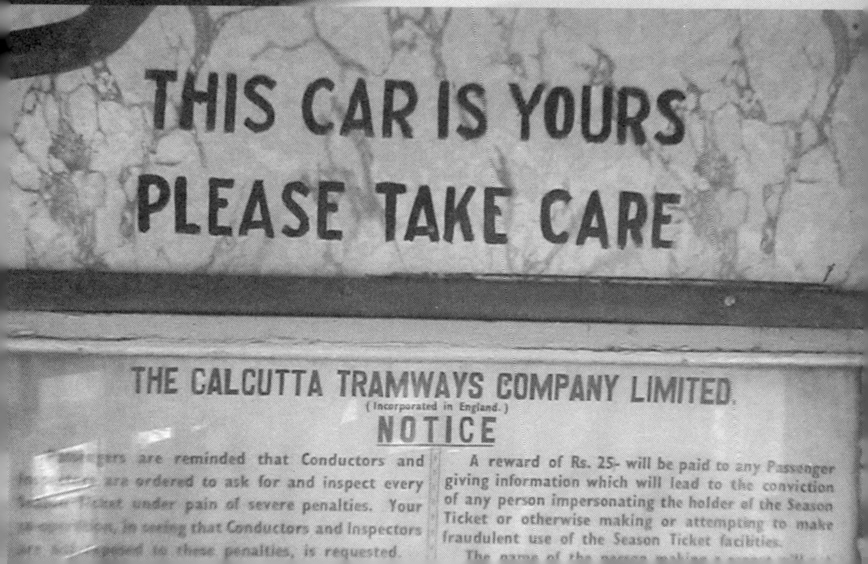
THIS CAR IS YOURS
PLEASE TAKE CARE
THE CALCUTTA TRAMWAYS COMPANY LIMITED.
(Incorporated in England.)
NOTICE
are reminded that Conductors and
are ordered to ask for and inspect every
Ticket under pain of severe penalties. Your
in seeing that Conductors and Inspectors
to these penalties, is requested.
A reward of Rs. 25- will be paid to any Passenger
giving information which will lead to the conviction
of any person impersonating the holder of the Season
Ticket or otherwise making or attempting to make
fraudulent use of the Season Ticket facilities.

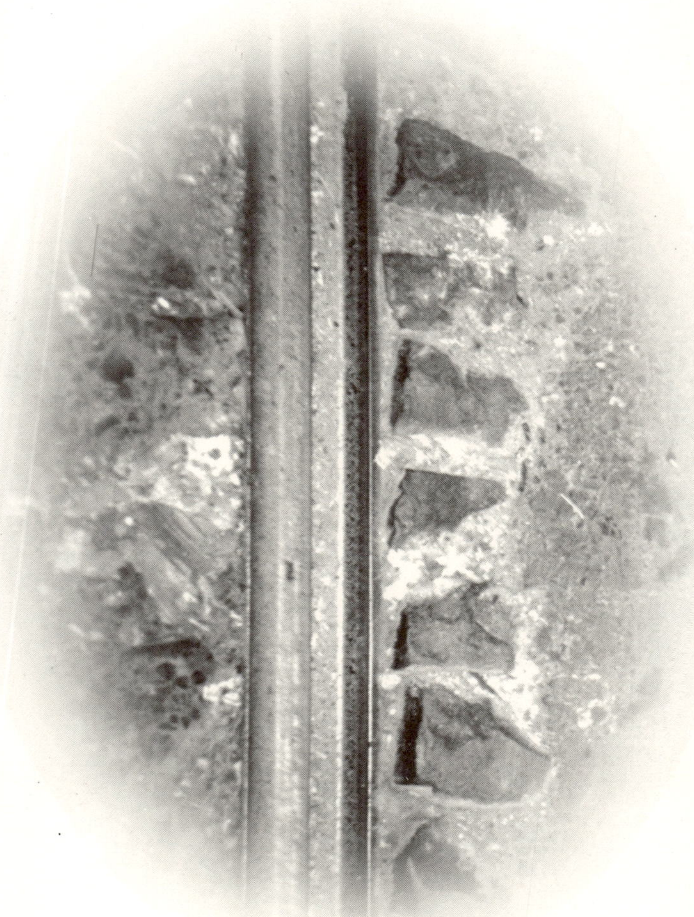

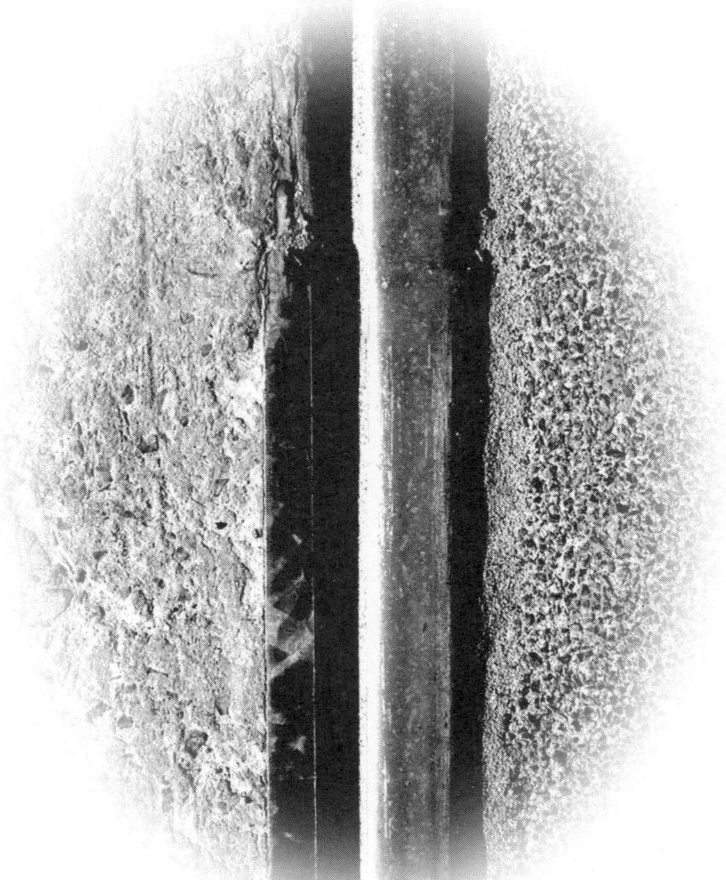

2

## *Conduct*

*Prabir Kumar Goswami*

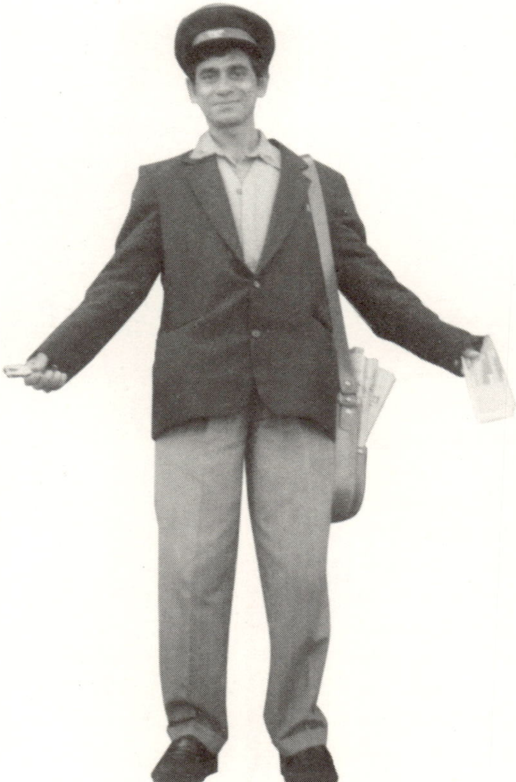

↓

2

# Conduct

Roberto D'Andrea

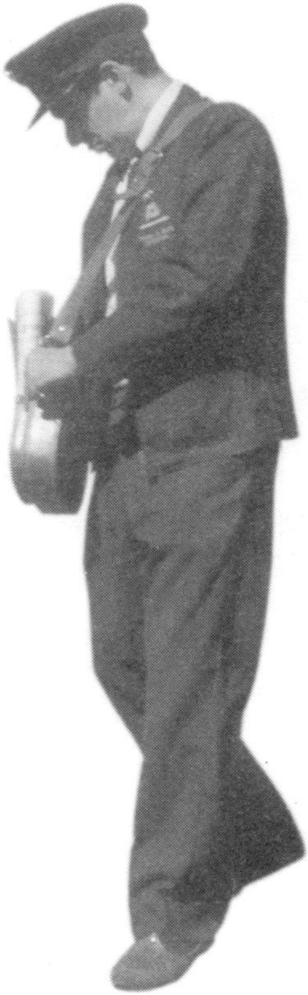

↓

K

## *Conducting Kolkata*

*Prabir Kumar Goswami*

*My father was a tram conductor since 1948. I am the second generation in tram service. I have grown up with the tram in my blood. I shall tell you about my being a tram conductor and my role as union representative in the Calcutta Tramways Workers & Employees Union, affiliated to CITU.*

*A tramways workers union was formed in 1922, but it was on 25 February 1975 that Calcutta Tramways Workers & Employees Union started its work, when the then right (Congress) party was ruling the state of West Bengal and central India government. They never looked at tram industry and its employees in sympathetic manner. They didn't have good faith in the public transport system or the interest of the commuters. The number of tramcars and employees came down poorly. The management and government was not ready to hear from the union. At this crucial moment we started work against this anti-public-interest policy.*

*At last in 1977 the Left Front government came into power in the state of West Bengal, led by Communist Party of India (Marxist). After this, two new routes were introduced – Esplanade to Joka and Esplanade to Bidhannagar; and the number of tramcars increased and so new recruitment was also made. Our union gained the opportunity to express opinions to government for betterment of the industry and employees. Still, sections of our administration and government are not taking proper initiatives in the interest of the industry. We have monetary problems along with the problem of space on the road, automobile association problem*

↓

M

## Conducting Melbourne

Roberto D'Andrea

Trams by nature are socialising entities. I joined as a tram conductor in 1989. I'm a product of the eccentric South Melbourne Tram Depot. Secular in character, entertaining and larrikin in spirit, South was always conscious and active, a talkative place with different nationalities, sexes and ages – a melting pot of intellectuals, travellers, students and the working class – all in the one place and uniform, serving the jungle of humanity. The trammie family would return home after working a shift to the depot sharing the stories of the day's events around the conductors' pay-in tables or canteen. Uniform for many of us turned into costume. We had tram poets, singers and storytellers who loved trams and the people who patronised them. There's a great tradition of bonding that's developed over time between the trammie and the local, often enhanced when the trammies add a bit of activism.

Witness Frenchie – an eccentric and entertaining tram conductor from the Malvern Tram Depot who added to his duties acrobatics and magic tricks. Born to a family of French circus troupe performers he left his mark and memory on generations of Melbourne's tram-loving community. Dressed immaculately in the Tramways blue and red striped uniform he plied the middle and upper-class tram routes of south-east suburban Melbourne, and along with the likes of Domenic – the singing Italian connie from Brunswick Depot – were loved by the locals. But the bond between the trammie and the local is best described in moments when governments or tram authorities have wanted to enact negative

↓

K

*and pressure from private bus owners. But the Left Front government is in power. Our Chief Minister assured us again in October 2002 that tram will continue with the city as it has been going more than 100 years. He tells us that government is thinking to expand tramways.*

*Mahatma Gandhi once told that if any one should want to learn discipline and unity then go to tram union. Whenever there is any possibility of riot we tramways workers try hard to prevent it. I learnt about the massive riots of 1946 before independence and partition through my father and senior tramways colleagues. Violence was spreading throughout India and in Calcutta. No one was believing other people. For long years people were living together, then Muslims were killing Hindus, Hindus were killing Muslims. Tramways workers took a social responsibility to form a big rally going to sensitive corners of the city (particularly Muslim areas) to protect people. This was a totally unarmed security force to give assurance to the Muslim and Hindu – they didn't even have a piece of stick. The tramway workers stayed for twenty-four hours a day changing in three shifts, standing between Hindu and Muslim people so they could not damage others, until after fifteen to twenty days they could slowly withdraw. This is my inheritance of social responsibility as a tramways worker's son.*

*In the year 1992 after the demolition of the Babri Masjid [mosque] in Ayodhya, Uttar Pradesh, there was more communal riot all over India. In Calcutta there was a curfew where more than four or five people could not congregate, there was a power blackout in the evening and services stopped. Just at the moment riots began starting in Calcutta, a few organisations took the*

↓

change. Two defining events have been the Loney Report of 1982 and the tram conductors dispute from 1989/90.

Loney expressed the state government thinking that proposed closure of approximately one-third of the tram network. Trammies, through the workers' union – the Australian Tramways and Motor Omnibus Employees Association – argued publicly against government and took the issue to the locals with a series of trammie petitions, stop-work meetings and colourful public demonstrations in a pre-election environment. The Liberal Government was defeated and a freshly elected Labor Government was given a mandate to improve rather than cut the tramways. In the following years the ticketing system was changed to be 'multi-modal', allowing passengers to purchase one ticket for trams, trains and buses. Also new trams and trains were purchased and with this modernisation, patronage increased.

By 1989 we faced another tram issue – Melbourne's tram conductors were to be replaced by a proposed system of 'scratch tickets', where passengers had to pre-purchase tickets and self-validate them to travel. A colourful series of protests followed. To highlight the issue to Victorians, from September to late December a series of stop-work meetings was held in central Melbourne. With Tramway Union direction, trammies would 'stable' the trams near the city square and walk behind colourful banners chanting 'Trammies united will never be defeated'. I had joined up as a connie in July. Fascinated and in fear of the Americanisation of Australian society I became quite involved. Each of Melbourne's eight tram depots came together forming the 'save conductors' committees. We prepared petitions which the connies took to

↓

K

*decision to stop this communal violence. Five to six thousand tramways workers wearing uniform gathered near Kiddepore and started chanting with slogans. When we entered the streets and lanes, people at first closed their doors and windows – their eyes were in disbelief.*

Hindu Muslim bhai bhai,
sabone humlogone ekta chay.
*Hindu Muslim are two brothers,*
*All want to live.*

Hindu Muslim bhai bhai,
sabai umra banchter chai.
*Hindu Muslim are two brothers,*
*We want to stay all together.*

Hindu Muslim bhai bhai,
kano amra oparer rokta chai?
*Hindu Muslim are two brothers,*
*So why do we need to have blood of each other?*

*The chants followed a line of Bengali poet Kazi Nazrul Islam: 'Ek brinte duti ful, Hindu Musalman' which translated means something like 'There are two flowers in same tree, which represent and reflect the two communities. The two flowers live apart from one another, but their origin is one.'*

↓

M

passengers, asking 'Fares please and would you like to sign the petition?' Our motto was 'Safety, service, security'.

By mid-December we had tens of thousands of signed petitions, all packed into babies' prams as a symbolic gesture and placed on the steps of Parliament House during one of the city stop-work meetings – accompanied by that chant 'Trammies united will never be defeated'. Each depot delivered the pro-connie message in their own way. South Melbourne Depot produced t-shirts and badges to give to passengers with a variety of pro-connie and tram messages. Most trammies helped with the work being done on-site at the depot. Renown Melbourne poet Michael Leunig wrote the famous tram-connie poem based on the Lord's Prayer:

Dear God,
Save the tram conductors.
Protect them for they are our protectors and
help them for they are our helpers.
Preserve the human touch they bring and the
human presence they provide.
Save us too from the follies and brutalities of
governments and all those who dehumanise
our world in the name of cost efficiency.
They have forgotten what life is for and why we are here.
Help them to remember.
Help us all to remember …

On the last day of 1989 trammies were to sign a paper which would see the connies gradually replaced by scratch tickets.

↓

K

*One after another people opened doors and windows and came forward to us and requested: 'Please stay as much as you can.' We were able to assure peace and harmony in their mind – that's why they came forward to us. That's the dependability and credibility the tramways workers have, generation after generation.*

*We cannot damage this credibility given to us by the common people. We have our limited duty, in my case as tram conductor this is to sell the ticket. But we are not just handing over ticket and money, we are always handing over thoughts and ideas – we are a social creature! The tramway worker extends his hand and cooperation to others. People seek information from the tram people because it will come genuinely. That's the vital role we play, day after day, year after year, whether they be my passenger or not. Maybe in one hour or one day you will be my passenger.*

↓

M

31 December and things were at boiling point. The newspapers, radio and television had covered the connies' dispute as one of the headlines – it was known Australia-wide, much of this due to the trammies' public campaign. The drivers had been offered a pay rise to tempt a 'split in the ranks'. No one of the 2,600 trammies signed or accepted the pay rise. The trammie family had stayed united.

On 1 January 1990, like the Barcelona trammies sixty years earlier fighting Franco in Spain, we took over the system and ran the services ourselves – without pay but with majority public support. That evening we were told that our 600 DC electricity was to be cut! Trammies, some dressed in pyjamas, decided 'to run the trams into the city'. For the next thirty-three days trams were on display, static in the central streets of Melbourne. When the dispute settled the connies were retained and Transport Minister Jim Kennan was replaced.

Governments change, and in 1993 with the newly elected Liberal Government connies were under attack again. By 1997 the privatisation of the tram network was on the agenda. The government arguing that an automated ticketing system would bring cost savings. We disagreed! – and took our reasons for connie retention back to the locals. We argued that conductors not only sold and checked tickets but were integral in assisting and nurturing the elderly, mothers and children; kept the tram safe, graffiti and vandalism free; that we looked after a vibrant tourism trade and that we were a part of Melbourne. Any savings made through staff wages would be social costs elsewhere! The connies' campaign involved workers, artists, tram poets, and singing

↓

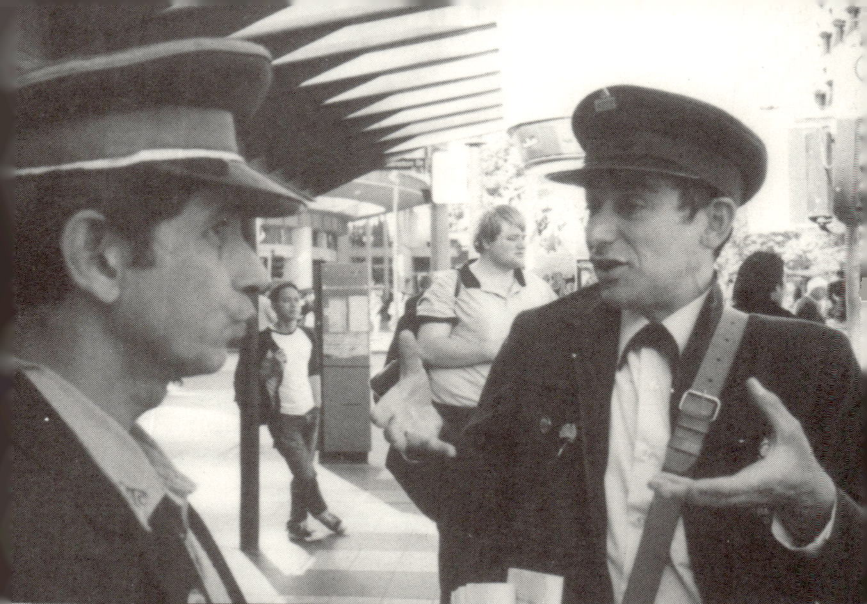
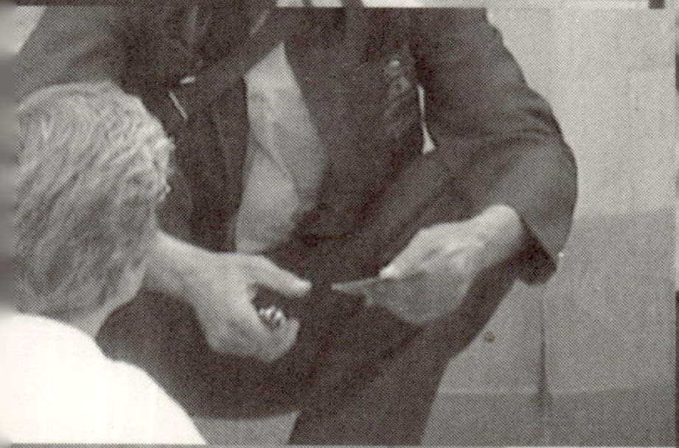
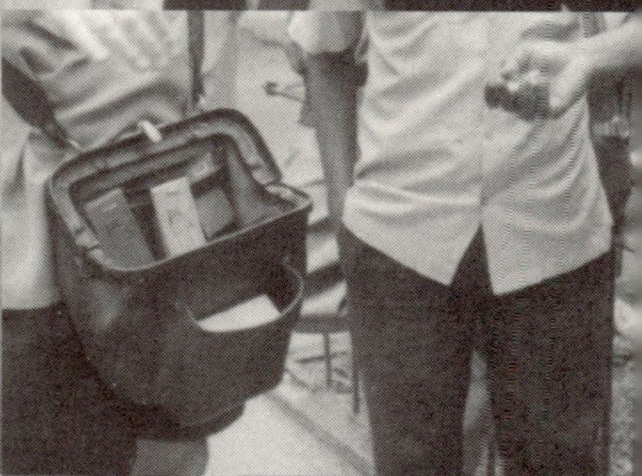
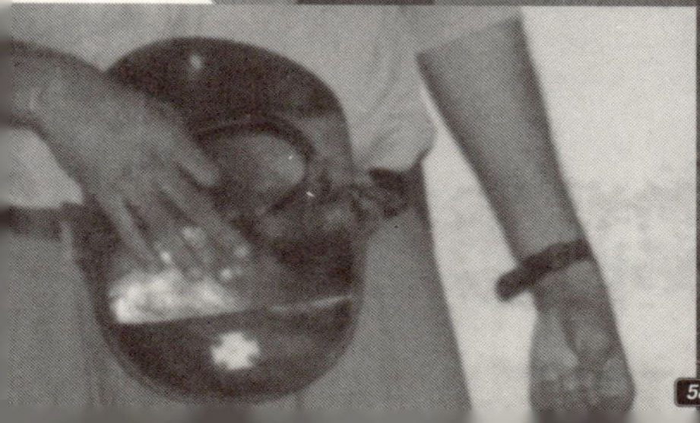
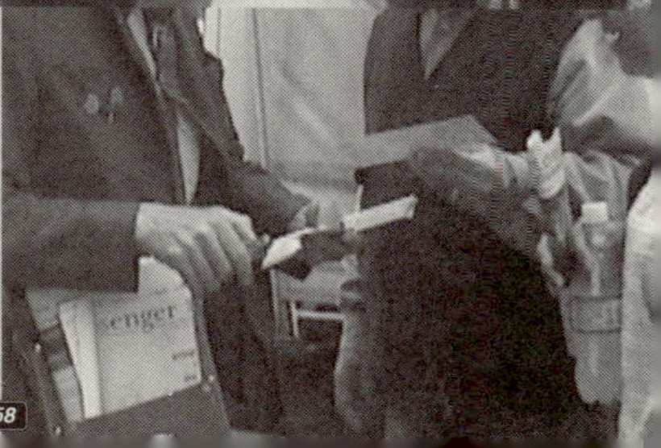

M

connies. We later formed the 'I Prefer a Tram Conductor Coalition'. The media was attracted by the connies' colourfully arguing our point and giving our community a diversity of opinion.

Melbourne had won the rights to host the Formula One Grand Prix motor racing event. Building up to the event in 1997 it was the time of 'enterprise bargaining' and the trammies were called to a stop-work meeting at the Collingwood Town Hall by the union. We were told that on a number of occasions an agreement with government was ready to sign but that government continually withdrew the agreements at the eleventh hour. Boiling point once again. Many of us trammies believe that it was a smoke screen to hide the unpopular introduction of the ticketing system, to blacken the reputation of your local trammie and to justify the unpopular introduction of a privatisation model born and used in Thatcherite England and the United States: private ownership of public assets.

Authority did eventually get its way, but at a large cost to community. The last tram conductor in Melbourne finished on 23 May 1998. We now have a smaller number of ticket inspectors, oddly titled 'customer service employees' who get around in big groups and are sometimes aggressive authority figures seeking people to punish with a fine! The relationship between them and the passenger grows cold and on occasions has been violent and ugly. Fare evasion has been at epidemic proportions whether it be through civil disobedience, simply confusion or an attitude of 'No staff, so let's take a free ride'. Graffiti and ripped seats, unassisted elderly and confused tourists. Locals still miss the connies and media still talks of the disaster that is Automated Ticketing.

Connies have not given up the fight to stay on board the moving platform. Now we are in exile. The protest has continued, aided by

↓

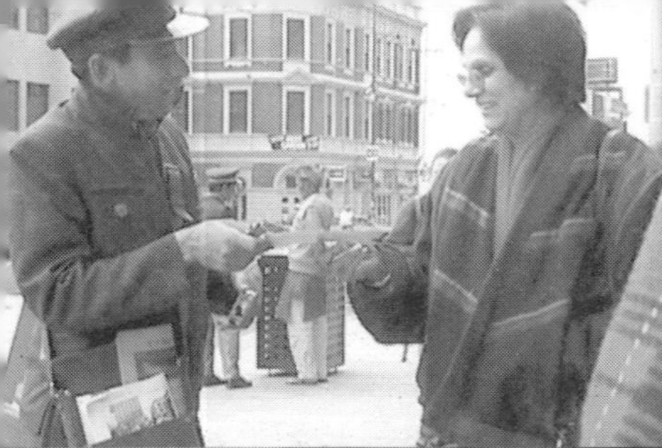

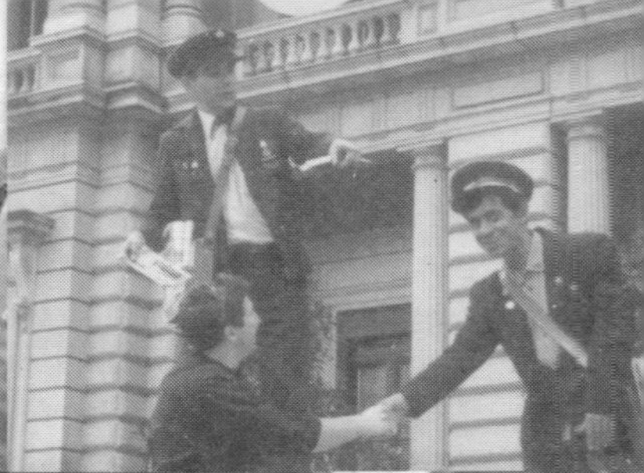

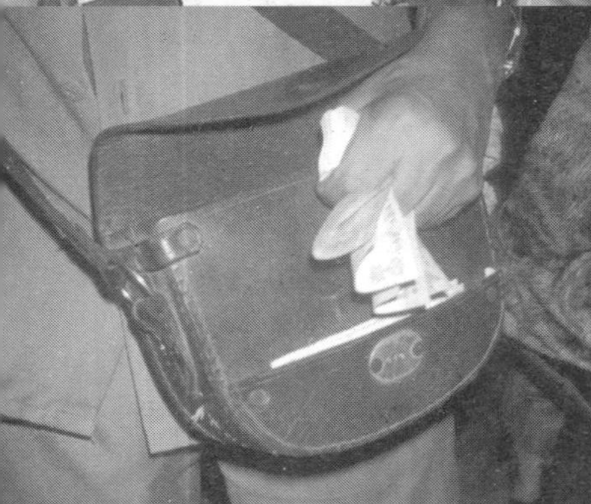

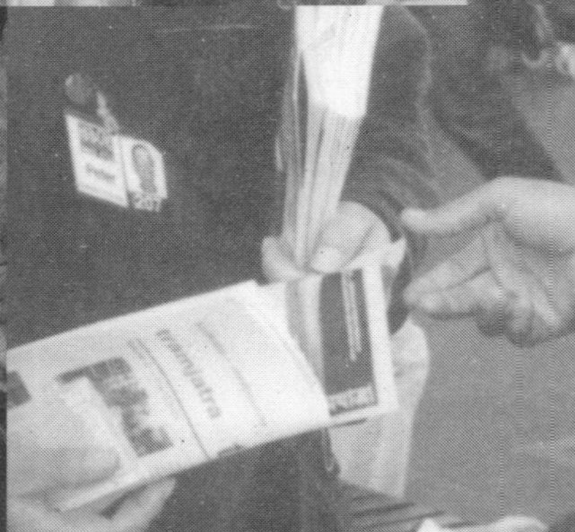

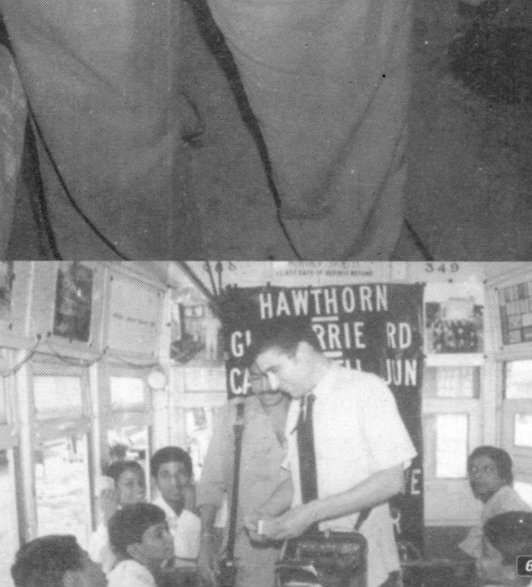
349
HAWTHORN

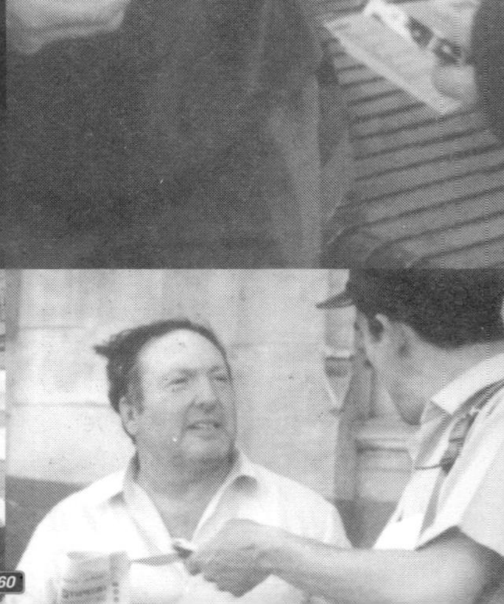

M

a ticketing system that is clumsy, unfriendly and unpopular. Building on our 112-year Melbourne tram tradition of human-to-human service, former connies have come together with tram-loving locals to form our own connies' performance troupe. No Melbourne tram to work on, but plenty of festivals and gatherings to attend. Connies won first prize at Melbourne's 1999 Moomba Festival for most popular parade float, have worked with Australia's Circus Oz, and have had world-wide media coverage by stripping off and doing a 'full monty' on the steps of Melbourne GPO. We continue the rites of bag and tickets, and dress in uniforms that span the many eras of tram fashion. We keep alive a trammie tradition of yarning, storytelling, poetry and singing. Out of our beautiful leather conductor's bag pops a series of collectable swap cards, origami or perhaps a magic trick. We go to festivals, country and city.

Part of keeping our conducting skills alive has been to join with trammies in West Bengal on board trams in Kolkata – a place where we can keep the ticket punch clicking and our linguistic and performative traditions intact. Back inside the trammie family next to our Indian friends we compare our similarities and differences, and help Kolkata celebrate its unique tramways tradition while supporting the vulnerable tramways to survive and rejuvenate.

Trams bring together many people. At the moment you've got rivalry and hate brewing around the world. What I think is very dear to what connies do is that we can bring people together. As we still say to the locals, 'We're not dead yet!' We await a return to our rightful place on board Melbourne's trams.

↓

K

*Prabir Kumar Goswami is a Kolkata tram and bus conductor who was invited to participate in the* tramjatra *Melbourne activities of November 2001. At the time he was a Tollygunge Depot delegate of the Calcutta Tramways Workers & Employees Union (CTW&EU), affiliated with the Centre of India Trade Union (CITU) that is itself affiliated with the ruling West Bengal state Communist Party of India (Marxist) government. In early 2002 Prabir was elected as one of five Assistant Secretaries of the CTW&EU. He reports to Shri Prajay Dasgupta, General Secretary, and Shri Rajdeo Goala, currently President of CTW&EU, formerly secretary of that union for ten years, and also since 2003 the Chairman of the state-government-run Calcutta Tramways Company Inc. According to Prabir, 75 per cent of Kolkata tramways workers are members of the CTW&EU.*

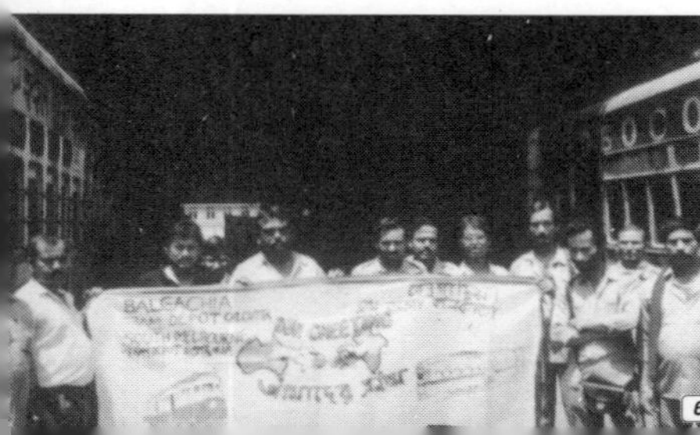

M

Roberto D'Andrea worked as a Melbourne tram conductor from 1989 until 1999 when the role of conductor was ceased. He has been a South Melbourne Depot proxy delegate of the Tramways Union, a committee member of the 1990 Met Ticket Task Force, the Public Transport Users Association and the National Trust 'Friends of W Class Trams'. Roberto has agitated for the value of tram conductors as a leading organiser of the 'I Prefer a Tram Conductor–Connie Coalition' lobby group since February 1998, and by standing for parliamentary election as an independent candidate in the seat of Monash in the 1999 Victorian state elections with 'tram party' and 'tram ticket' policies. He initiated and performed in the exhibition 'Trammies' at the Melbourne Immigration Museum in 2003. He currently leads the Connies Performance Troupe and works on environment and landcare projects throughout Victoria.

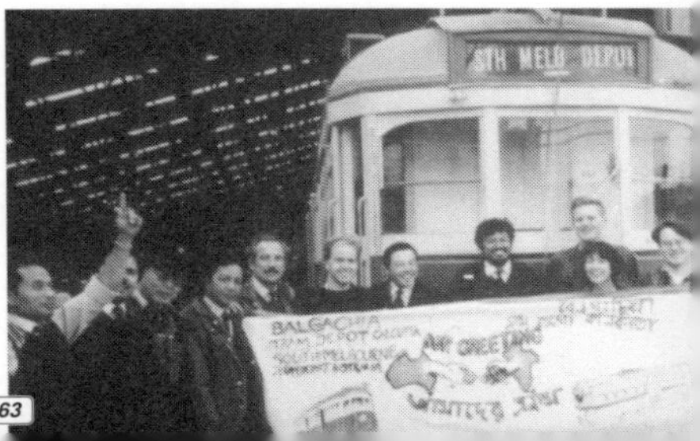

3

## still, getting there

Soumitra Das

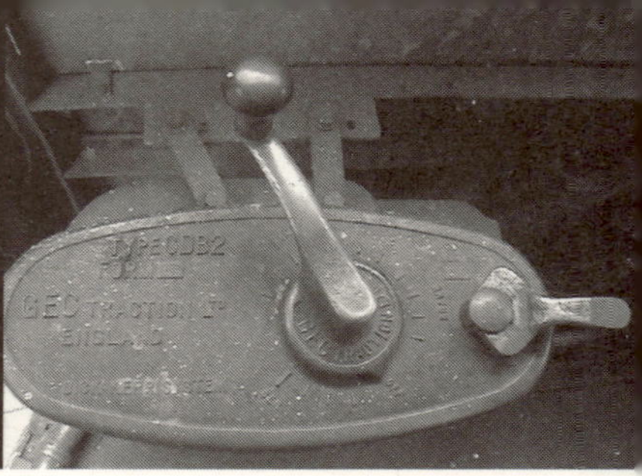

If cities could dream what would Calcutta have dreamt of? Assuming that we dream of the stuff our minds and memories are made of, the city would be on a rewind mode, and if it stops at its not-so-distant past to dredge up images that lie immersed in its subconscious, the tramcar is bound to be one of them.

A horse-drawn tram led the procession in Dalhousie Square in the central hub of the city to celebrate what was perceived to be the tercentenary of Calcutta in 1990. All because these horse-drawn vehicles moving on fixed tracks started operating in the city in 1880, and have thereby become a part of the city's heritage. But like so much that is of value in Calcutta's rich heritage, the tram too is endangered today, undermined by callousness and worse, wrong-headedness.

A news item that appeared on 7 March 1901 in *The Statesman*, one of the earliest English language dailies published from Calcutta, heralds the arrival of electric tramways: 'The electric plant for the Calcutta Tramway Company is being put up rapidly, the lines have been relayed all over the city, and it is expected that by the end of the month a start will be made to running cars by electricity on the Kidderpore and Kalighat sections.'

Since 1901, the tram has become a part of the repository of

images that constitutes the collective memory of Calcutta. Their tracks still lie intact under layers of tar macadam along erstwhile routes. During the sun-scorched days of summer, the steel lines gleam through the tar as squishy as melting chocolate. The tram ride along the wide-open parkland known as the Maidan in the heart of the city is one of the most cool and refreshing anywhere. Not surprisingly, a collection of photographs taken by an unknown GI in 1947 of the sights of Calcutta, that has recently been acquired by the University of Pennsylvania in the USA, shows a man wriggling into a tram through a rear window, the easiest means of accessing an empty seat in the vehicle when the door is overcrowded. On a more tragic note, Bengal's best-known modern poet, Jibanananda Das, was run over and killed by a tram.

Trams frequently feature in films shot in Calcutta and Bengali literature. For though trams were eased out of other metros such as Bombay and Madras long ago, they still trundle down the streets of Calcutta. Trams are woven into the fabric and cultural ethos of this city. Their tracks are battered with age and neglect but they still bravely lurch down old-world Chitpur, the city's arterial road, rattling the houses built along its fixed course. What Rabindranath Tagore, the poet philosopher no Bengali is ever tired of quoting, had written about the feelings of a highway as if it were a sentient being, holds true about tram tracks too. 'I lie forever still and unmoving yet I never get a moment's respite...I am nobody's destination, I am only their means of getting there.'

Perhaps this is one of the attributes of tram tracks – immobility that facilitates mobility – that brought artist-designer Mick Douglas to Calcutta from Melbourne, the only Australian city where tramways have survived. Initially he experimented with such motifs as the three eyes of Hindu deities, engaging the body of a Calcutta tram to give shape to his striking design. Then he decided to organise and curate *tramjatra* here in 2001, where the two cities, literally and metaphorically hemispheres apart, were intended to be engaged in a dialogue that would involve the diverse voices of artists, activists and tramways workers from both countries struggling to keep the tramways alive as an alternative means of public transport.

A *tramjatra* curatorial ticket, one of a swatch Douglas had designed, carried a legend that said it all: 'What if *tramjatra* were to enable its participants and its passengers to act upon their creative and critical potential?' In Calcutta, a variety of free tram tickets were distributed among tram passengers by the other man whose vision and persistence made *tramjatra* possible. Meet Roberto D'Andrea, the ex-tram conductor from Melbourne who worked in Calcutta's trams on and off from 1995 in a Melbourne tram conductor's uniform. D'Andrea, an inveterate show-biz type, kept *tramjatra* alive and kicking, literally, with his clowning. Only in one respect do Calcutta trams have an edge over their Melbourne counterparts: they can still boast conductors who have in Australia been replaced by a mechanised system to collect fares. D'Andrea's Indian counterpart was Prabir Kumar Goswami, a Calcutta Tram Company conductor who is also a tram company labour union leader. Like D'Andrea, he distributed the free *tramjatra* tickets among passers-by. Jumping on the *tramjatra* bandwagon he visited Melbourne.

To initiate a dialogue with the unfamiliar, even before *tramjatra*, legends in English as well as in Bengali script were juxtaposed with photographs D'Andrea had taken of his interactions with Calcutta tram workers and placed in advertising panels in Melbourne trams. These were culturally provocative because in Melbourne civic elements are always in English. Nonetheless, D'Andrea drew a strong reaction from Calcutta's mayor Subrata Mukherjee, who is hostile to trams. In a letter to the editor of *The Telegraph* newspaper published from Calcutta, he dismissed *tramjatra* as a 'joke', and the participants, mostly people in the peak of their careers, as a bunch of 'retired' people.

The truth is that like almost everything else in Calcutta, *tramjatra* ran the risk of being politicised. West Bengal Transport Minister Subhas Chakraborty, at the opening of *tramjatra* Kolkata in March 2001, declared that Calcutta's tram network would be extended. And Mukherjee reacted by writing, 'It's another gimmick by the transport minister to attract attention.' However unjustified Mukherjee's criticism may have been, it must be admitted that the transport minister's public professions of support for this mode of transport were little better than an eyewash. He wanted to get a good press before elections. Not unsurprisingly, even after four whole years back in power, the minister has done nothing to improve the tramways infrastructure. On the contrary, the tracks are gradually being truncated. The longest tram route in Calcutta used to once extend from Galiff Street in the deep north to Tollygunge, furthest south. Now the mid-section in central Calcutta is missing. The same is the case with Ballygunge and Gariahat in south Calcutta where a monstrous flyover was erected recently. Thereafter, tram tracks on that section, too, had to be lopped off. Some others will follow suit.

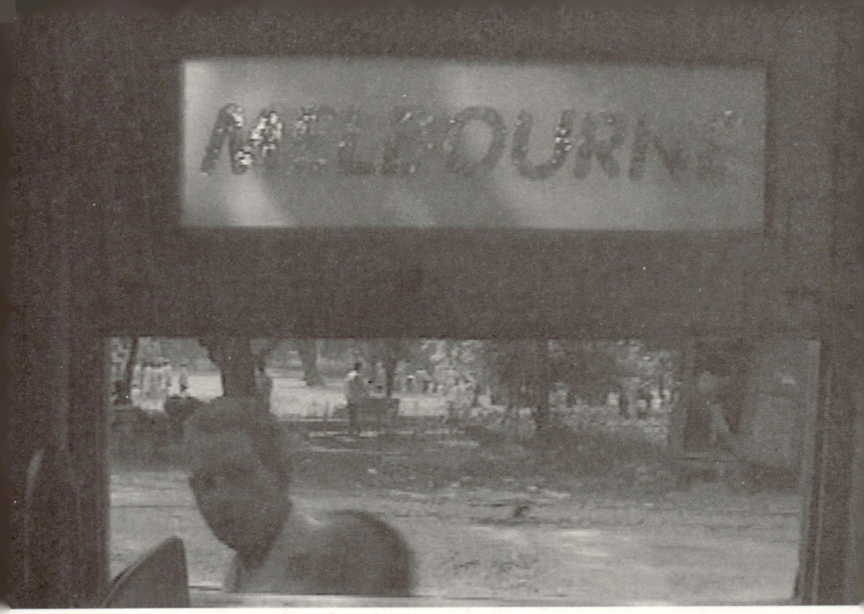

But why, in the first place, did Douglas and D'Andrea think of bringing together Calcutta and Melbourne, albeit symbolically? No two cities could have been so unlike each other. Calcutta, ironically known as the City of Joy, has earned the reputation of being a pigsty, on which, from time to time, members of the affluent international community descend to buy penitence on the cheap. Whereas Melbourne has been labelled the 'most livable' city. A thing they have in common is their tramways. However, unlike Calcutta, trams of Melbourne do not face any existential crisis.

Doubtless, neither D'Andrea nor Douglas was fired by any reformatory zeal. They wanted to tell Calcutta that streetcars are still desirable. Douglas' primary concern was 'exploration and expression of the environmentally sustaining and culturally enriching potential tramways hold for their cities'.

For Douglas and the rest of the participants it was a trans-continental and cross-cultural journey that involved their dreams and memories, where even personal responses and feelings had symbolic and generic connotations. Receptacles of personal histories that we are, these take on a more expansive dimension when we embark on the path to relate to others. For even our most intensely personal reactions and feelings have resonances transcending geographical and cultural barriers that can be transferred from one to another. This is possible in aesthetic terms through storytelling and representation and collaborative efforts. In this case, tramways animated the thoughts and feelings of participants. So it mattered not for the participants that these vehicles have turned into bone-rattlers in Calcutta, whereas in Melbourne they are sophisticated. For them it was a dream vehicle that traversed the territories of the mind over a fixed route, periodically repeating its journey.

The participants came from varying backgrounds and even among the Indians there were yawning gaps in their social and economic status. From the lowest rungs came the patuas or scroll painters who belong to remote villages: Dukhushyam Chitrakar, Sarna Chitrakar and Moyna Chitrakar. In the social hierarchy, tram conductor Prabir Kumar Goswami is definitely above them. And participants like artist Jayashree Chakravarty and filmmaker Mahadeb Shi are a class apart. There were two other Indians who never made it to Australia but who were, nonetheless, involved in catalysing *tramjatra* – tram activists Debasish Bhattacharya and

Jayanta Basu, both vocal in their demand for retaining tramways. The Australians belong to the local community of artists and designers, of which D'Andrea now counts himself.

What the *tramjatra* participants created collaboratively was akin to a palimpsest where individual inputs were the various layers recording their different personal narratives, constructs and landscapes of memories as they travelled through time and space, literally and metaphorically. Their individual cultural inheritances played off against each other forming the facets of a collective whole. This was not a simple case of studies in contrasts, of the urban being juxtaposed with the folkloric, of the Third World with the First, or of the local with the global. *Tramjatra* attained a complex structure where the contrasts and the individual narratives complemented each other, each enriching the other and being nurtured in a symbiotic relationship. The objective was to stimulate public imagination as *tramjatra* was staged over a period of time in the public domain of streets, tram terminuses, the tram tracks themselves, in newspapers and the RMIT gallery.

When *tramjatra* began in Calcutta in February 2001, Mark Misic, an artist and former tram conductor from Australia, created diamonds with the colours of spring at the intersections of tram tracks. Except for the itinerant street plays organised to celebrate the anniversary of Tagore's birth, such public performances are rare in Calcutta. But street artists (actually vagabonds with a flair for drawing the likenesses of Hindu gods and goddesses) who use the street or pavement as their canvas are quite a common sight in all Indian cities. India also has a strong tradition of rangoli in the south and alpona in eastern India. Very similar to Misic's conception,

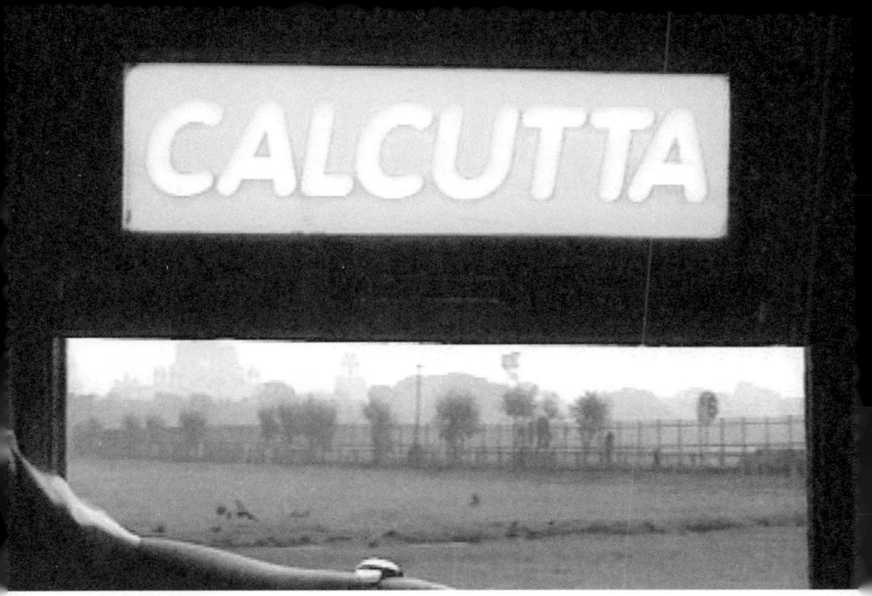


women use green, red and yellow powder to trace on floors colourful patterns called rangoli during festivals. In Orissa and Bengal, women make lotuses and creepers bloom spontaneously on floors with white ground rice, using their fingers fluidly like a brush.

While the aesthetic concerns of Misic may have been quite different from those of street artists and the women who execute rangoli and alpona, their works have one thing in common: these patterns are by nature ephemeral, meant to disappear in twenty-four hours or less – soon after the party is over. Such a common thread running through two apparently dissimilar cultures could be traced quite easily. It was not by accident that a 'decorator', better known for erecting pandals in Calcutta street corners during Durga puja, the city's biggest festival, had been engaged by Melbourne architect James Legge to erect at the Esplanade tram depot a structure of matting and plywood that was a copy of *Vault* by Ron Robertson-Swann, Melbourne's most vilified public sculpture. *Vault* had so outraged public sensibility after its initial installation that it was difficult for it to find a permanent place for itself. It has been, like a tram, a Melbourne icon shunted to different parts of the city. In Calcutta, Mahadeb Shi's film featuring Kolkata's tram 'Kather Bakso' (Wooden Box) was projected on the *Vault* replica. The film was also shown at the RMIT gallery in Melbourne, a venue that had turned into a hub for *tramjatra* akin to a tramways depot. However, perhaps even the weather gods had something against *Vault*. For soon after its replica was erected, an unseasonal nor'-wester crashed on the city from nowhere and wreaked havoc with the exhibits.

If one thought that the folk painters and performers from Midnapore would react with naivete when called upon to relate to trams one could not have been more mistaken. The element of fantasy in their pre-cinematic linear image sequence (which they accompany with singing) is what linked them to Douglas' earlier video artwork *Tracking* and Jayashree Chakravarty's imaginary maps that she had traced both in Calcutta and with eloquent effect on PVC sheets in Melbourne. Lisa Young's remarkable installation *Curious Yellow*, too, reverberated with this sense of fantasy slipping in and out of the realm of the unconscious.

In earlier days, Douglas, driven by his interest in art in the public realm, developed a 'speculative image' in his mind of a non-passenger tracking vehicle created with audio-visual technology. It was imagined to be an 'ephemeral civic museum' that would transmit images and sounds in streets. But he feared that the idea would be appropriated by the market. He produced a video installation where the tram was a phantasmagoric vehicle circulating non-stop through ever-changing vistas of Melbourne dreaming. In 1997, when Douglas visited Calcutta, he had 'stumbled upon' the scroll performing patuas. The fantastical linear image sequence is what attracted him to them. The bizarre lengths that the semi-literate Moyna Chitrakar had to go to get hold of her passport could easily inspire a magic realism novel. Which is nothing unusual for her, given the mythical and folkloric nature of the pats (scrolls) she creates. She and Dukhu, like others of their kind, have proved their surprising adaptability by producing propaganda material on issues such as adult literacy and prevention of common diseases. Their antediluvian aeroplanes were like men with bulging midriffs and their trams were humanoid vehicles with smiling faces in keeping with their belief that it is a kinder and gentler mode of transport that never ignores people in distress. It is, after all, cheaper and slower than any other.

In Calcutta, the pats had been enlarged and displayed at the tram depot, interfacing with Jayashree Chakravarty's seven panels that looked like a cross between graffiti and maps. On this mental landscape Chakravarty delineated imaginary tram tracks. So the folkloric encountered the contemporary. In Melbourne she had discovered a perfect vehicle for realising her concept in the transparent PVC sheet. This screen stretched across the pathway seemed to be the gateway to the real world of actual road and passage that one accessed through the realm of imagination – her painted tracks running through labelled territories she has, and has not visited. 'It was meant to give the impression that it was either being unfolded or being rolled up,' says Chakravarty – the element of ambivalence being crucial in her scheme of things.

The same undertow of uncertainty informed Lisa Young's installation *Curious Yellow* – a bright yellow W-class tram sticking out of a Melbourne sidewalk. It left viewers wondering whether it was emerging or submerging, appearing or disappearing. A bright toy that, nonetheless, carried dark undertones and played on our lurking fears of the subterranean world. Festive yet unsettling. That this feeling was intentional was indicated by the title of the work that referred to the controversial Swedish film of 1967. In those days the film was not allowed to be screened in the USA.

Familiar everyday objects gain the attributes of the strange and extraordinary once they are taken out of their quotidian context. Douglas appropriated the 'prow', a device unique to Melbourne roads that allows tram passengers to get on and off safely at mid-street stops. As its name suggests, this front-of-boat shaped structure tips up vehicles that do not leave any leeway for tram-ways infrastructure. Calcutta's tramways need them desperately. Douglas relocated bright yellow prows made of concrete from their roadside posts and re-engaged them in new positions in the cityscape as a temporary location for *tramjatra* projects. It was a leitmotif that facilitated and enabled the dialogue between the several works. Not every member of the citizenry was, however, pleased with this use that the familiar prow had been put to. A passerby expressed his displeasure in a letter to a Melbourne newspaper.

Mark Misic's magnetic portraits of tram drivers in Melbourne pasted on poles carrying the network of overhead wiring, too, seemed to have outraged somebody's sense of propriety. For the stickers carrying smiling faces used to be systematically removed. Misic maintained that 'a smiling trammy face might very well be a threat to the municipal powers that run silver town's hygienic empty public spaces'. Calcuttans used to seeing walls being vandalised with graffiti and posters would be mystified and amused by such a reaction. Misic nostalgically craved Calcutta's hurly burly:

'I long for the dust of Kolkata, you can see everything there – even the space.' *Tramjatra* creates a space – albeit mental – where two apparently disparate cultures can emote. We are still getting there but a beginning has been made. The tracks have been re-laid in our memory.

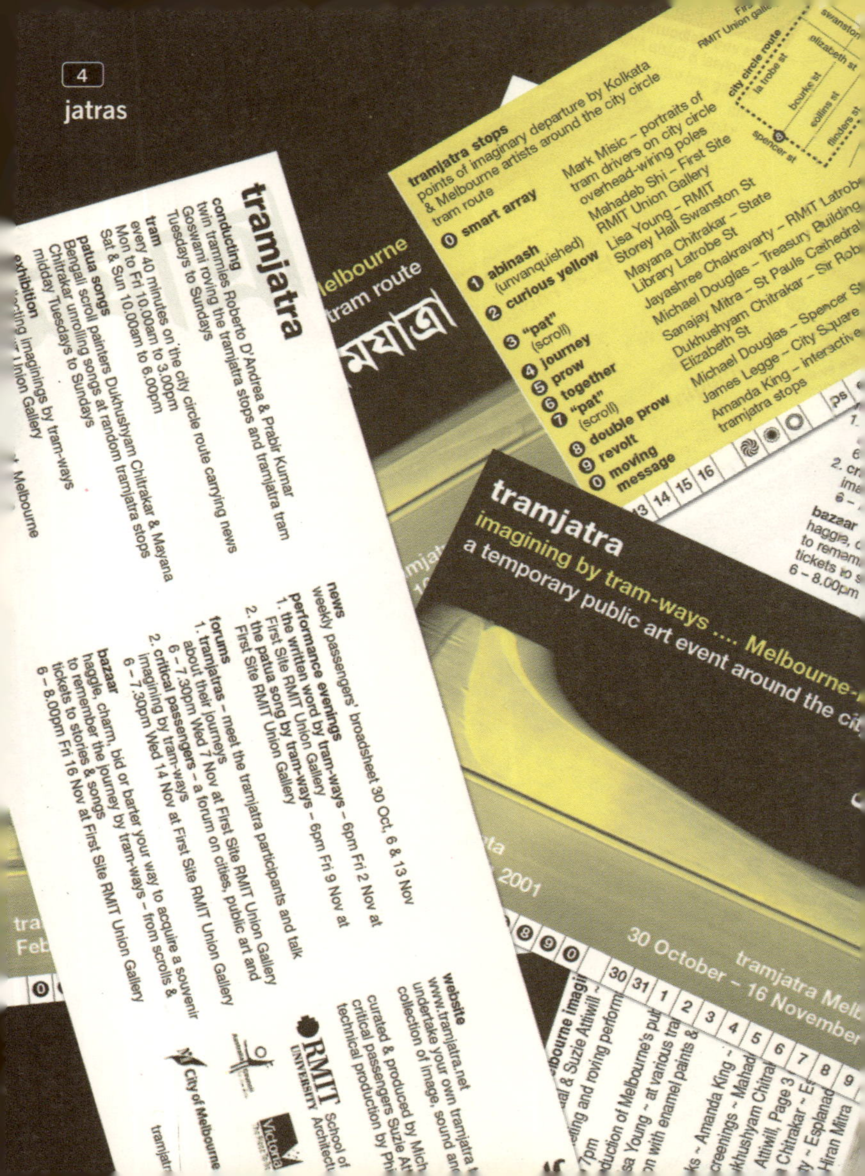
tramjatra
conducting
twin trammies Roberto D'Andrea & Prabir Kumar Goswami roving the tramjatra stops and tramjatra tram
Tuesdays to Sundays
tram
every 40 minutes on the city circle route carrying news
Mon to Fri 10.00am to 3.00pm
Sat & Sun 10.00am to 6.00pm
patua songs
Bengali scroll painters Dukhushyam Chitrakar & Mayana Chitrakar unrolling songs at random tramjatra stops
midday Tuesdays to Sundays
news
weekly passengers' broadsheet 30 Oct, 6 & 13 Nov
performance evenings
1. the written word by tram-ways – 6pm Fri 2 Nov at First Site RMIT Union Gallery
2. the patua song by tram-ways – 6pm Fri 9 Nov at First Site RMIT Union Gallery
forums
1. tramjatras – meet the tramjatra participants and talk about their journeys
6 – 7.30pm Wed 7 Nov at First Site RMIT Union Gallery
2. critical passengers – a forum on cities, public art and imagining by tram-ways
6 – 7.30pm Wed 14 Nov at First Site RMIT Union Gallery
bazaar
haggle, charm, bid or barter your way to acquire a souvenir to remember the journey by tram-ways – from scrolls & tickets to stories & songs
6 – 8.00pm Fri 16 Nov at First Site RMIT Union Gallery
website
www.tramjatra.net
tramjatra stops
points of imaginary departure by Kolkata & Melbourne artists around the city circle tram route
0 smart array – Mark Misic – portraits of tram drivers on city circle overhead-wiring poles
1 abinash (unvanquished) – Mahadeb Shi – First Site RMIT Union Gallery
2 curious yellow – Lisa Young – RMIT Storey Hall Swanston St
3 "pat" (scroll) – Mayana Chitrakar – State Library Latrobe St
city circle route
spencer st
bourke st
collins st
elizabeth st
tramjatra
imagining by tram-ways .... Melbourne
a temporary public art event around the
30 October – 16 November
2001
City of Melbourne

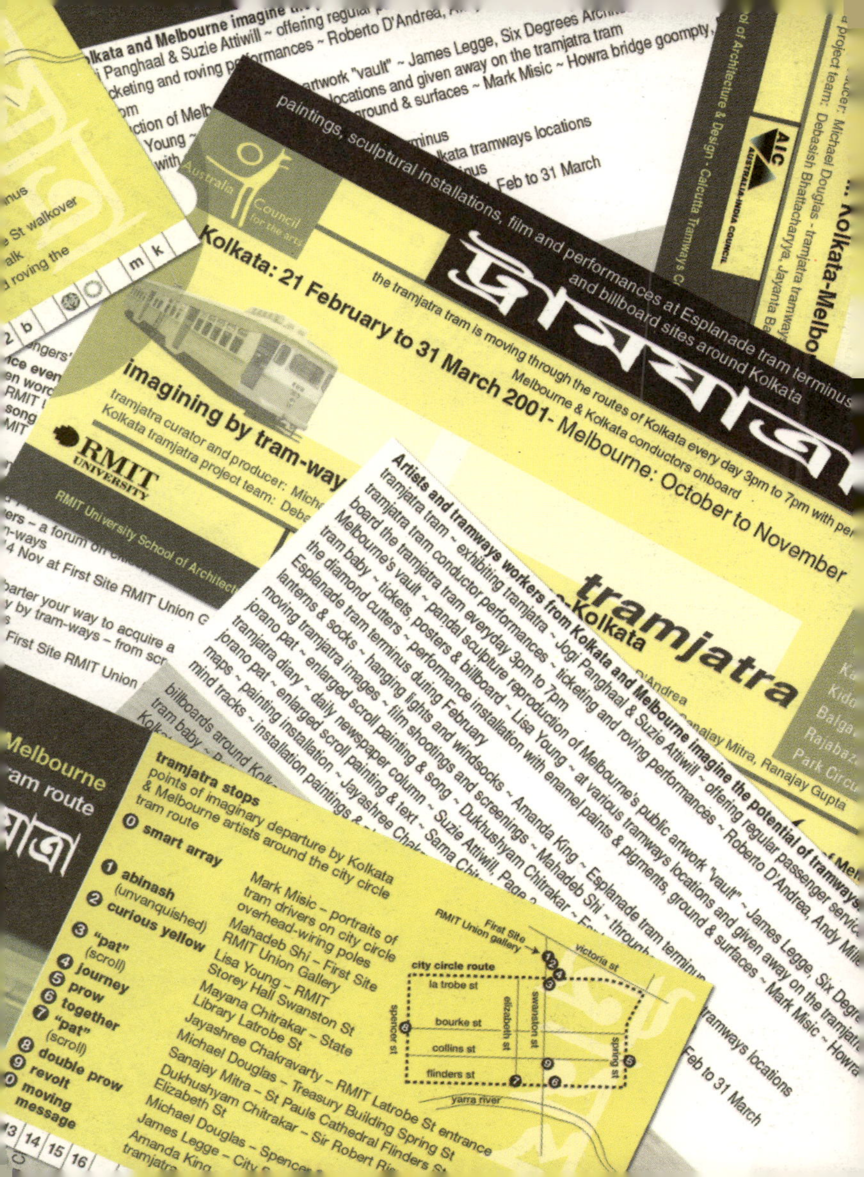
paintings, sculptural installations, film and performances at Esplanade tram terminus
and billboard sites around Kolkata
Kolkata: 21 February to 31 March 2001- Melbourne: October to November
the tramjatra tram is moving through the routes of Kolkata every day 3pm to 7pm with
Melbourne & Kolkata conductors onboard
imagining by tram-way
tramjatra curator and producer: Mich
Kolkata tramjatra project team: Deba
RMIT UNIVERSITY
RMIT University School of Architecture
Australia Council for the arts
tramjatra
Artists and tramways workers from Kolkata and Melbourne imagine the potential of tramways
tramjatra tram ~ exhibiting tramjatra ~ Jogi Panghaal & Suzie Attiwill ~ offering regular passenger servic
tramjatra tram conductor performances ~ ticketing and roving performances ~ Roberto D'Andrea, Andy Mil
board the tramjatra tram everyday 3pm to 7pm
Melbourne's vault ~ pandal sculpture reproduction of Melbourne's public artwork "vault" ~ James Legge, Six Degre
tram baby ~ tickets, posters & billboard ~ Lisa Young ~ at various tramways locations and given away on the tramjatr
the diamond cutters ~ performance installation with enamel paints & pigments, ground & surfaces ~ Mark Misic ~ Howra
Esplanade tram terminus during February
lanterns & socks ~ hanging lights and windsocks ~ Amanda King ~ Esplanade tram terminus
moving tramjatra images ~ film shootings and screenings ~ Mahadeb Shi ~ through
jorano pat ~ enlarged scroll painting & song ~ Dukhushyam Chitrakar
tramjatra diary ~ daily newspaper column ~ Suzie Attiwill
jorano pat ~ enlarged scroll painting & text ~ Sama Chi
maps ~ painting installation ~ Jayashree Cha
mind tracks ~ installation paintings
Melbourne
tram route
tramjatra stops
points of imaginary departure by Kolkata & Melbourne artists around the city circle tram route
0 smart array
1 abinash (unvanquished) — Mark Misic – portraits of tram drivers on city circle overhead-wiring poles
2 curious yellow — Mahadeb Shi – First Site RMIT Union Gallery
3 "pat" (scroll) — Lisa Young – RMIT Storey Hall Swanston St
4 journey — Mayana Chitrakar – State Library Latrobe St
5 prow — Jayashree Chakravarty – RMIT Latrobe St entrance
6 together — Michael Douglas – Treasury Building Spring St
7 "pat" (scroll) — Sanajay Mitra – St Pauls Cathedral Flinders St
8 double prow — Dukhushyam Chitrakar – Sir Robert Ris
9 revolt — Elizabeth St
0 moving message — Michael Douglas – Spencer
James Legge – City
Amanda King
city circle route
First Site RMIT Union gallery
victoria st
la trobe st
bourke st
collins st
flinders st
spencer st
elizabeth st
swanston st
spring st
yarra river
Kolkata-Melbo
project team: Debasish Bhattacharyya, Jayanta Ba
AIC AUSTRALIA-INDIA COUNCIL
School of Architecture & Design - Calcutta Tramways C
Kolkata and Melbourne imagine
Panghaal & Suzie Attiwill ~ offering regular
ticketing and roving performances ~ Roberto D'Andrea
artwork "vault" ~ James Legge, Six Degrees Arch
locations and given away on the tramjatra tram
ground & surfaces ~ Mark Misic ~ Howra bridge goompty
kata tramways locations
Feb to 31 March
ers – a forum on
4 Nov at First Site RMIT Union G
barter your way to acquire a
y by tram-ways – from scr
First Site RMIT Union
billboards around Kol
tram baby
St walkover
roving the
Sanajay Mitra, Ranajay Gupta
tramways locations
Feb to 31 March

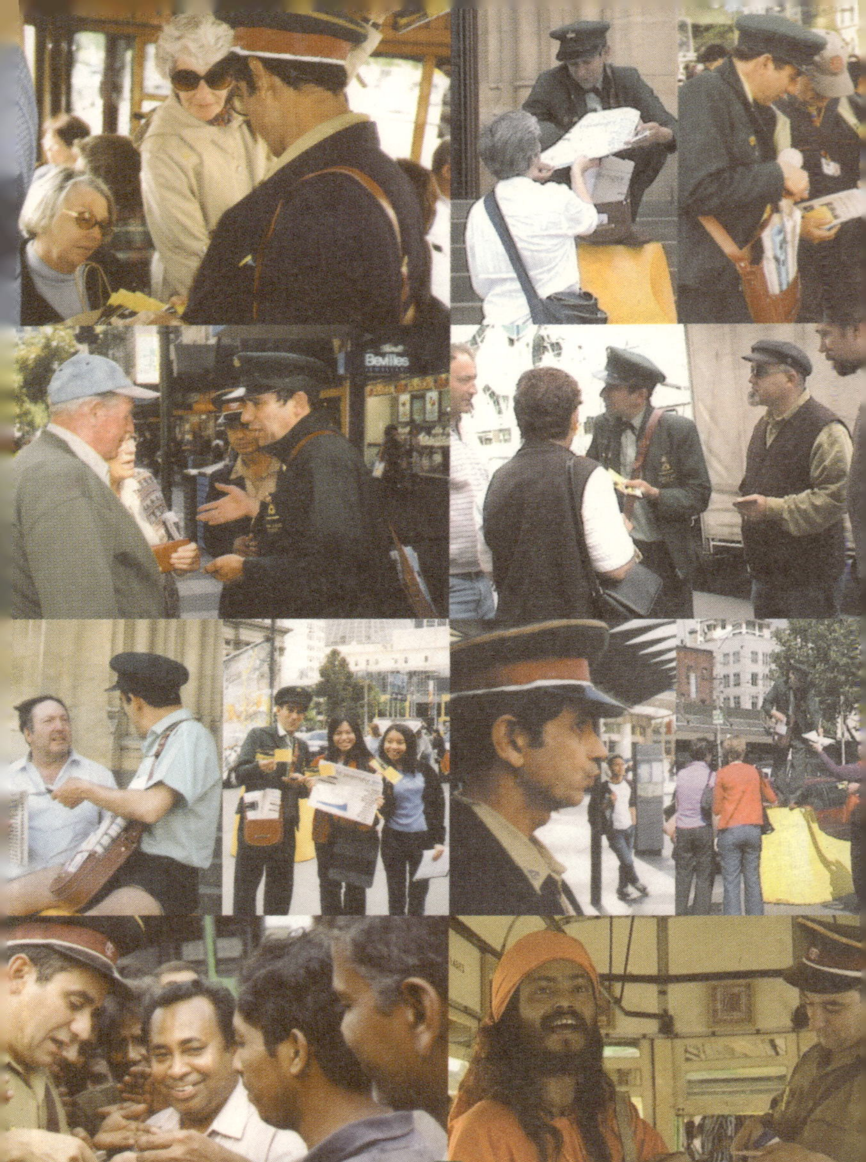
Bevilles

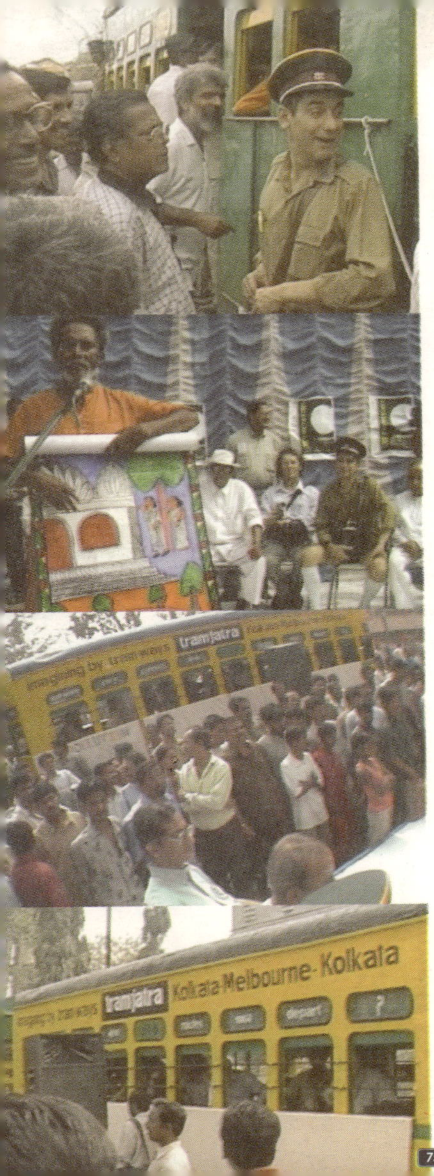


Often you need just to find someone in the crowd that accepts a ticket for the first thing, and you start a dialogue, and that dialogue then is overheard by the rest of the tram travellers, and it warms the crowd up, so all of a sudden you start a bridging with a little bit of a storytelling and yarning. In the space of ten minutes you're conducting the tram.
*Roberto D'Andrea*

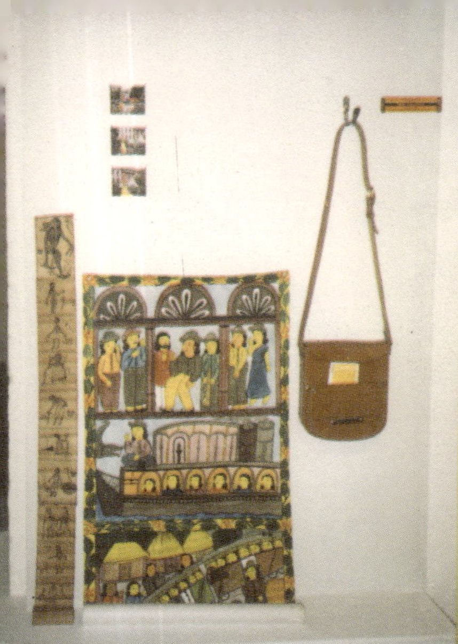
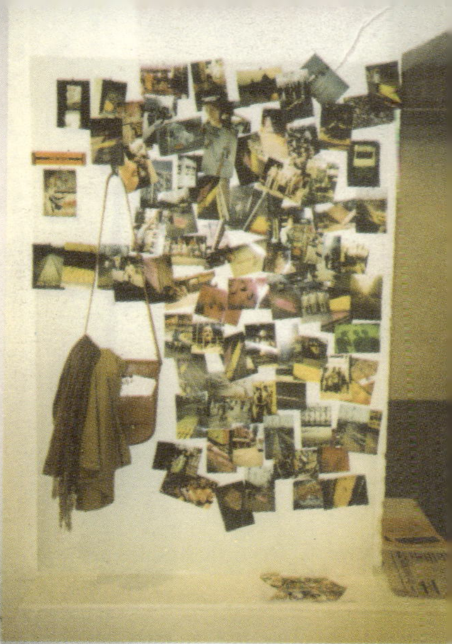
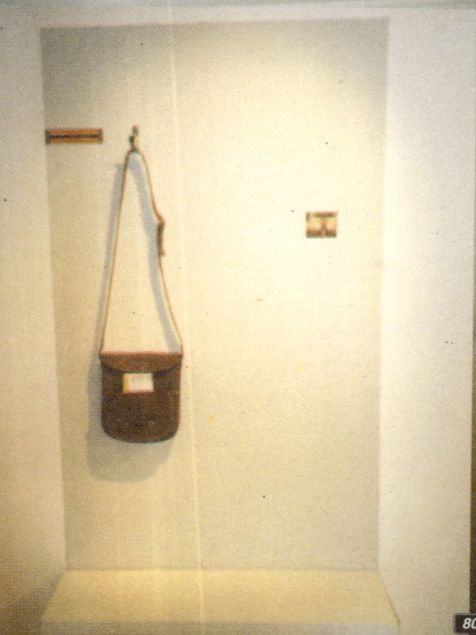
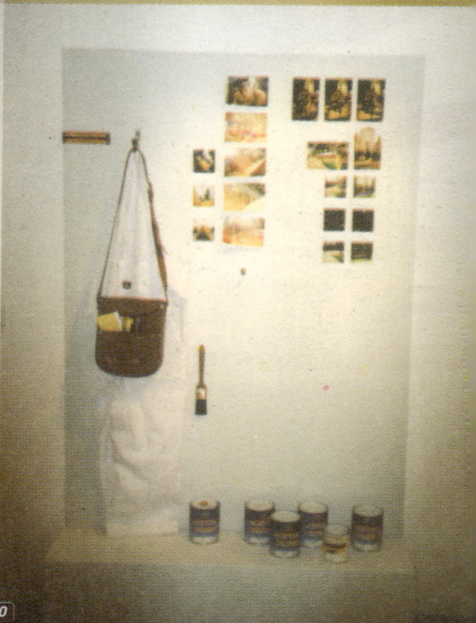

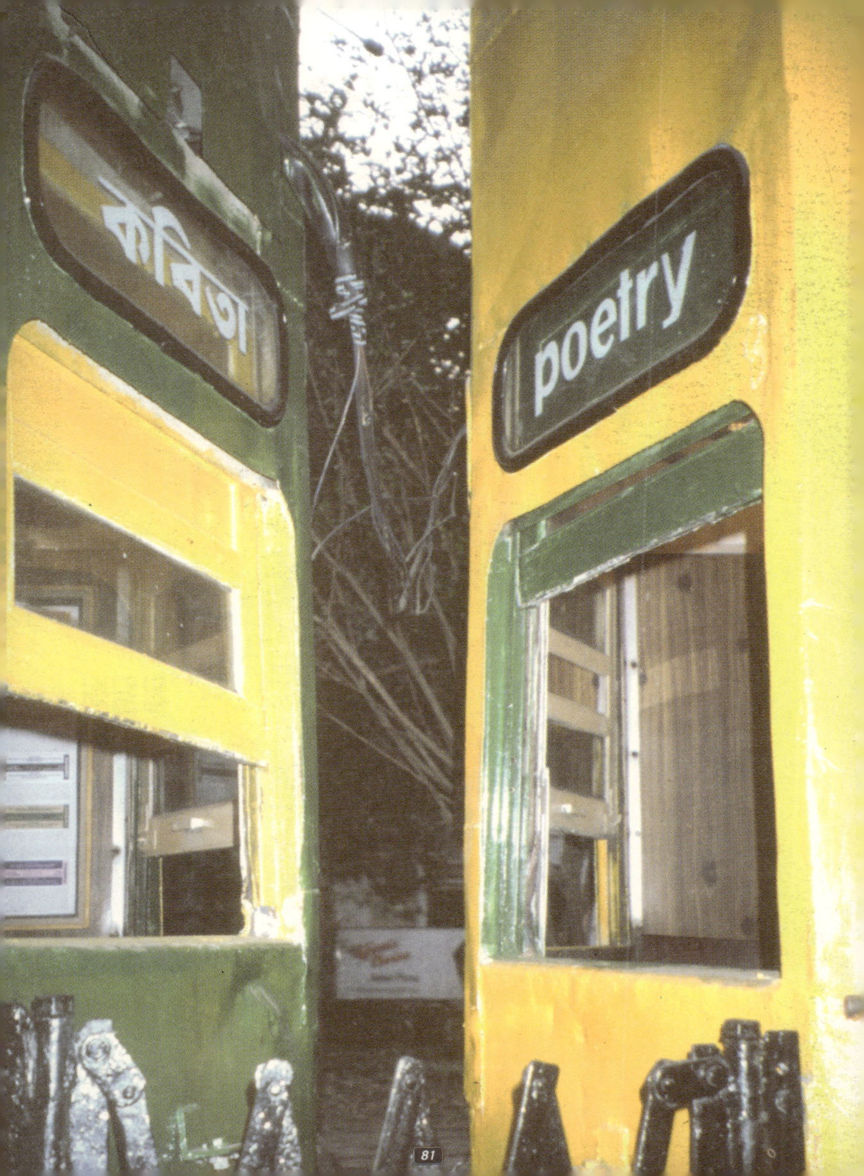
কবিতা
poetry

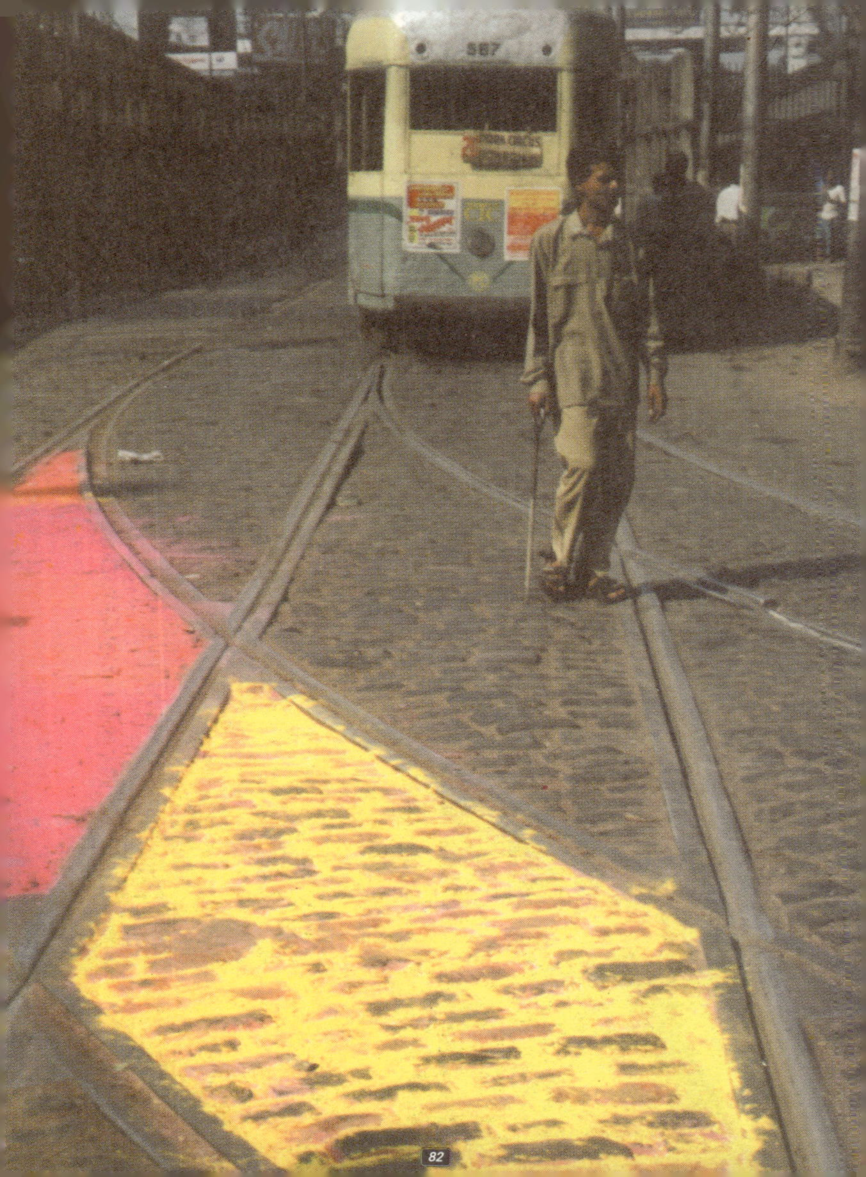

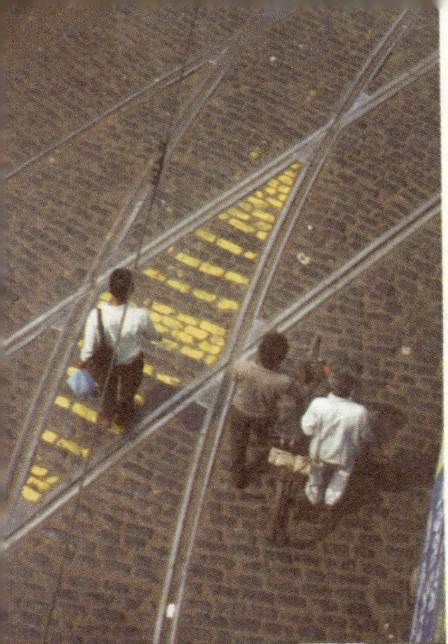

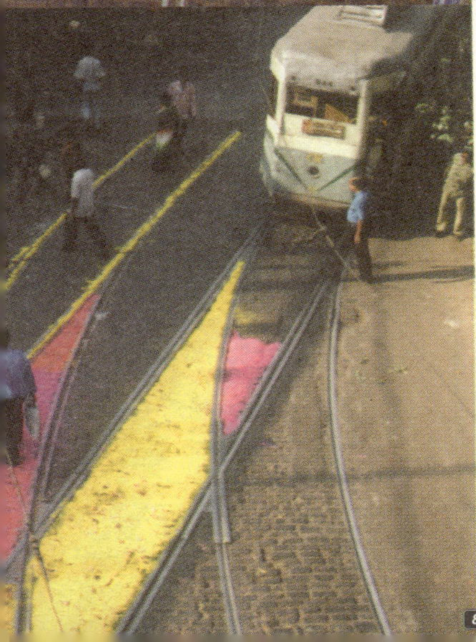

The pigment project was motivated by a desire to play with people; to be able to get out there and show off and see what came of it in the streets of Calcutta.
I worked with the trammies in the Howrah terminus. The tram tracks with their unique lines became the zone to make the temporary pigment installation performances. I could not have done anything like this in Melbourne. I remember seeing the policeman doing hand directions at the corner, then cars hurling towards me driving all over the pigment. I think: do I get off, or do I continue the performance? Fortunately the motor beasts narrowly miss me and their tyres carry the bright green pigment into the city as I hear local people saying in Bengali 'Pagla' ('He's a bit mad!').
*Mark Misic*

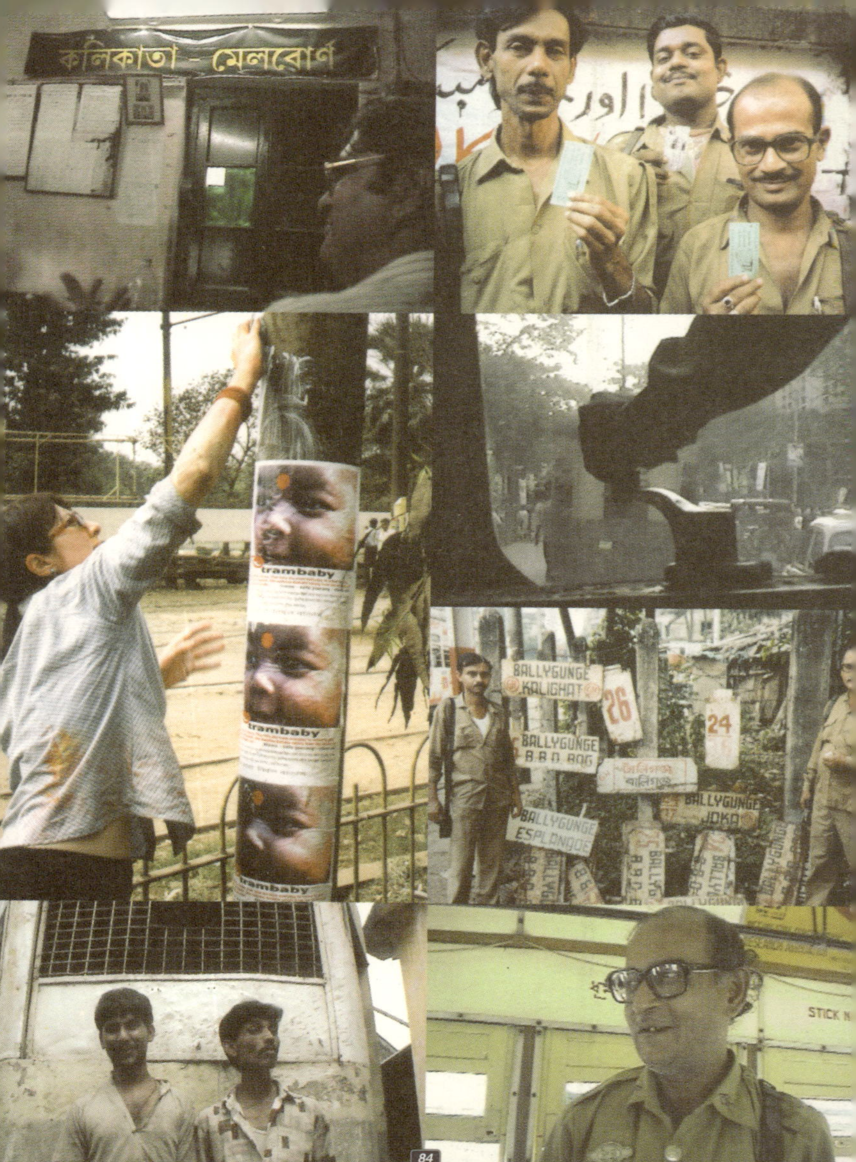
কলিকাতা - মেলবোর্ণ
trambaby
trambaby
trambaby
BALLYGUNGE KALIGHAT
26
24
BALLYGUNGE B.B.D. BAG
BALLYGUNGE JOKA
BALLYGUNGE ESPLANADE
STICK N

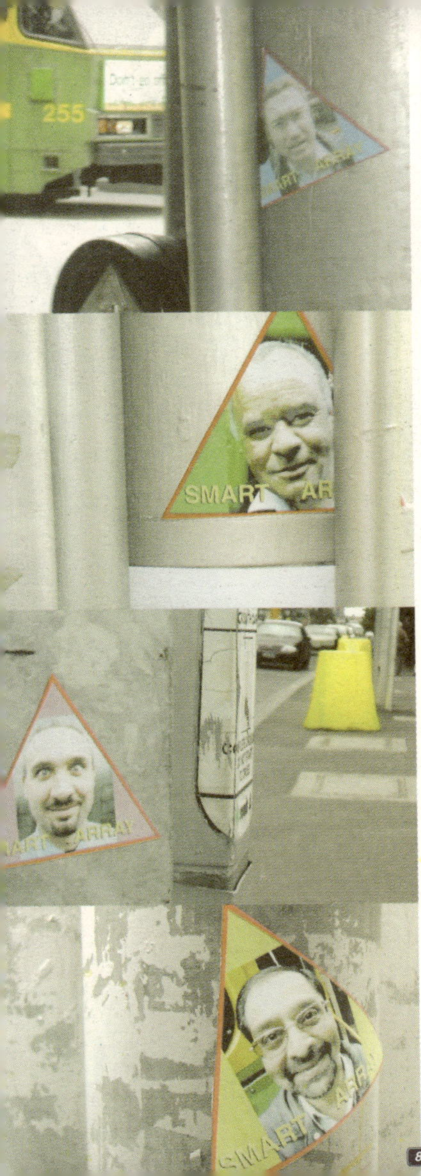


An array of smiling tram drivers' faces are being stuck on and picked off tramway poles in Melbourne. I like the way stickers travel in this city, jokers on this serious town.
*Mark Misic*

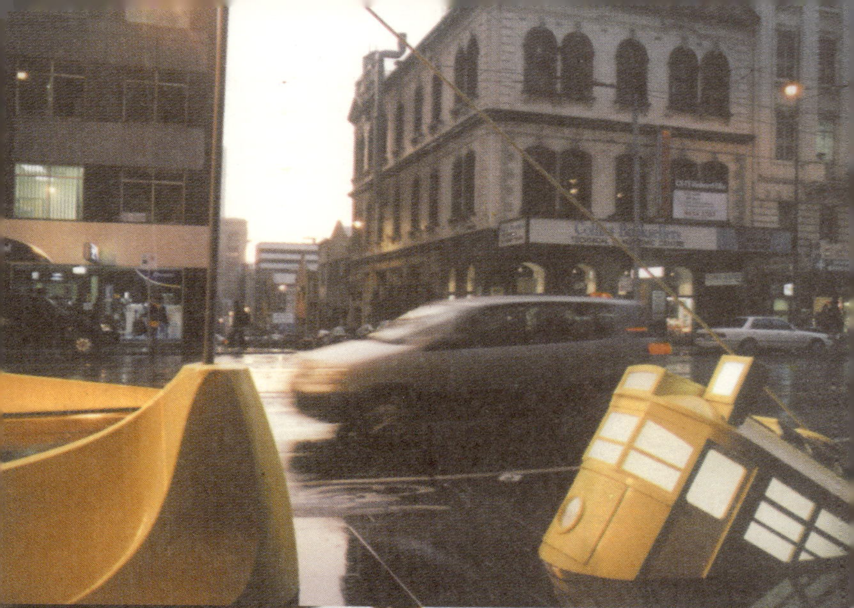

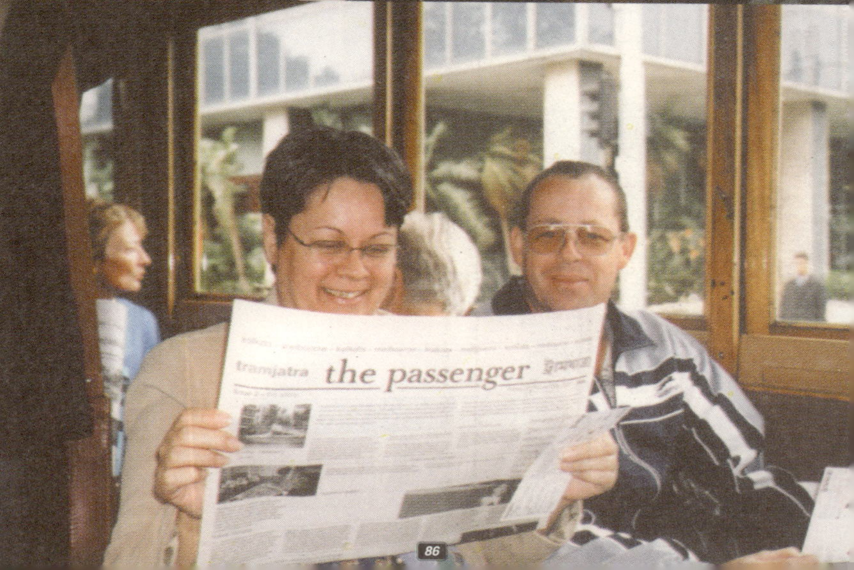
tramjatra
the passenger

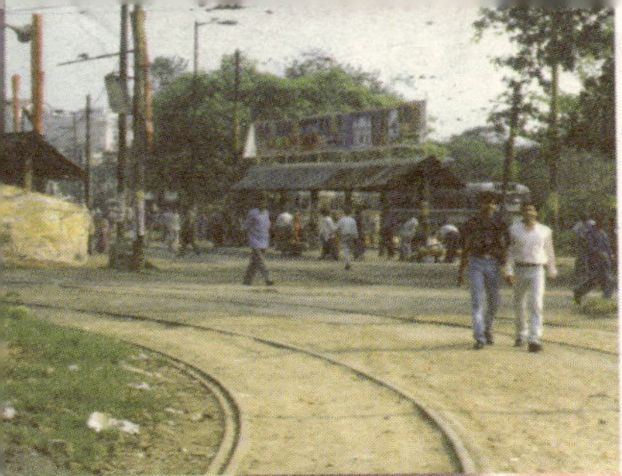

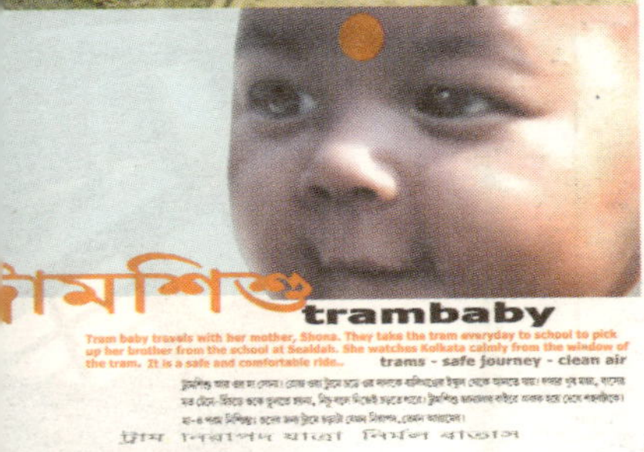


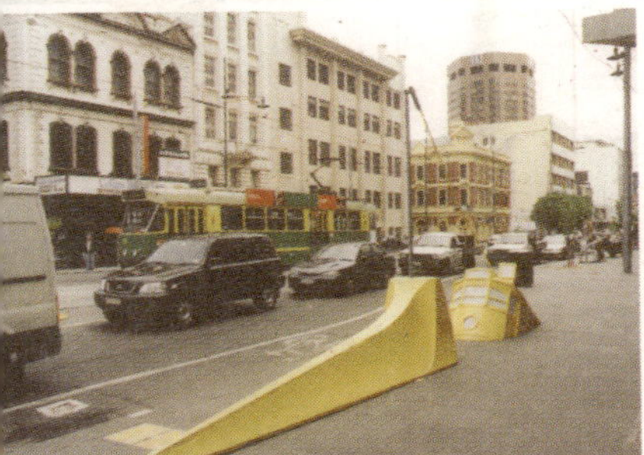

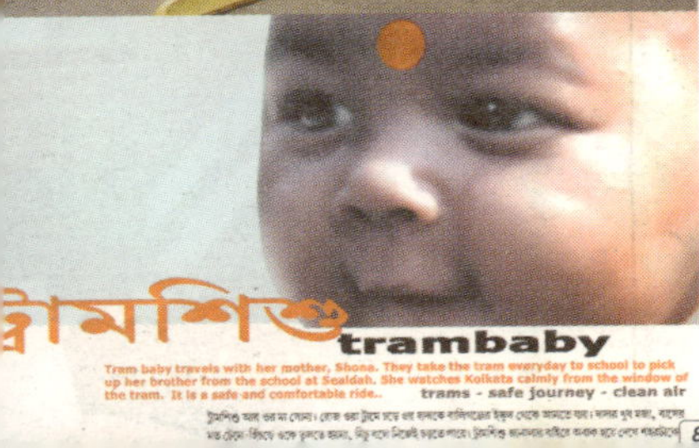


In a city I am in awe of and overwhelmed by, I do not feel I can comment. I am no expert – about trams or about Indian trams or about India or about cities or about Calcutta or about Art or about Art in this context. Total crisis! What am I to do? I imagine a series of cards to be given away – the cards would speak of the small ways that everyday people use the trams, the ordinary process of moving around that occurs anywhere. The one card we do celebrates Sarna's new and delightful baby girl – amazingly named Trambaby! She is Sarna's fourth child and was born during an earlier phase of the project. She represented for me a future entitlement – to safe travel and clean air which she would witness with her calm and beautiful eyes.

*Lisa Young*

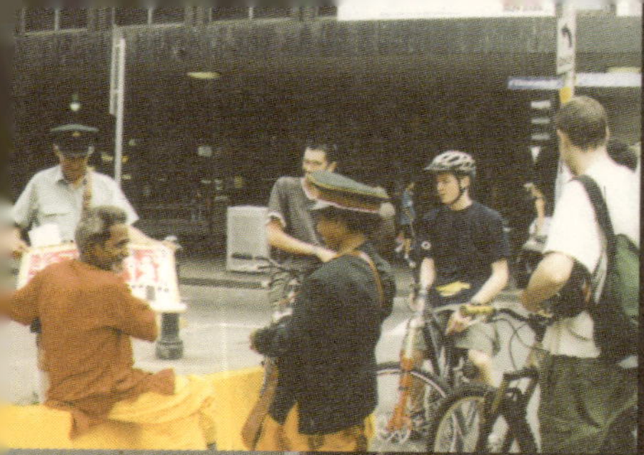

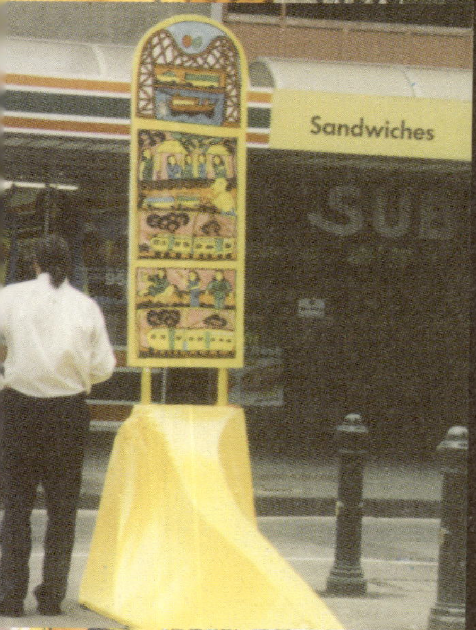
Sandwiches
SUB

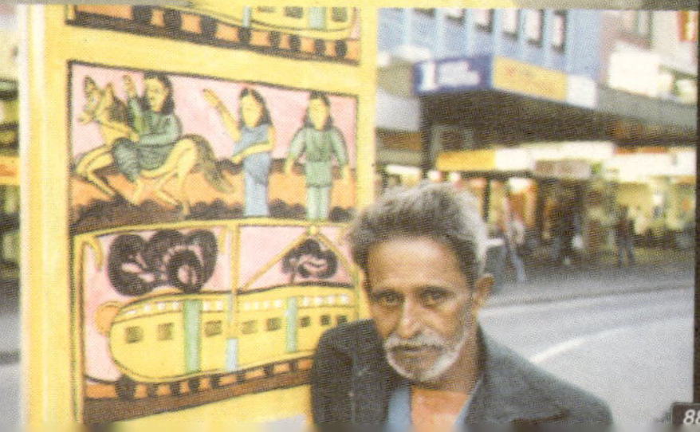

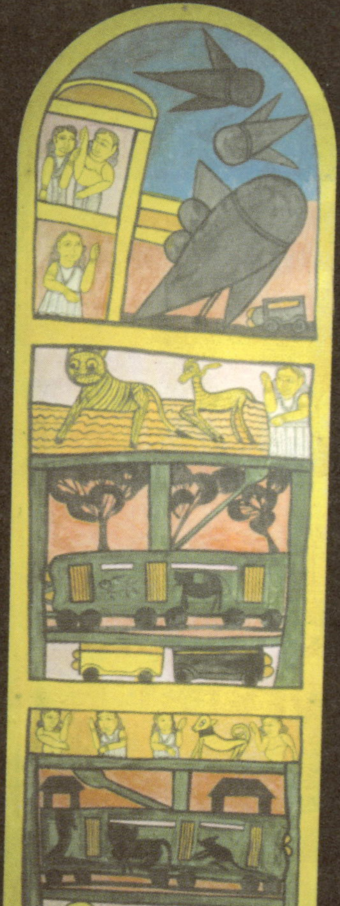

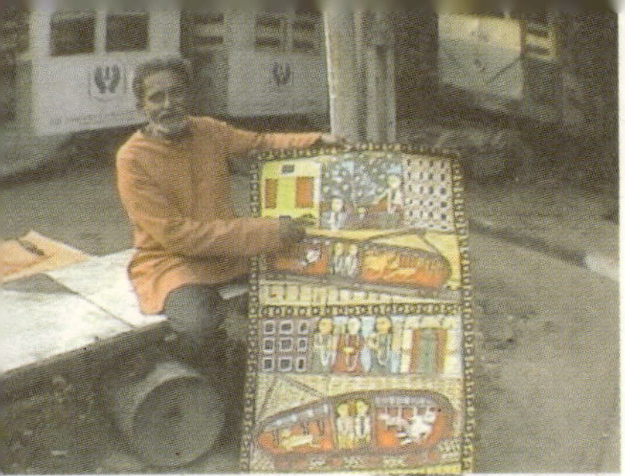

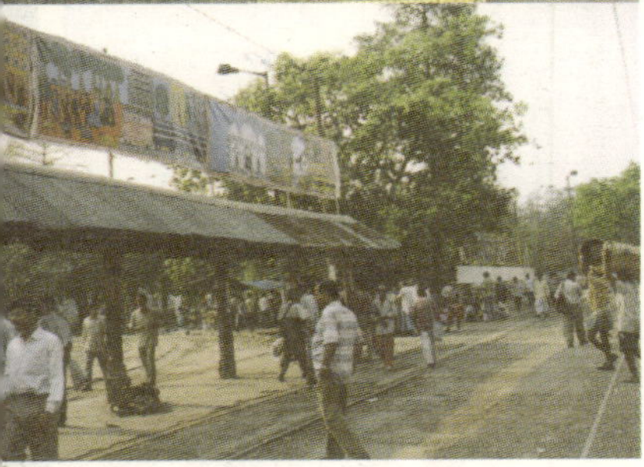

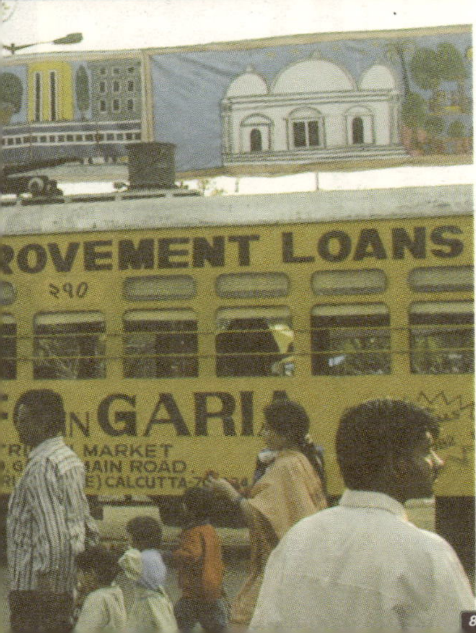


At Naya is my home

My home is within
Medinipur's Pingla Thana,
at Naya

My home is within
Medinipur's Pingla Thana,
at Naya

Thirty families of patuas
live there

We are thirty families
of patuas

Michael Douglas
came from Melbourne

With Mahadev
came Aparna Das

Came Aparna Das

Spoke about
trams eloquently

They spoke about
trams eloquently

I move ahead with trams

*Dukhushyam Chitrakar*

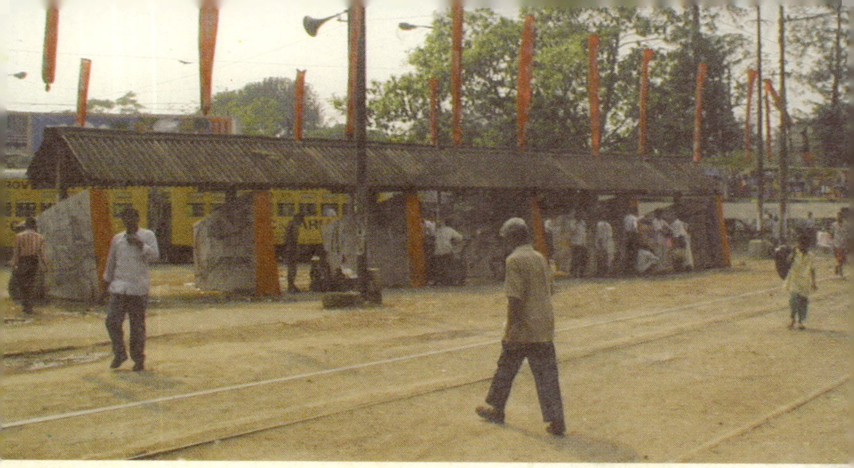

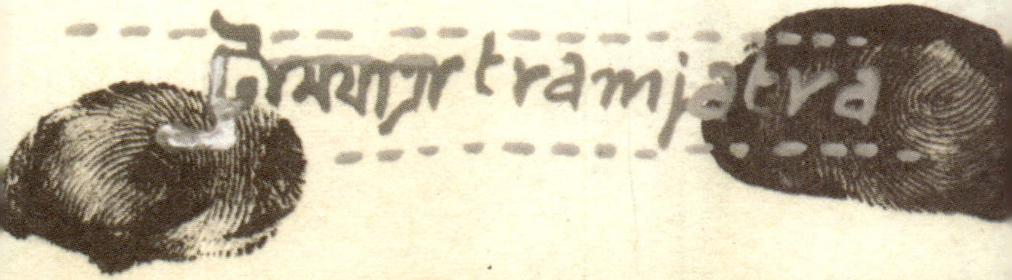
tramjatra

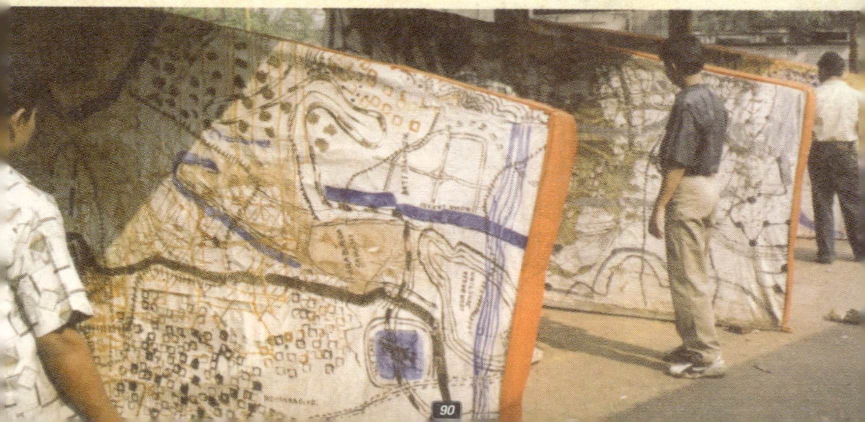

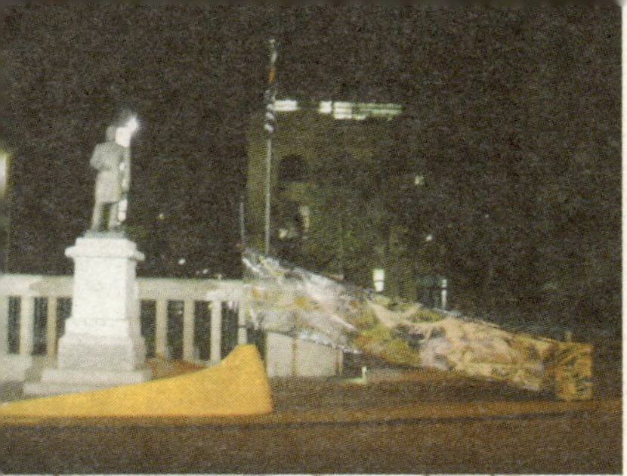

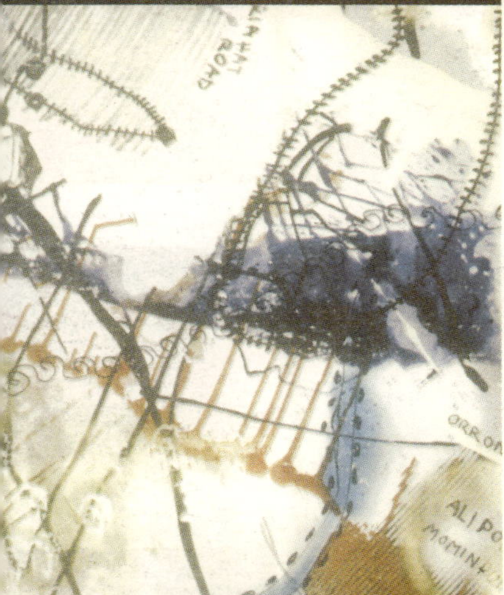

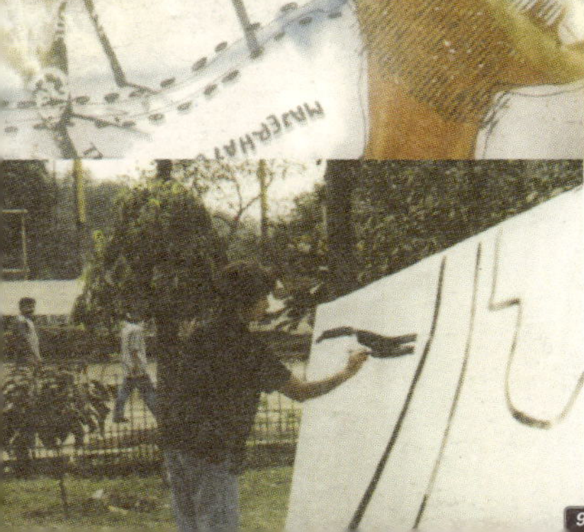

I work on maps, different sorts of maps. I am used to making work that goes into the gallery, within four walls. To see my work standing in public where people catch the tram – I never knew I could do anything like that.
*Jayashree Chakravarty*

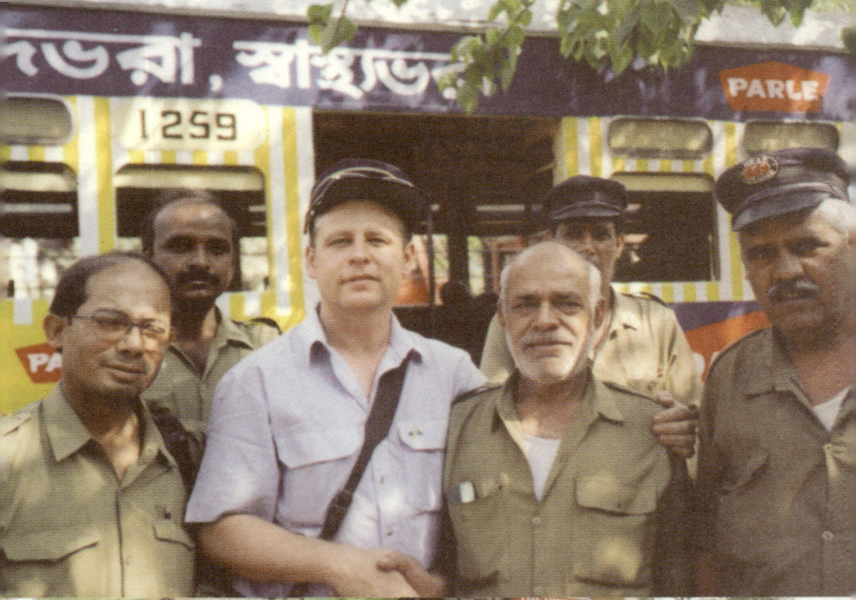
1259
PARLE

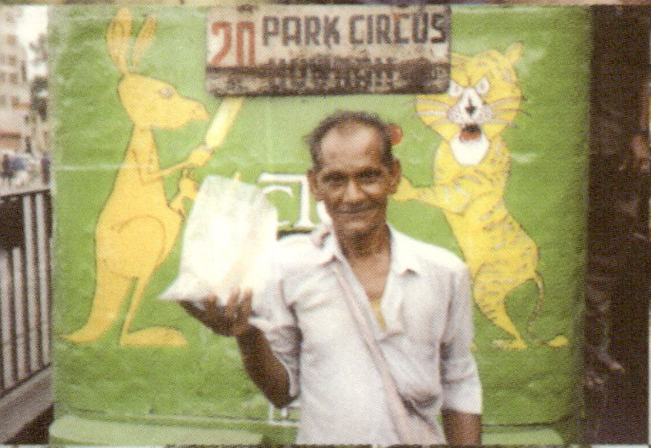
20 PARK CIRCUS

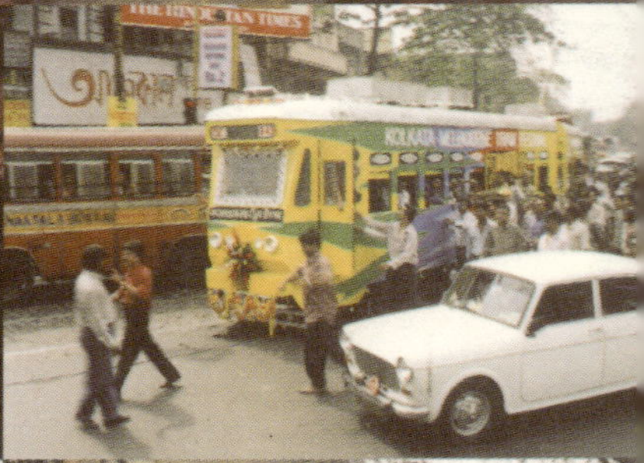

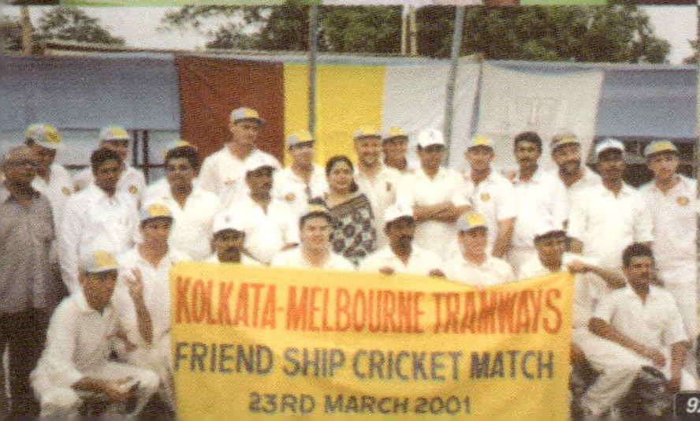
KOLKATA-MELBOURNE TRAMWAYS
FRIEND SHIP CRICKET MATCH
23RD MARCH 2001

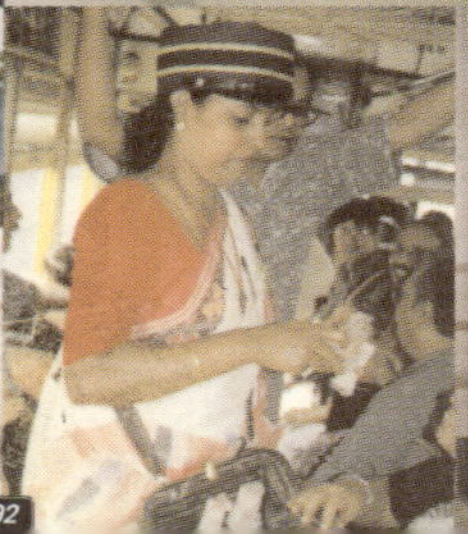

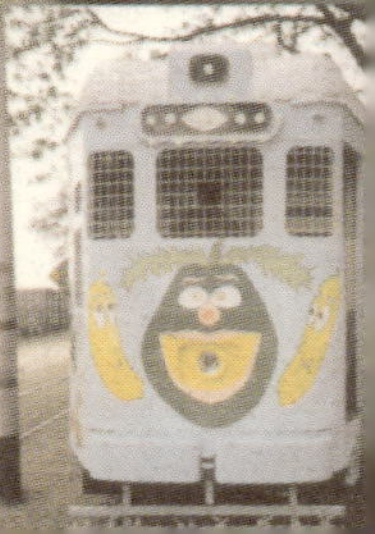

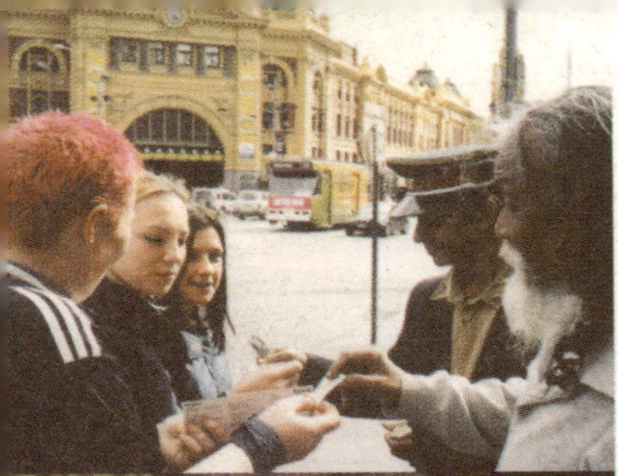

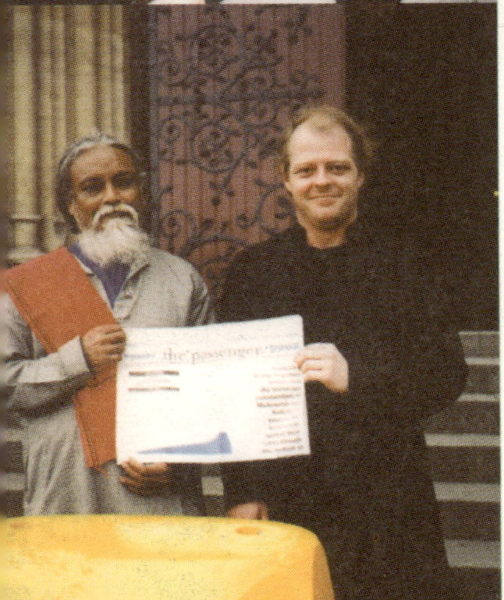



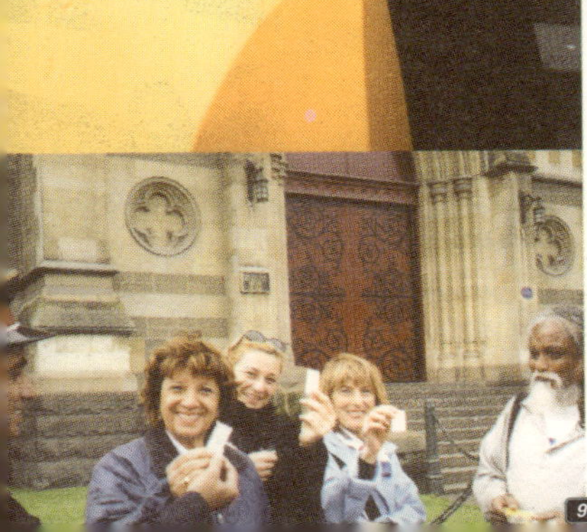

The simple word of friendship and a ticket to exchange can make a real sense of value.
*Andy Miller*

My work is to bring people together. My approach is based on being interactive with people and on the process of integrating the individual into the whole.
*Sanjay Mitra*

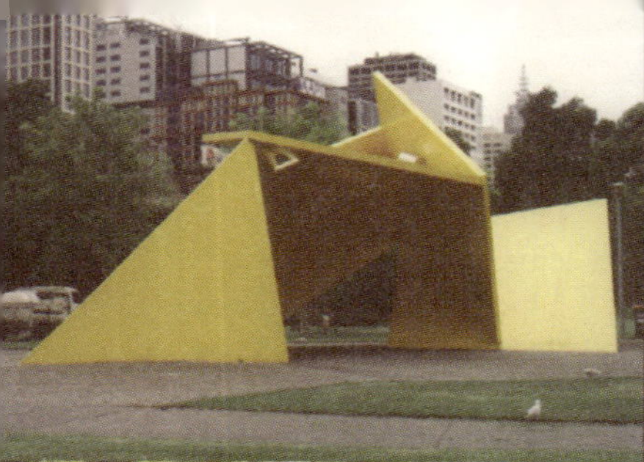

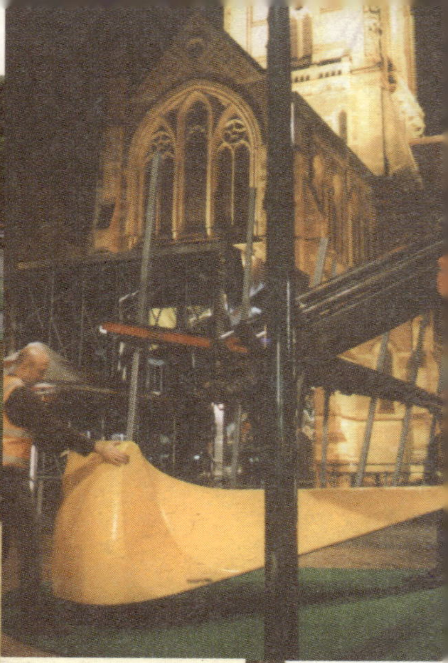

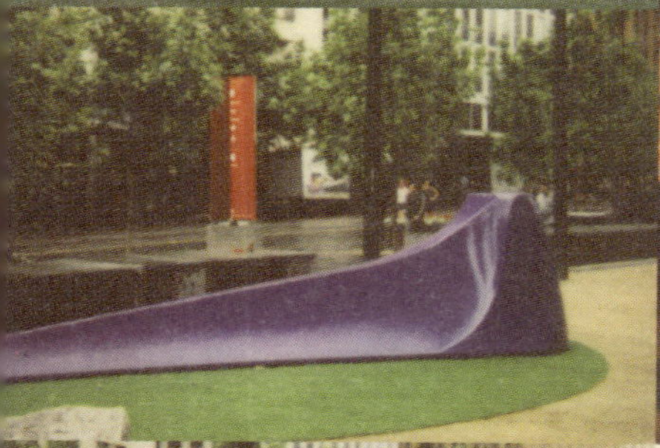

**THE AGE**
THURSDAY NOVEMBER 8, 2001
*BREAKING NEWS* theage.com.au

NOEL RYAN, Wollongong

## Tram protectors off the rails

The bright yellow tram-stop protectors, which have recently been put on the steps of both St Paul's and the Old Treasury, are inappropriate and disrespectful.

Why can't we all honor the heritage that has been given to us and leave safety barriers where they belong — on the road?

ROBERT SWAN, Fitzroy

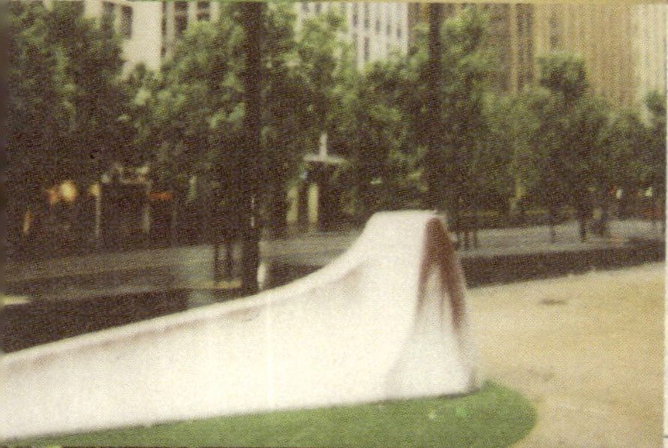

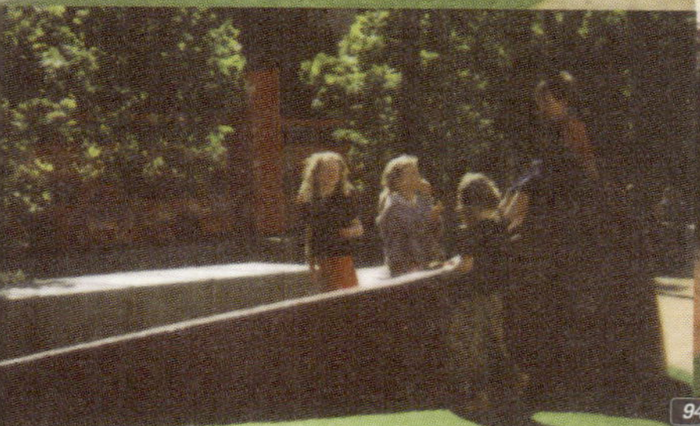

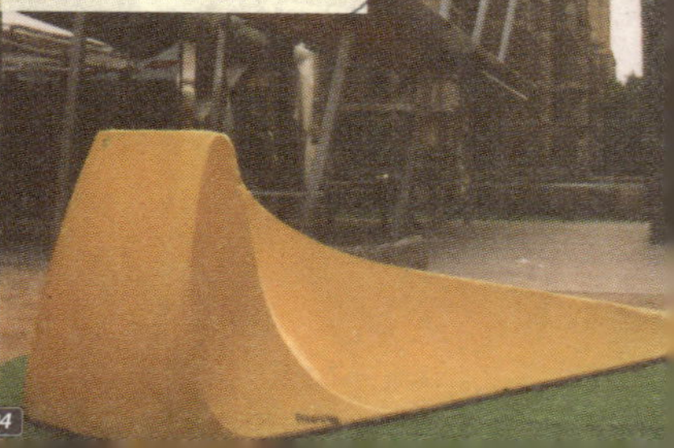

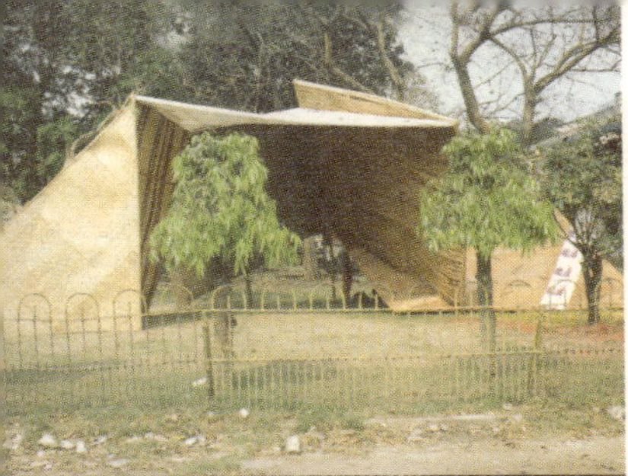

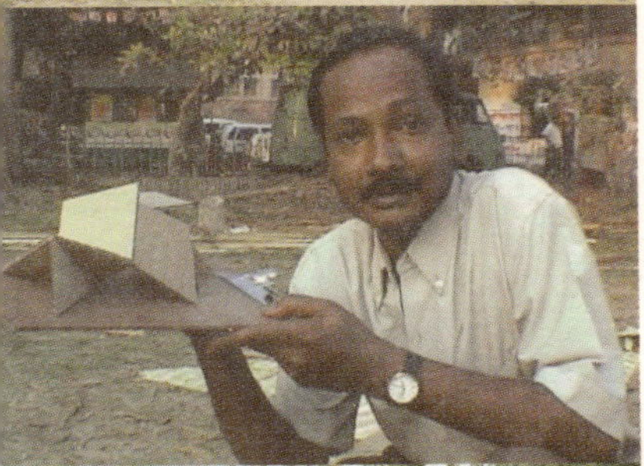

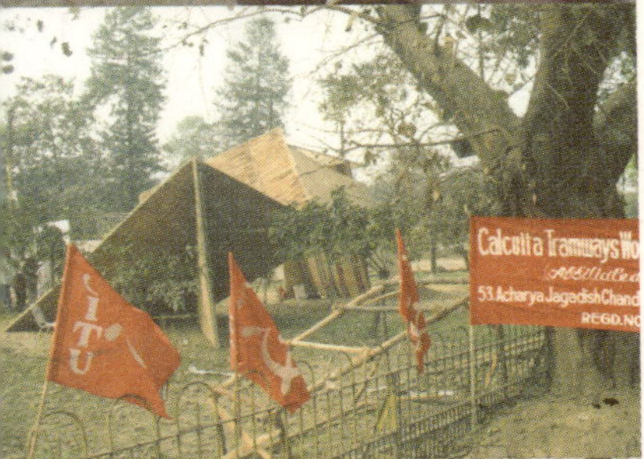


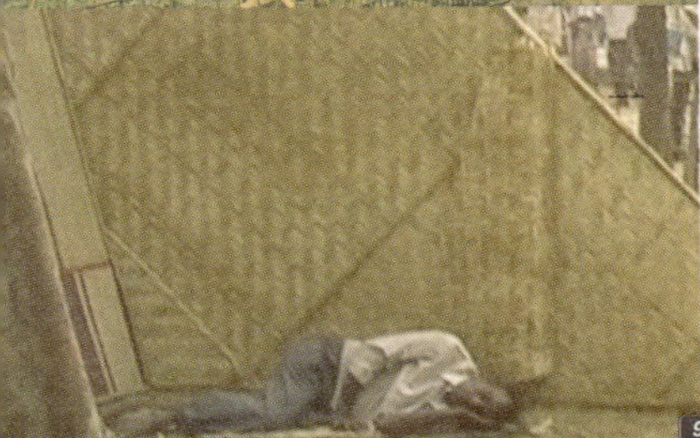

I tried to create something that was both strange and familiar to the people of both cities. Pandal makers are artisans who build intricate canvas and bamboo temporary buildings (pandals) for weddings and festivals. They tend to replicate a building that is well known and construct it in a matter of days with all the detail and colours of the original. I selected Ron Robertson-Swann's abstract sculpture called *Vault* – a 1970s sculpture with a chequered history of glory and rejection that has become a Melbourne icon – to be made at full scale at the Esplanade tram terminus.
In Melbourne a tram prow – bright yellow like *Vault* – was placed at the site of the original *Vault* and painted a different colour every couple of days, including primary and heritage colours. This work titled *Re:Vault* draws attention to the contradictions that exist in our civic spaces and the perceived value of colour and form in these spaces.
*James Legge*

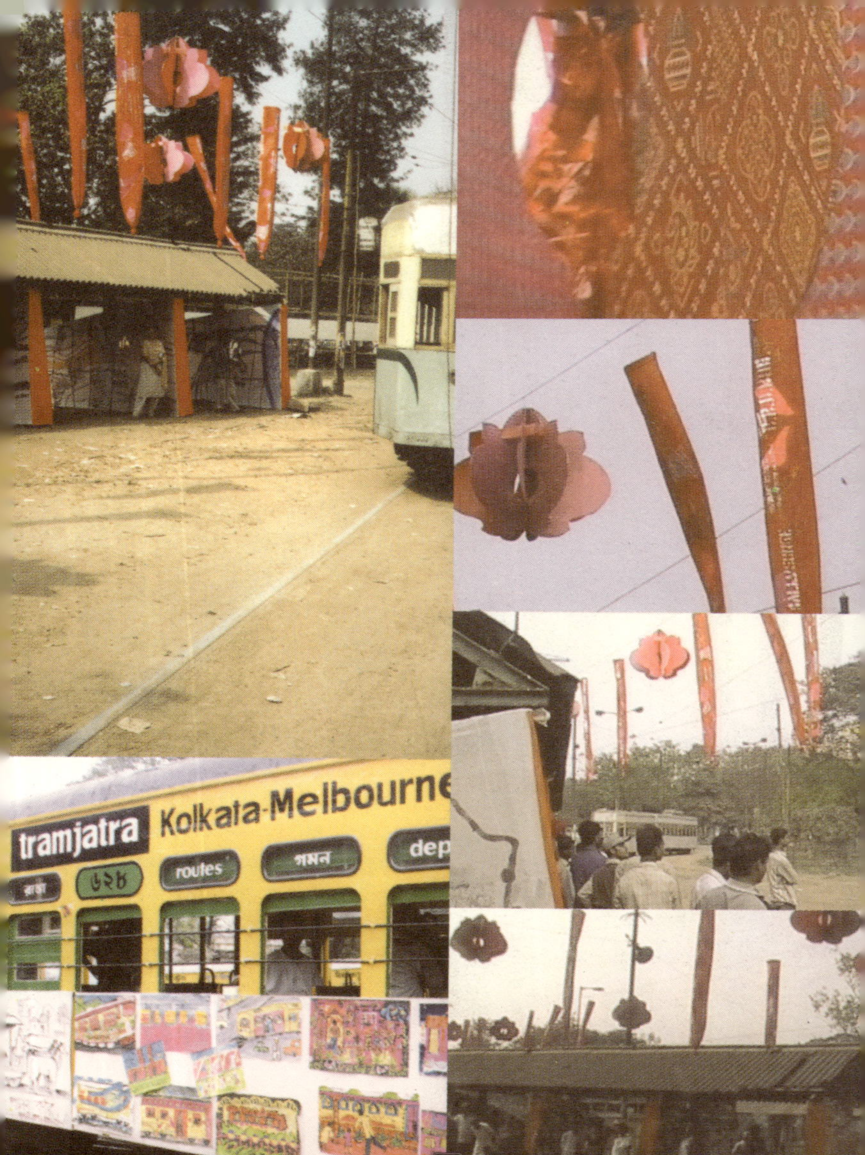
tramjatra
Kolkata-Melbourne
routes
গমন

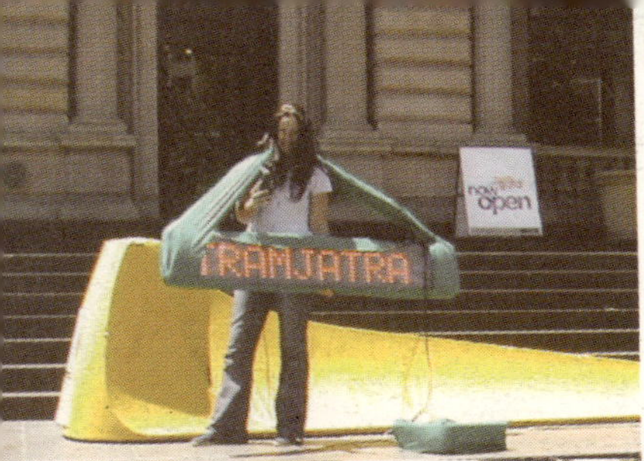


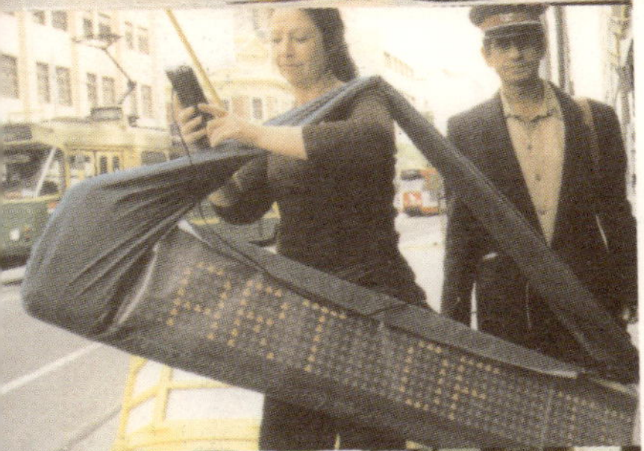

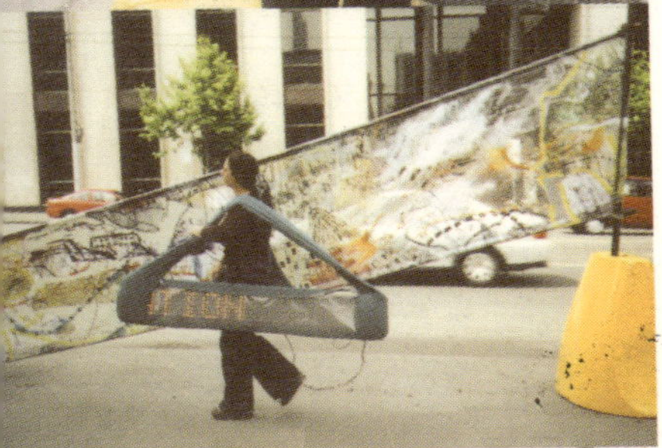

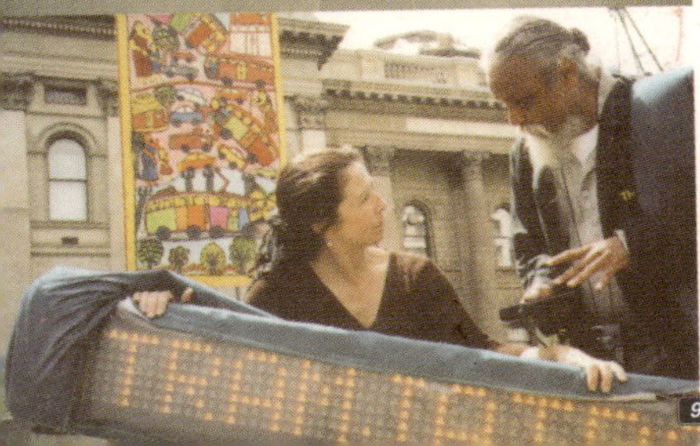

Ordered empty spaces.
Delicate grids of tramlines
cross a clear blue sky.
Room to meditate.
Poetry perhaps, a line of
philosophy, ideas, lightbulbs
lighting up, the light of day...
This mobile electronic
'moving message' board
roves around the trams and
tramstops of the City Circle
line, telling tales, making
puns, and spouting
homespun philosophy,
fully interactive for
passengers! If you are
waiting for a tram or
sitting aboard, tell us
your thoughts and they
could be written in lights!
*Amanda King*

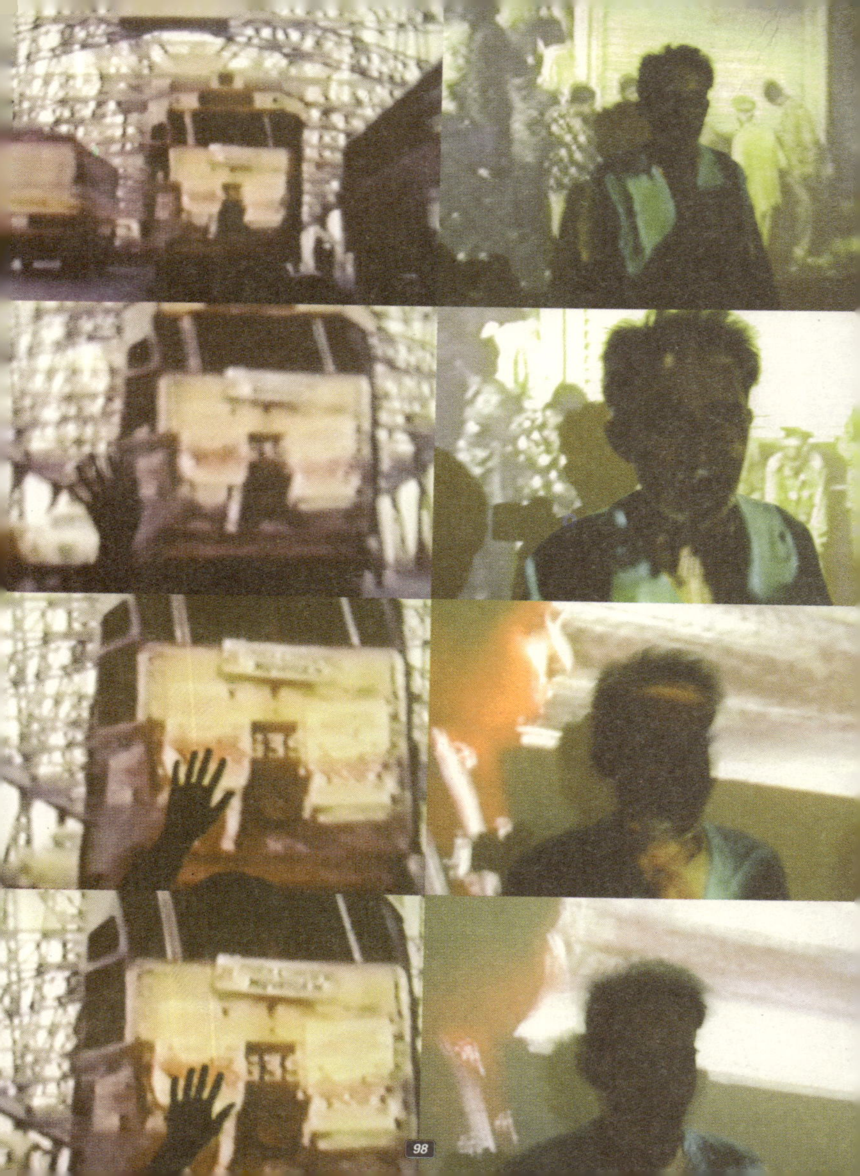

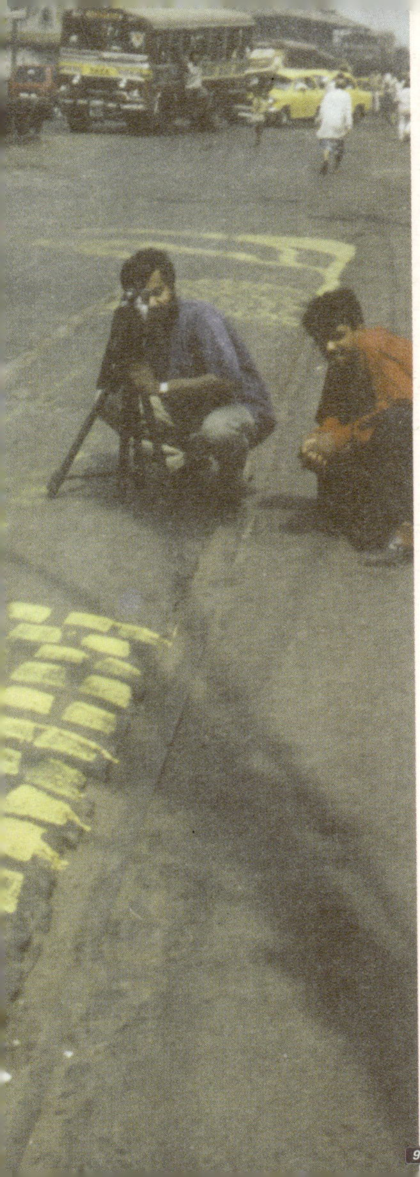

Every film has to create a new space. I work with tram and city through images captured on film.
*Mahadeb Shi*

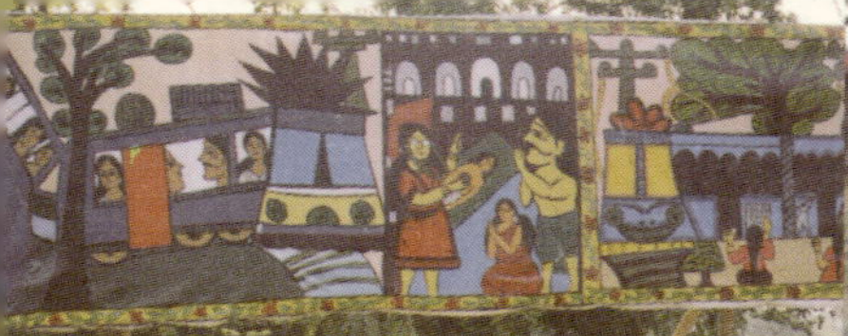
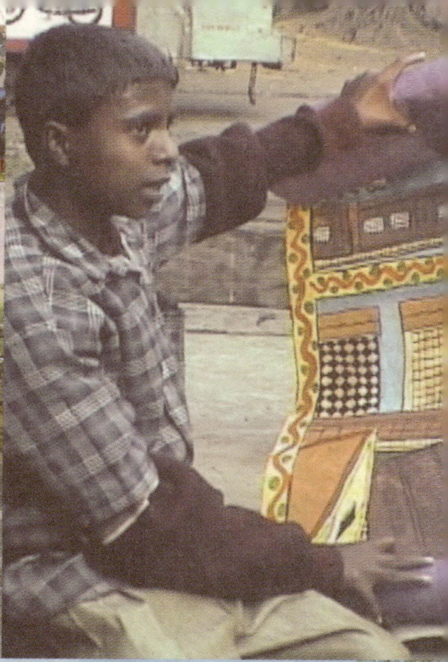
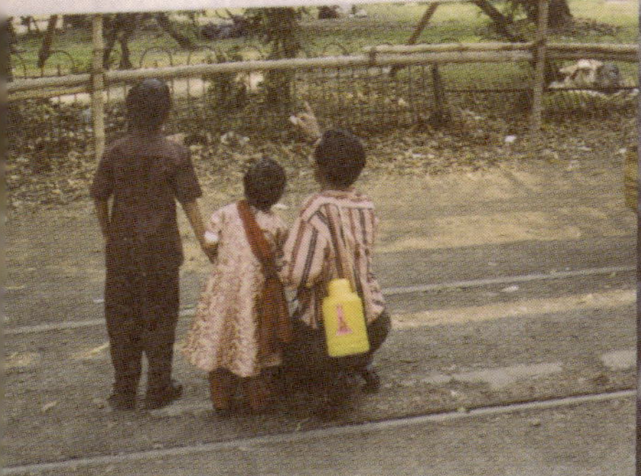
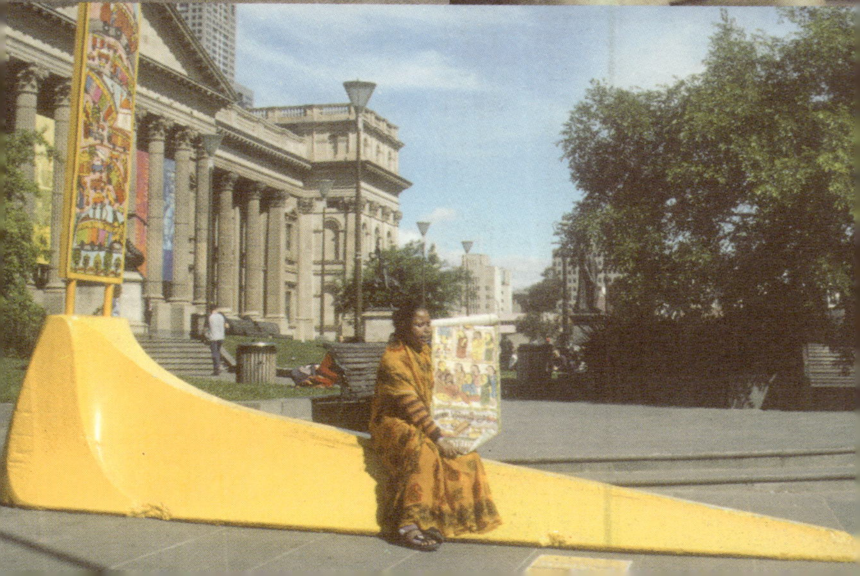

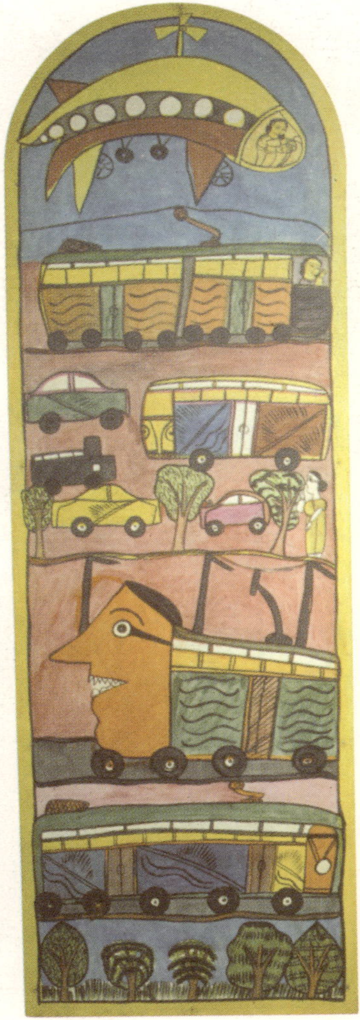

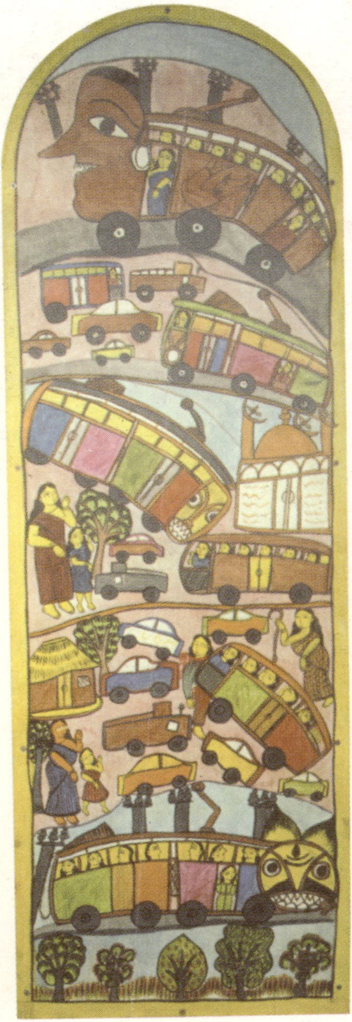

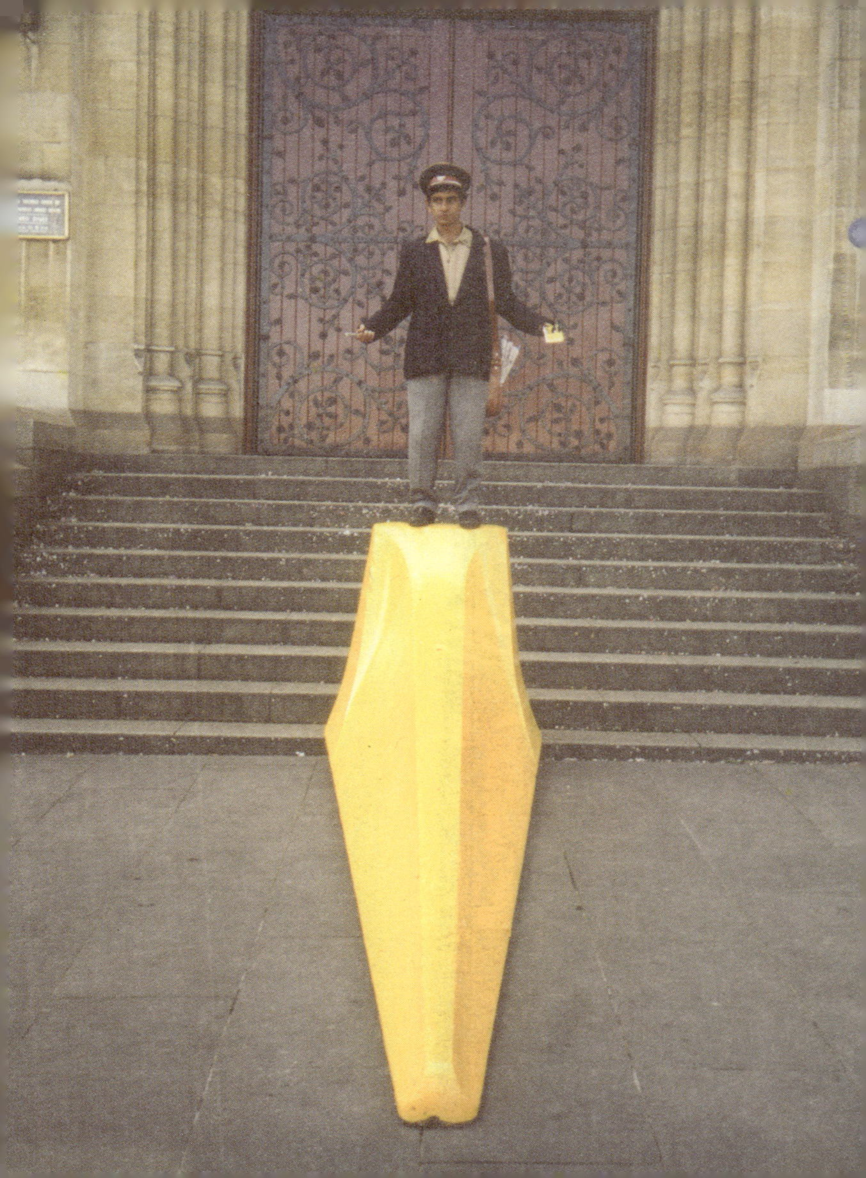

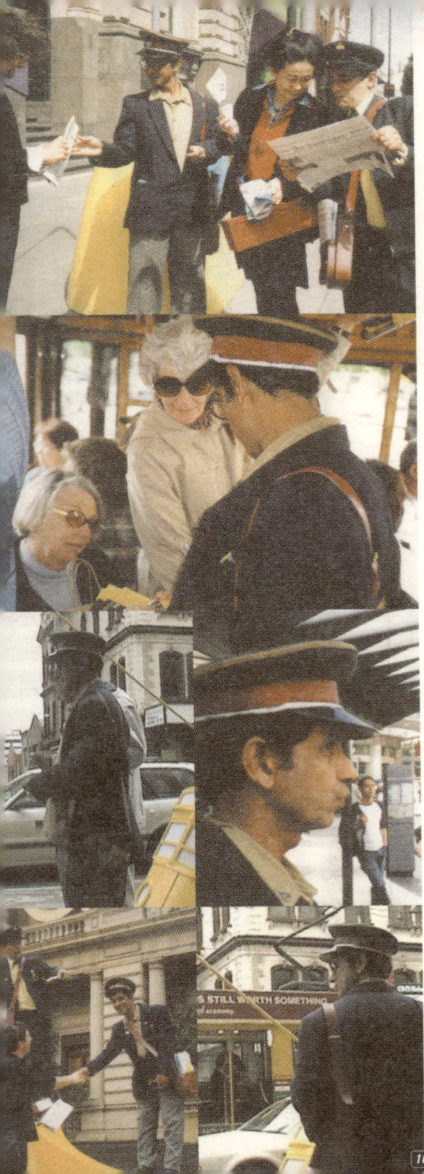

In Melbourne people were surprised to look at me. I told people that yes, there is the tram conductor in Kolkata. People tell me they are not satisfied with the machine that has been introduced. They are missing the presence of the tram conductor. Regular passengers tell me they miss the utility of the conductor as a human being.

*Prabir Kumar Goswami*

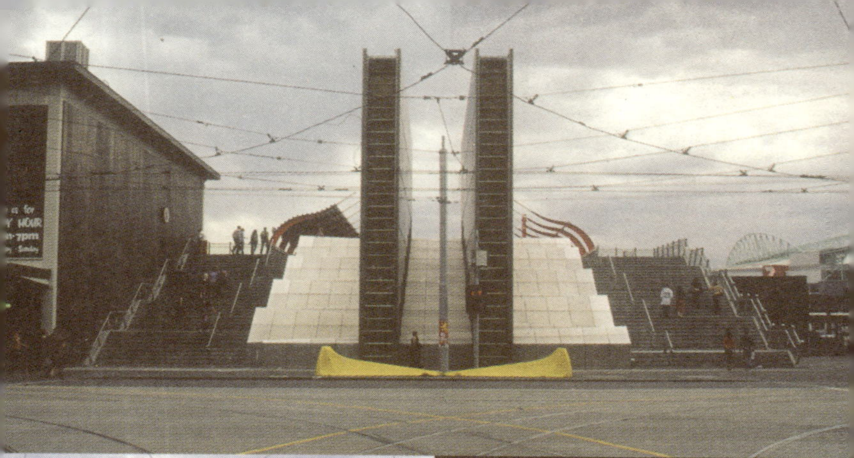

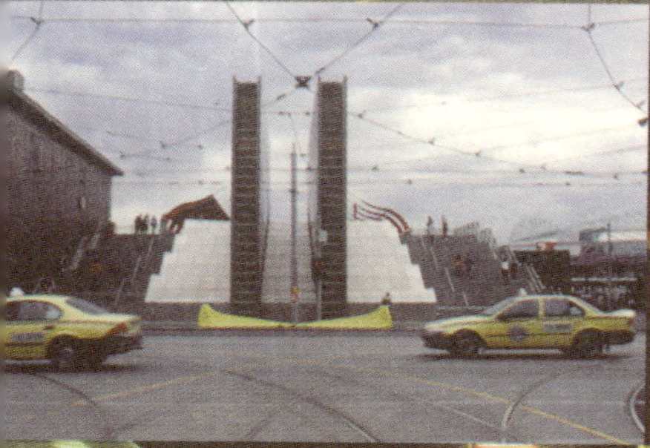

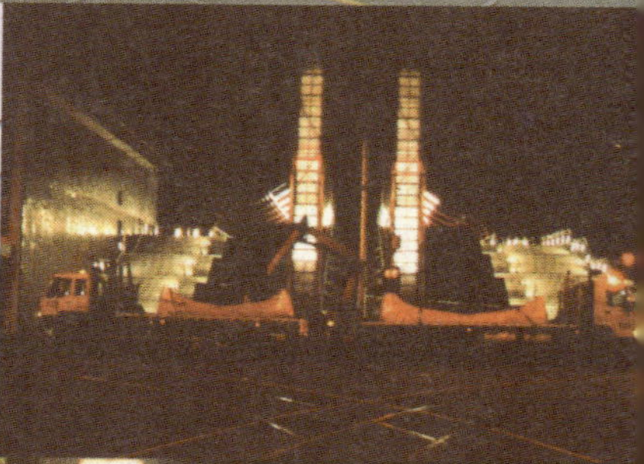

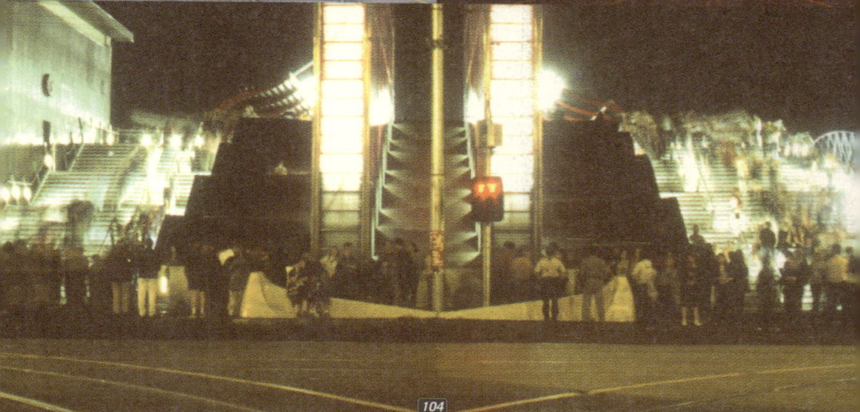

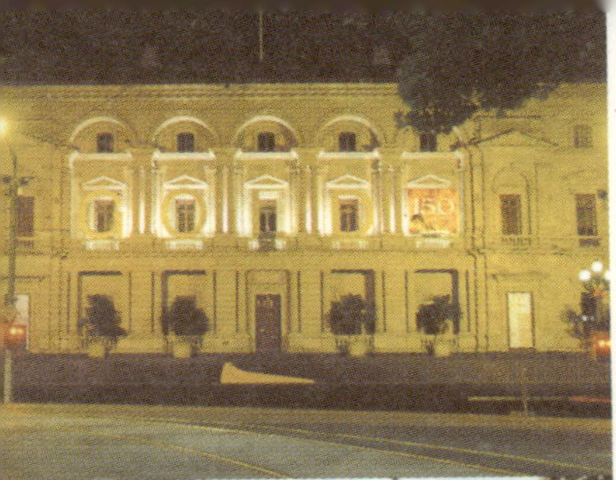
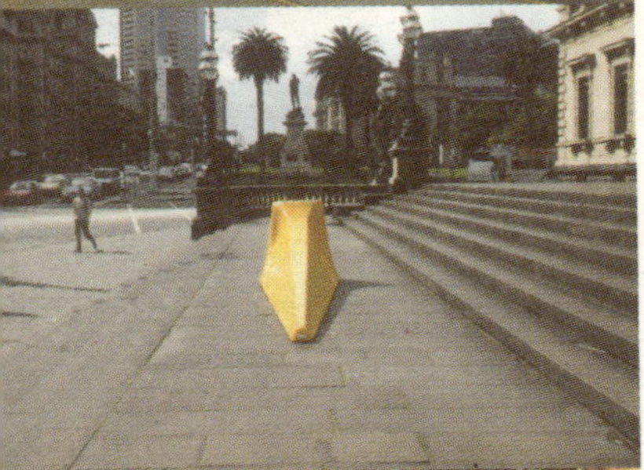
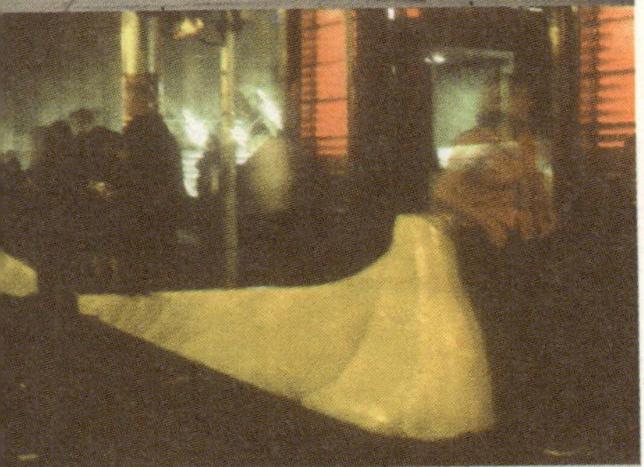
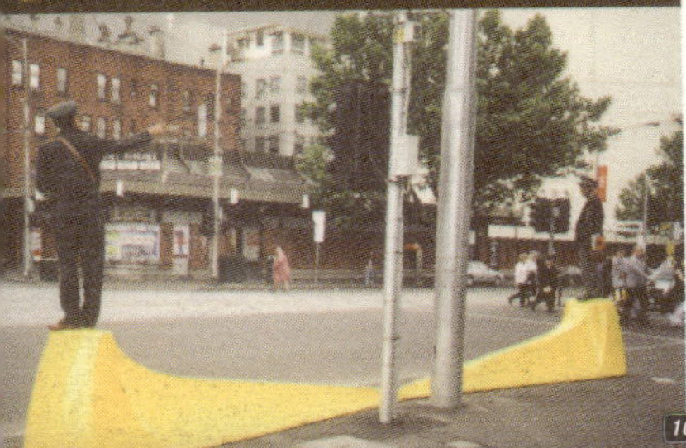

Tramways are a medium of social, civic and environmental relations, and hence are also a medium of artistic possibility. I've been making transformations to core elements of this medium (tram 'prow' safety barriers, conductors' bags, clothing and uniforms, tickets, instructional signage and the external image of the tram) so as to stimulate new lines of connection and questioning, and to provide an infrastructure for others to work with creatively. This is, for me, about the inter-connected relations of a network: the net-effect is to gather together and maintain dynamism in this project network that operates through the medium of tramways. This network of *tramjatra* is enabled by tools and events that foster social relationships, information sharing, artistic production and the generation of ideas and learning. It seeks to give carriage to open-ended and open-minded transport: to forms of travel that make multiple crossings between, across and beyond.

*Mick Douglas*

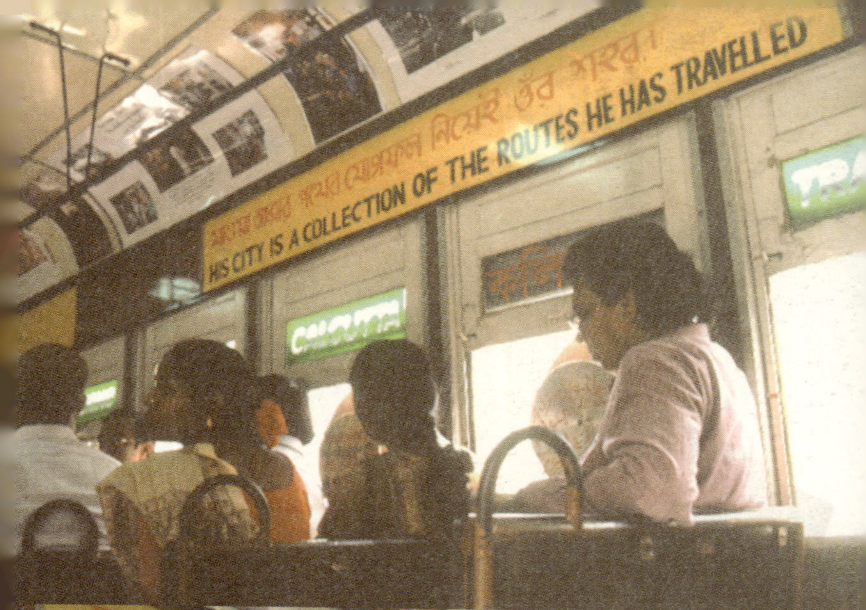
HIS CITY IS A COLLECTION OF THE ROUTES HE HAS TRAVELLED
CALCUTTA

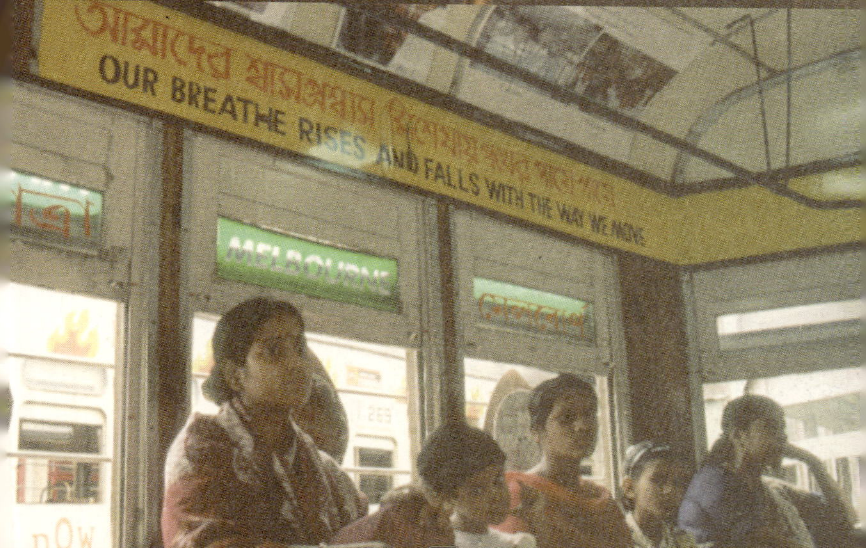
OUR BREATHE RISES AND FALLS WITH THE WAY WE MOVE
MELBOURNE

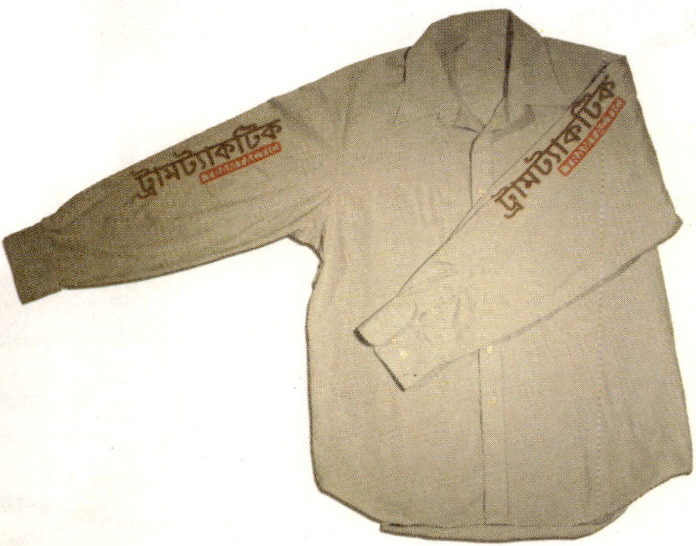
ট্রমট্যাকটিক

5

# Kolkata's tram conveys ordinary people

Sarna Chitrakar

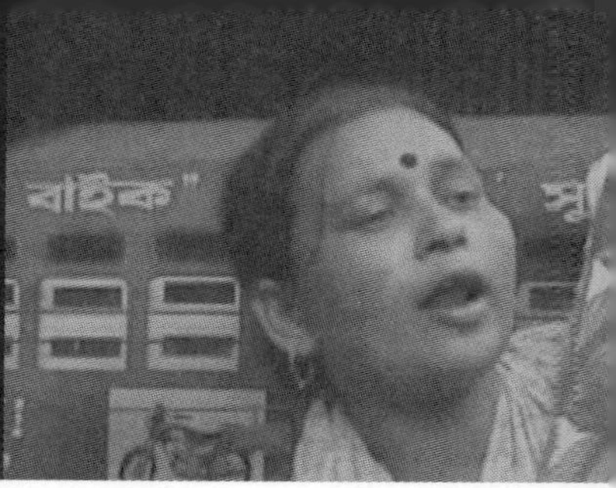

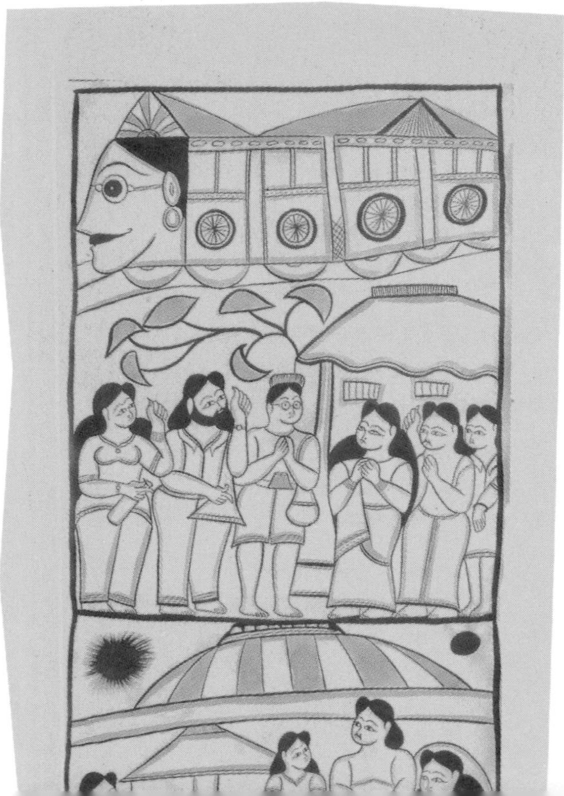

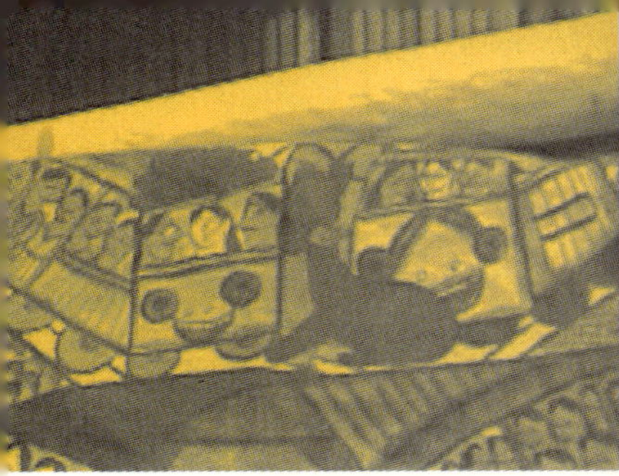

## কলকাতারই ট্রাম, করে লোক যানবাহন

স্বর্ণ চিত্রকর

Kolkata's tram conveys ordinary people.
Go from Ballygunge Phandi to Tollygunge Station.
It is Kolkata's tram!

Mick Douglas with Mahadev and Aparna Das came to Naya.
We got to know each other. I requested them to be seated.
And then we got to talk.

Kolkata's tram conveys ordinary people.
Go from Ballygunge Phandi to Tollygunge Station.
It is Kolkata's tram!

কলকাতারই ট্রাম, করে লোক যানবাহন
বালিগঞ্জ ফাঁড়ি থেকে (থিকে) টালিগঞ্জে স্টেশনে যান।
কলকাতারই ট্রাম।।

মইকেল ডগলাস, সঙ্গে মহাদেব আর অপর্ণা দাস
আলাপ করে দেয়, বসতে আসন দিই
তারপরে হইল আলোচনা।

কলকাতারই ট্রাম, করে লোক যানবাহন
বালিগঞ্জ ফাঁড়ি থিকে টালিগঞ্জ চলে যান।
কলকাতারই ট্রাম।।

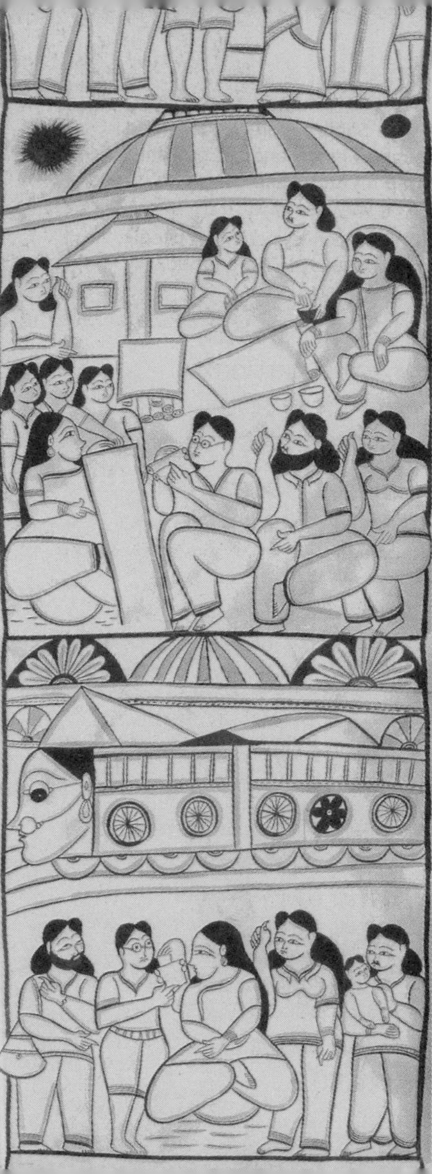

Meeting the Sahib we are all delighted.
One brought a mat... another brought water.
I displayed my scroll and sang with it.
We were all very happy.

Kolkata's tram conveys ordinary people.
Go from Nonapukur to Khiddirpur.
It is Kolkata's tram!

সাহেবকে দেখে আমরা অতি উল্লাস
কেউ মাদুর দেয় কেউ জল নিয়ে আয়
পটের গান করি আমি পট দেখিয়ে
আনন্দে আমরা ছিলাম সবাই।

কলকাতারই ট্রাম, করে লোক যানবাহন
নোনাপুকুর থিকে খিদিরপুর চলে যান।
কলকাতারই ট্রাম।।

After listening to the refrain and the song Mick said,
'Very good. Very good. You will have to make a scroll on the tram;
compose your song! If it is good there will be an exhibition
at The Touring Guest House in Kolkata.'

Kolkata's tram conveys ordinary people.
Go from Nonapukur to Khiddirpur.
It is Kolkata's tram!

পটের গান শুনে মাইকেল বলে ভালো ভালো
ট্রামের পট করতে হবে গান রচনা কর
ভালো হইলে পরে, এগ্‌জিবিশন হবে পরে
ট্যুরিং গেষ্ট হাউস, কলিকাতায়।

কলকাতারই ট্রাম, করে লোক যানবাহন
নোনাপুকুর থিকে খিদিরপুর চলে যান।
কলকাতারই ট্রাম।।

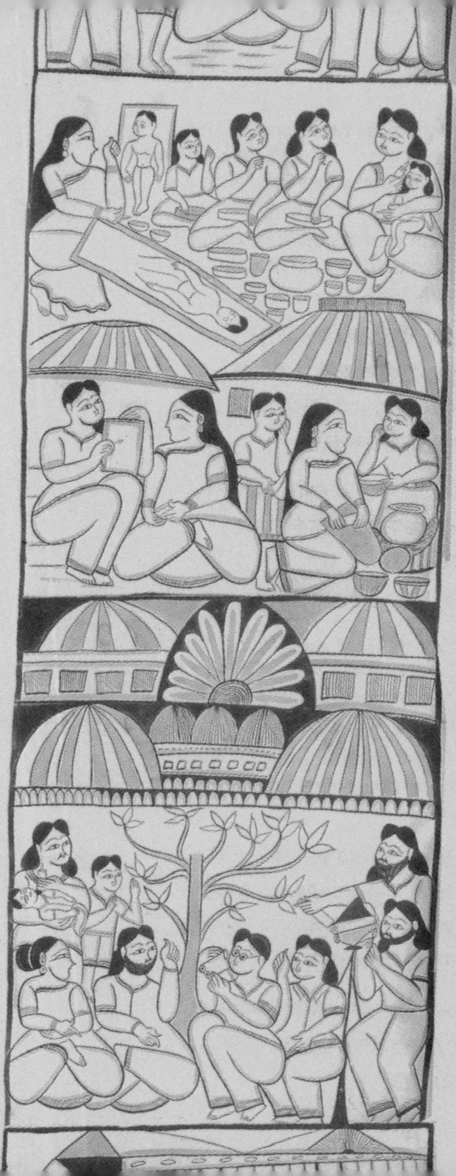

My brother composed the song.
And I learnt it.
I was kept busy the whole day.
We got much pleasure singing the song.

Kolkata's tram conveys ordinary people.
Go from Esplanade to Khidderpore.
It is Kolkata's tram!

রচনা করিল আমার ভাই
গান তুলি আমি সর্ব সদাই
সারাটি দিন আমি মেতে থাকি
গান করে আমরা আনন্দ পাই।

কলকাতারই ট্রাম, করে লোক যানবাহন,
এক্সাইল থেকে খিদিরপুর চলে যান।
কলকাতারই ট্রাম।।

The sahebs worked along with us.
I Sarna was there, also Dukhushyam.
We worked the whole day;
then had a meeting at Victoria.

Kolkata's tram conveys ordinary people.
Go from Esplanade to Khidderpore.
It is Kolkata's tram!

সাহেবরা আমাদের নিয়ে কাজ করিল
সঙ্গে আমি স্বর্ণ, দুখু শ্যামও ছিল
সারাটা দিন কাজ করি আমরা
মিটিং করি ভিক্টোরিয়ায়।

কলকাতারই ট্রাম, করে লোক যানবাহন,
এক্সাইল থেকে খিদিরপুর চলে যান।
কলকাতারই ট্রাম।।

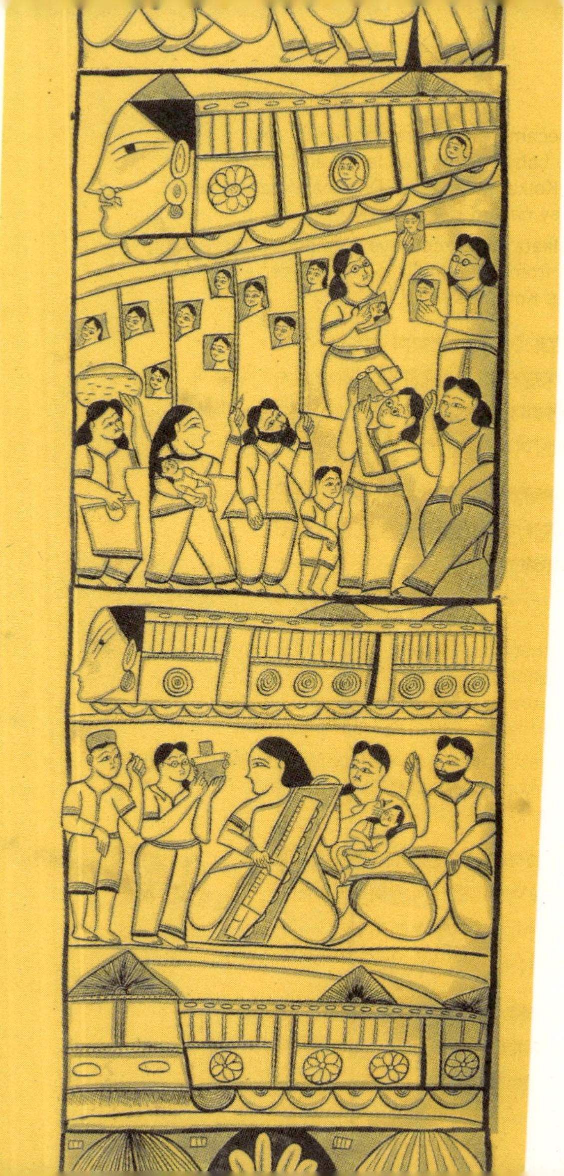

I became even more happy that day.
My baby's photo was taken and placed
in Kolkata's trams at Dharmatala and Ekshail.
They named it Trambaby.

Kolkata's tram conveys ordinary people.
Go from Nonapukur to Tollygunge.
It is Kolkata's tram!

আরো বেশী খুশি হলাম যেইদিন
আমরা বেবীর ফোটো নিয়ে টাঙায় সেই দিন
কলকাতার ট্রামে, ধর্মতলায়, এক্সাইলে
লিখে দিল ট্রাম শিশু।

কলকাতারই ট্রাম, করে লোক যানবাহন
নোনাপুকুর থিকে টালিগঞ্জ চলে যান।
কলকাতারই ট্রাম।।

Further, Roberto and Mick told us that our work
was not over with Kolkata.
We would have to go to Australia;
over there a *tramjatra* would be held.

Kolkata's tram conveys ordinary people.
Go from Dharamatala to Khiddirpur.
It is Kolkata's tram!

আরো বলেছিল রবার্টো, মাইকেল ডগলাস
কলকাতাতে আমাদের কাজের শেষ নেই
যেতে হবে অস্ট্রেলিয়া
সেখানে হবে ট্রামযাত্রা।

কলকাতরাই ট্রাম, করে লোক যানবাহন
ধর্মতলা থিকে খিদিরপুর চলে যান।
কলকাতারই ট্রাম।।

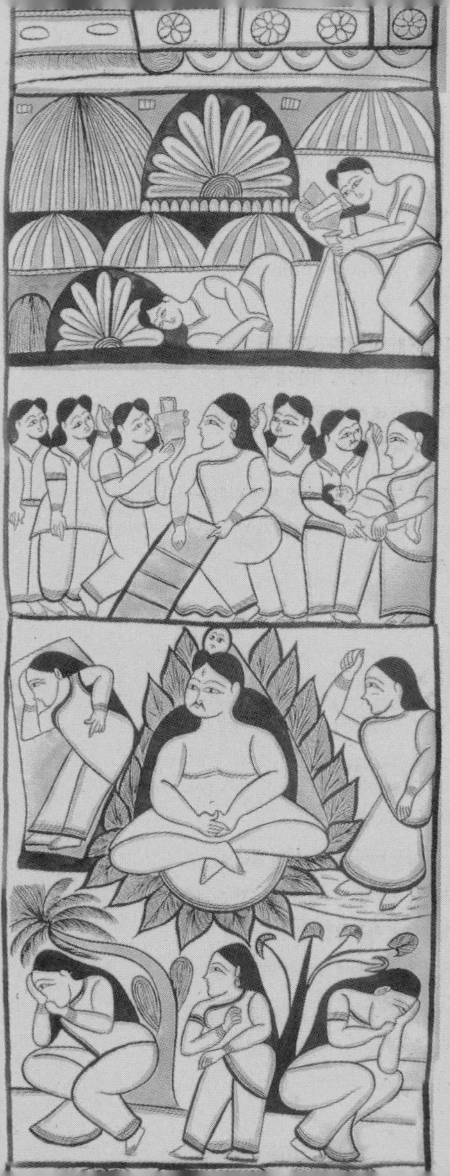

On hearing about Australia I started thinking about
when I would go to Australia.
I have learnt so much coming to Kolkata.
How much more I would get to know at Melbourne.

Kolkata's tram conveys ordinary people.
Go from Tollygunge to Ballygunge.
It is Kolkata's tram!

অস্ট্রেলিয়ার কথা শুনে আমার মন
ভাবছে অস্ট্রেলিয়া যাব আমি কখন
কলকাতায় এসে এত কিছু জানতে পারি
মেলবোর্ণেতে জানব কত কি।

কলকাতারই ট্রাম, করে লোক যানবাহন
টালিগঞ্জ থেকে বালিগঞ্জ চলে যান।
কলকাতারই ট্রাম।।

God could not accept my excessive joy.
Sirs, what Providence writes cannot be erased by anyone.

Kolkata's tram conveys ordinary people.
Go from Dharamatala to Khiddirpur.
It is Kolkata's tram!

আমার মনে এত আনন্দ
পারল না সইতে বিধাতা তখনো
বিধাতারই লিখা বাবু
পারে না তো কেউ খন্ডাতে কখনো।

কলকাতারই ট্রাম, করে লোক যানবাহন
ধর্মতলা থিকে খিদিরপুর চলে যান,
কলকাতারই ট্রাম।।

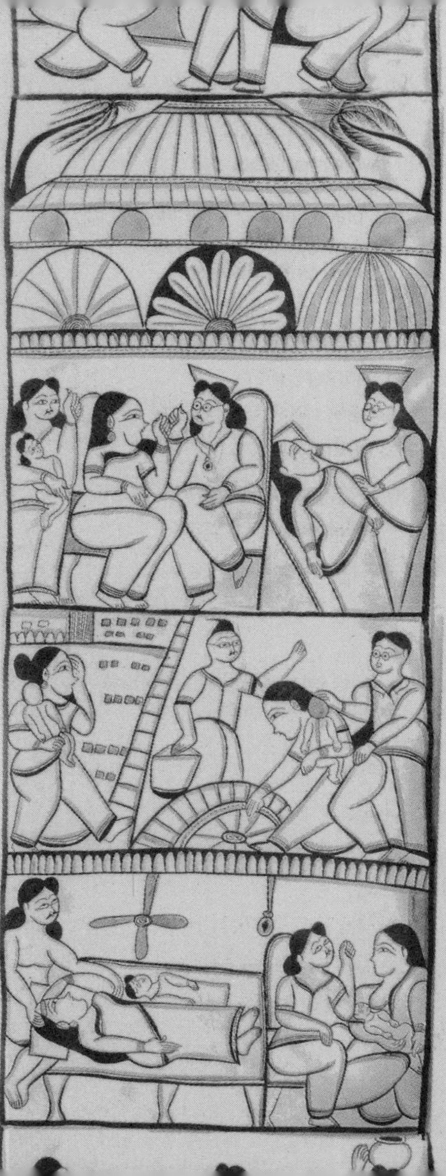

Inexplicably I became pregnant.
All my hopes were shattered.
It was the time for tears.
The birth took place and my tears flowed.

Kolkata's tram conveys ordinary people.
Go from Esplanade to Khidderpore.
It is Kolkata's tram!

বুঝতে না পেরে আমার গর্ভে সন্তান এল
সব আসা ভেঙ্গে চুরমার হল
শুরু হল চোখের জল
কানতে কানতে চলে গেল।

কলকাতারই ট্রাম, করে লোক যানবাহন
এক্‌সাইল থেকে খিদিরপুর চলে যান।
কলকাতারই ট্রাম।।

How hard I toiled.
Destiny could not bear so much of happiness:
which is why ultimately I was in tears.
My regret will extend over a lifetime.

Kolkata's tram conveys ordinary people.
Go from Esplanade to Khidderpore.
It is Kolkata's tram!

কষ্ট করিলাম আমি কত
সইল না সুখ কপালে এত
তাইতো অবশেষে কানতে হল
পস্তাতে হবে সারাটি জীবন।

কলকাতারই ট্রাম, করে লোক যানবাহন
এক্‌সাইল থেকে খিদিরপুর চলে যান।
কলকাতারই ট্রাম।।

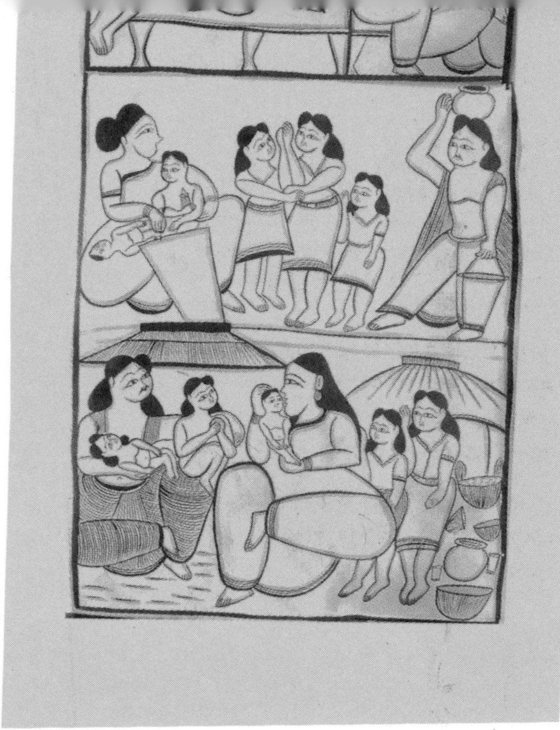

At present I am quite happy.
I live in joy with my family.
Sorrow exists, but so too joy;
therefore I still live my life.

Kolkata's tram conveys ordinary people.
Go from Tollygunge to Ballygunge.
It is Kolkata's tram!

Namaskar. I am Sarna Chitrakar.

এখন আমি খুবই খুশি
ফেমিলিকে নিয়ে বেশ আছি সুখে
দুখের মাঝে সুখও আছে
তইতো আমি আছি বেঁচে।

কলকাতারই ট্রাম, করে লোক যানবাহন
ধর্মতলা থিকে বালিগঞ্জ চলে যান।
কলকাতারই ট্রাম।।

নমস্কার ।। আমার নাম স্বর্ণ চিত্রকর

6

# journeying and seeing

Jogi Panghaal

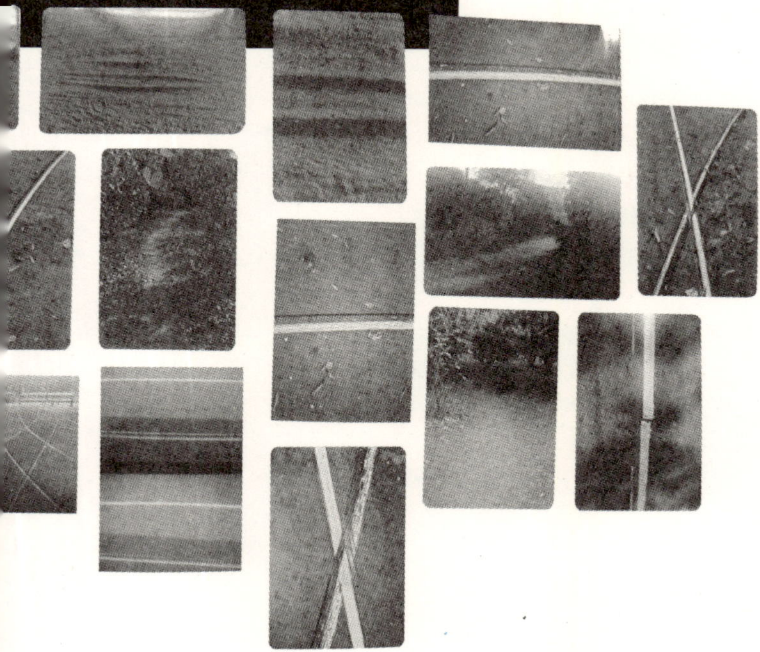

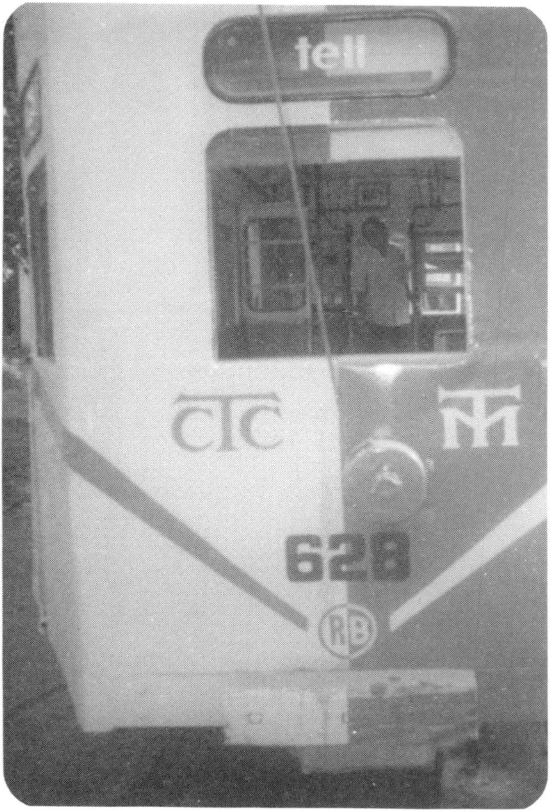
tell
CTC
628

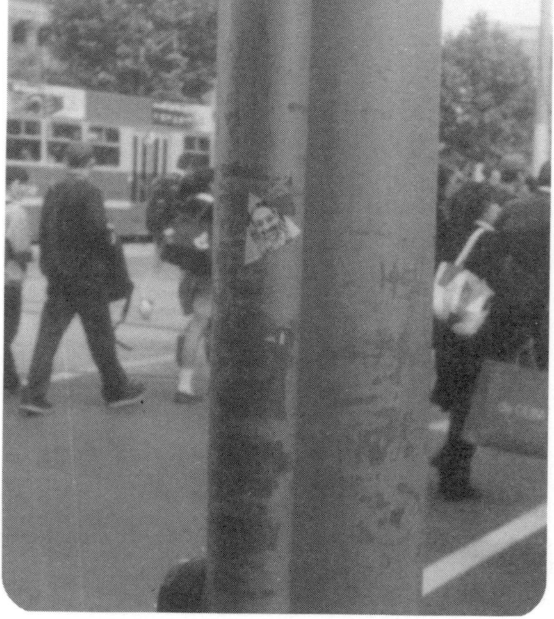

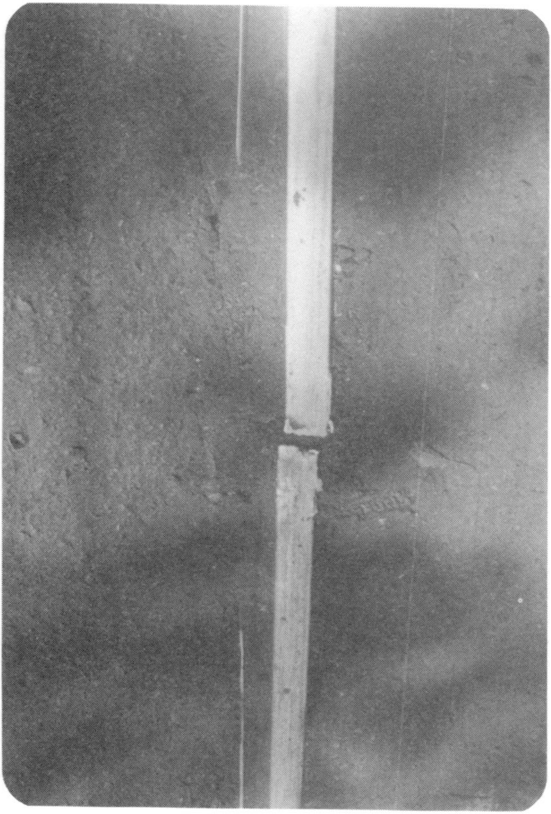

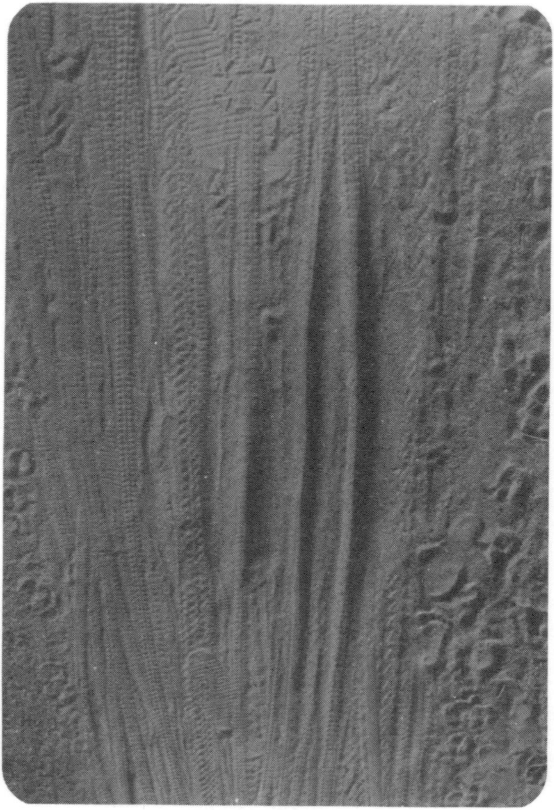

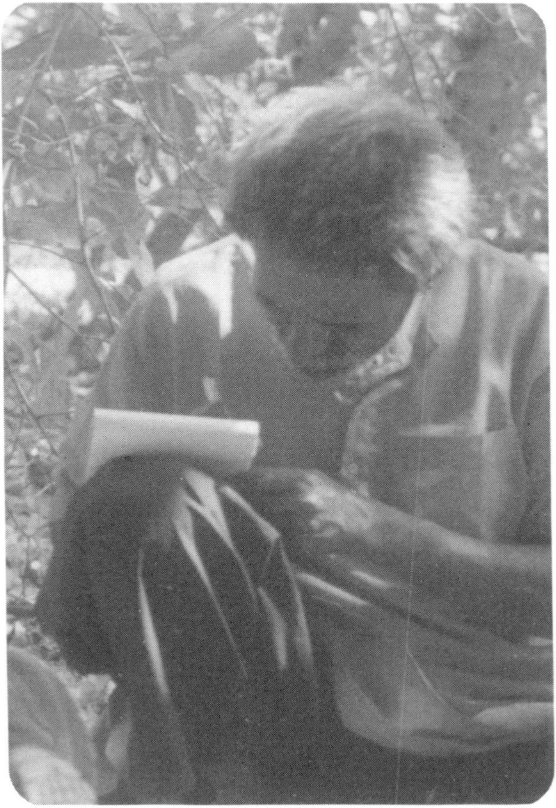

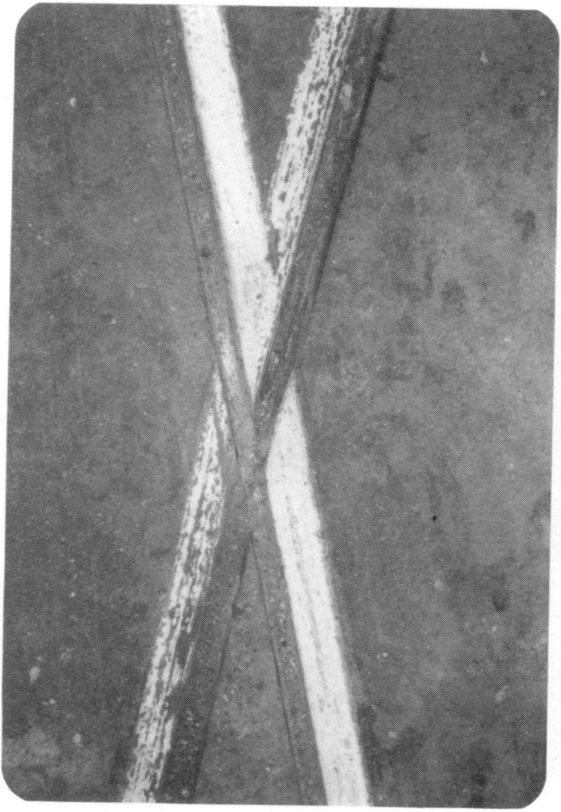

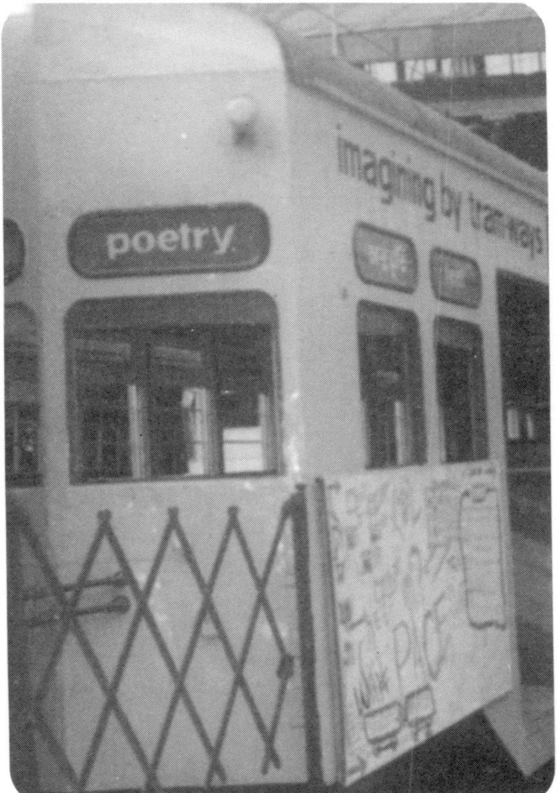
poetry
imagining by tramways

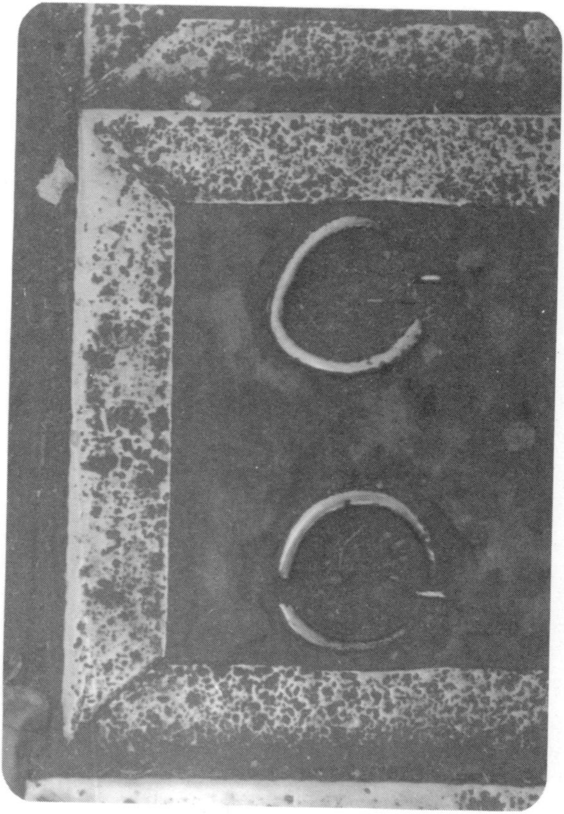

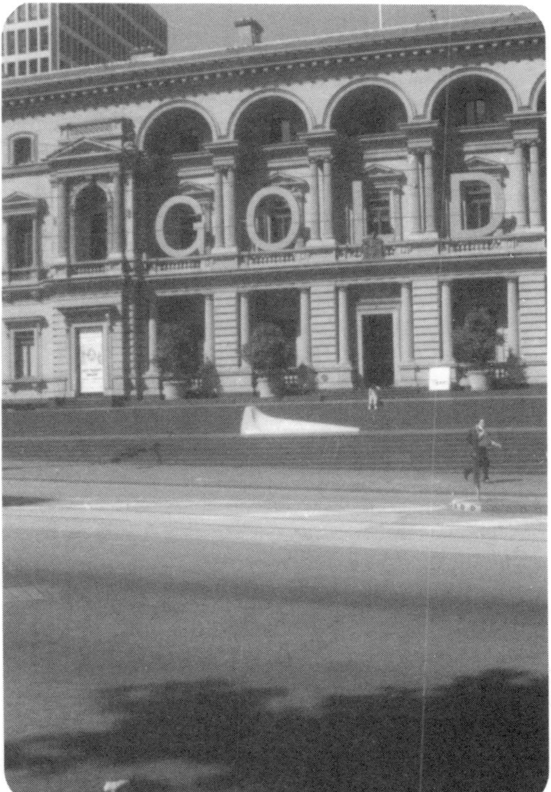
GOD

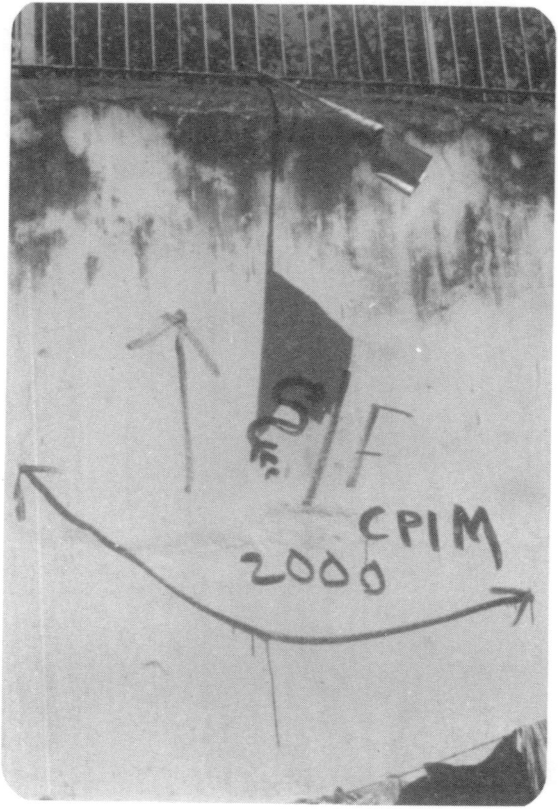
CPIM
2000

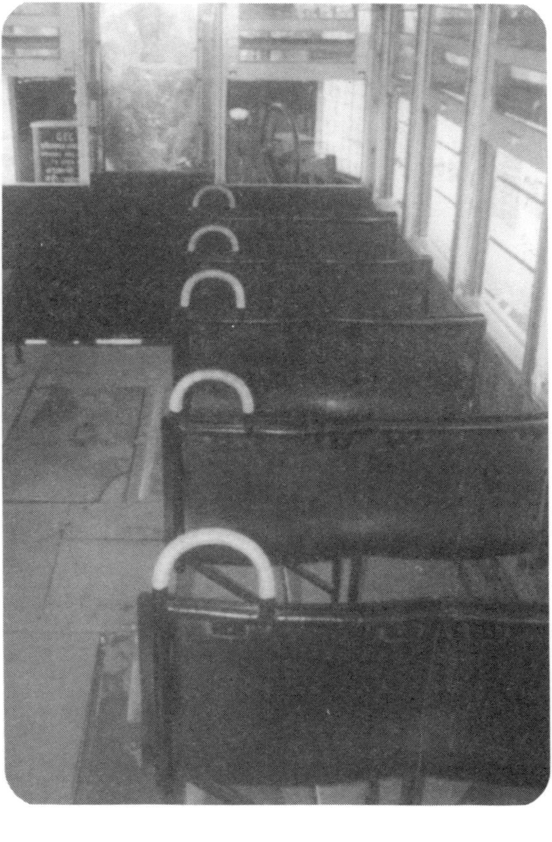

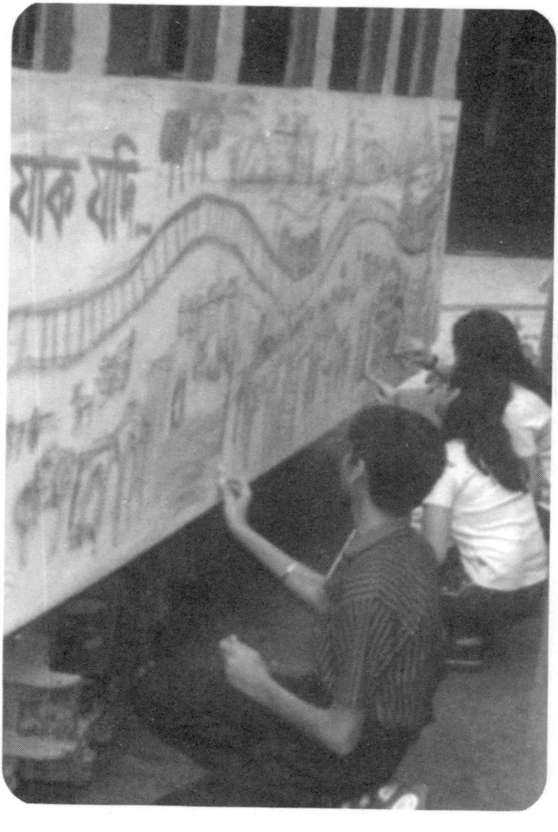

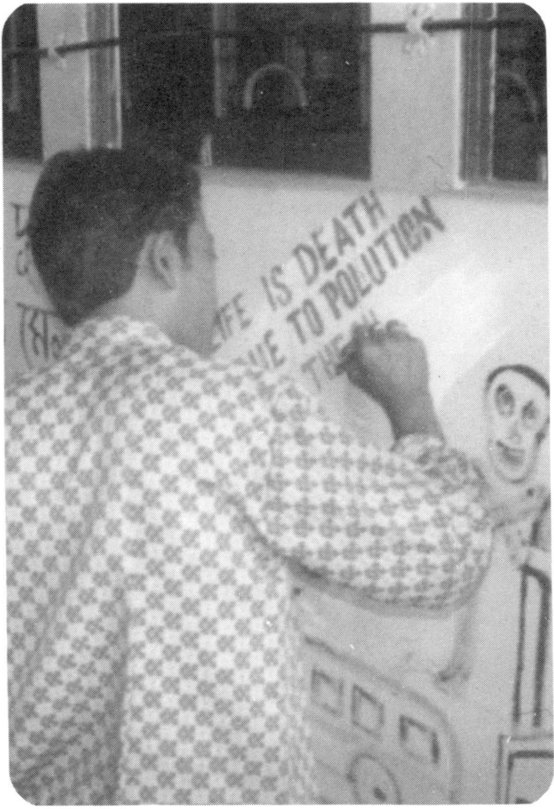
IS DEATH
TO POLLUTION

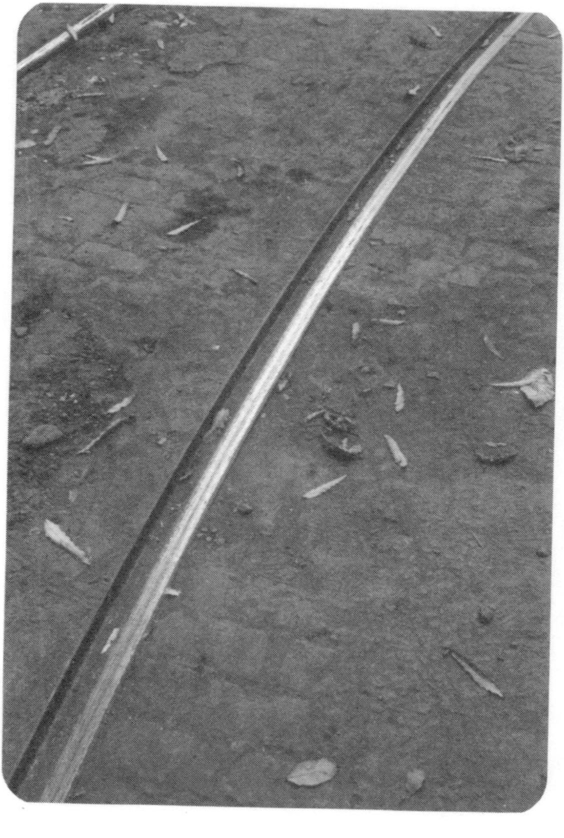

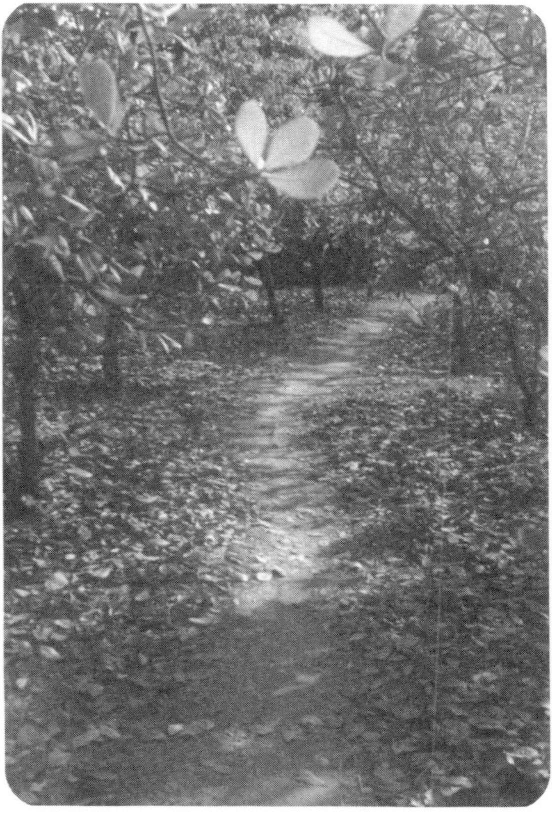

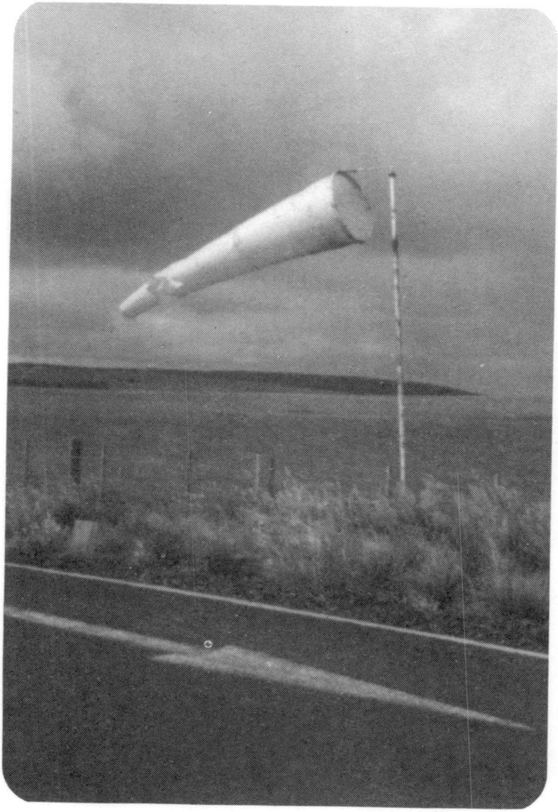

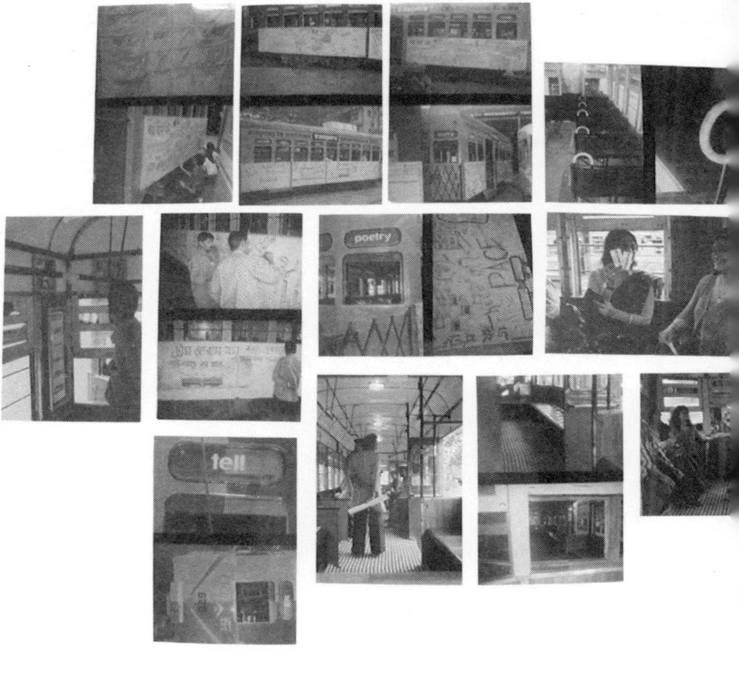
poetry
tell

7

# passage

Suzie Attiwill

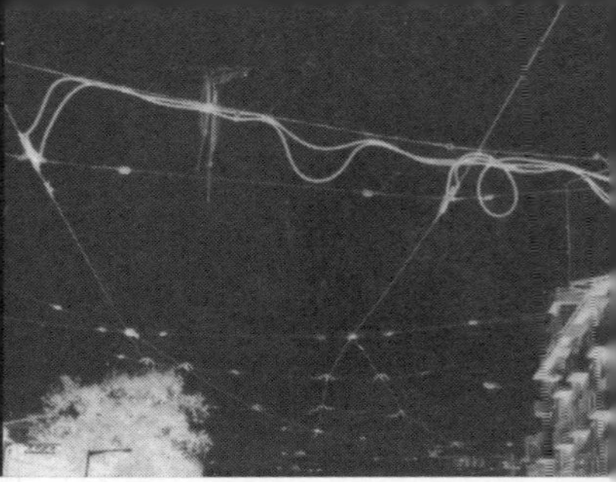

I was a passenger on *tramjatra* and while one could say that every one is a passenger in one way or another, the designation of my role as a 'critical passenger' articulated a specified place or seat on board *as a* passenger. Forces and velocities of trams and the project itself transported me along tracks and passages through cities encountering networks and artworks, loops and derailments, arrivals and departures.

I use the past tense as the journey of *tramjatra* reached a point of arrival when the loop between Kolkata and Melbourne was completed. However the invitation to write something for this book has given the project momentum again. Different tracks appear and gesture one to step back on board, to take up a seat again and, in the company of others, be transported along various paths. The distance that has opened up between the actual journey of *tramjatra* in 2001 and the present has made me aware of differences between writing while in the project and writing about it now. I am reluctant to take up a reflective position – looking back on the journey, summing it up, spreading out the postcards, projecting my own image onto a journey composed of many paths and trajectories. It was a position – a seat if you will – which I also resisted occupying during the project despite the implications of a critical passenger as one who might reflect upon something from a distance.

But as a passenger sometimes you cannot choose where you want to sit, let alone direction and speed. Sometimes you don't even have a seat and have to stand holding onto a handrail. For the same token, you cannot be too fussy about who sits next to you. Passengers are transported, escorted, guided, carried along tracks and passages by vehicles – in this case trams, *tramjatra* and art – and always in the company of others. A passenger is neither driver nor conductor. There is a passive aspect to being a passenger – a passenger is along for the ride (with the potential to be taken for a ride). 'Mmmm' – I hear you think – 'but aren't you a critical passenger? Wouldn't critical imply a more active, directional position on board *tramjatra*? Or at the very least, given that you are critical, you would be offered a seat.'

Well maybe not a seat but I was guaranteed a ticket each trip.

I am not suggesting that a passenger is not active in some way so much as articulating the sensation of passivity that is part of any journey. I am reminded of a passage someone sent to me at the *tramjatra* hotmail address and which was later published in *The Statesman* newspaper. 'The tram is usually a displacing experience. Before getting in you are thinking of your own business. When you get in the tram you understand that your presence interferes with the other passengers' thoughts and the passengers' presence interferes with your thoughts. I have often realised that, once entered in the tram, I have changed the thread of my thoughts. I start thinking of the others' thoughts. Many different thoughts... .'[1] This is the active aspect of being a passenger. Things happen along the way. One encounters forces and is caught up in the flow, making decisions and, in the process, producing singular trajectories and idiosyncratic passages within the determined passage.

The critical passengers' ticket – there were two of us, Jogi Panghaal and myself – posed a point of departure and passage of travel: 'What if a practice of critical selection, evaluation and re-presentation were to stimulate the potential of *tramjatra*?' With this ticket in hand we travelled the network of *tramjatra*. This continuity of travel throughout the project distinguished the critical passenger as someone who moved through all aspects of *tramjatra* making connections across its various spatial and temporal manifestations and between the people involved.

The word 'critical' in relation to its meaning as a limit of continuity at which transformation occurs – for example, critical temperature – is a definition which was useful in relation to evaluation – more so than critical as criticism. In this seat, evaluation took the form of evaluating displacements caught up in the flow and dynamics of the project. The seat of criticism however was the one that many people expected a critical passenger to occupy – judging, in this case, art from a critical distance. I think Jogi, like myself, found the position of critic and judge problematic in relation to a project like *tramjatra* with its emphasis on creativity and imagination. To be critical implies a distance from one's object of critique – a critical distance. For such a distance to be established, the critic is required to take up a position and to position the object of critique – the effect of this is the projection of one's own image onto others[2] and a prioritising of identity and identification. In contrast, a critical relation in constant movement and process is dynamic – producing and affecting positions, making them mobile and a question of becoming rather than being, 'and' not 'is'. When you think about it, anyway, it is not really possible for a passenger to take up a critical distance in relation to their passage as they will be left waiting at the point of departure – the tram stop.

But again this does not imply that anything goes. The philosopher Gilles Deleuze writes about decisions as distinct from judgement – one encounters forces and makes decisions, good and bad decisions as distinct from judging what is right or wrong. Decisions bring things into existence, invoke rather than explain or interpret. Deleuze wrote: 'it is not a matter of searching for an origin, but of evaluating displacements.'[3] This is a different seat to occupy than a seat of judgement. Evaluation becomes a process of making decisions in relation to distribution of forces and intensities rather than measuring and judging; isolating convergences, intersections and displacements; producing groups, arrangements and juxtapositions. As critical passengers we collected and arranged; gave shape and expression to the forces of *tramjatra*; created surfaces for others to add to, pass through and travel along.

As a critical passenger I became aware of being transported by *tramjatra* in different ways; I became sensitive to passage – 'ways of moving and being moved'[4] – and this affect of *tramjatra* continues to direct and move me.

I travelled through and along passages both real and imaginary – tram tracks and cities, *tramjatra* and art, lines of poetry and text, films and song. Michael Douglas described tramways as 'an array of particular spatial sequences and proximities with temporal passages and punctuations'.[5] *Tramjatra* was similarly composed of points and passages, sequences and punctuations. There were positions mapped out like tram stops in amongst the network of tracks – destinations and aims, points of departure and arrival.

To travel between points was useful at times as it enabled one to frame and focus points of view, fixing them like picture postcards in amongst the dynamics of the project. There was however something uneasy about taking a passage composed of points and positions – moving from one point to the next. It produced an underlining of colonialism that could be felt while seated, which in the context of *tramjatra* and the colonialist history of both cities meant this seat was well worn by people intent on getting from A to B. In contrast was the sensation of movement: the travel, the passage itself, the momentum, the velocity, and the forces that rushed along, stalled, derailed, lurched – affecting, propelling and halting one. Other forces and dynamics surfaced and produced passages made through improvised decisions and affects. In many ways, different kinds of passages distinguished the two cities. The grid of Melbourne almost demanded a passage composed of points and positions. Kolkata was more fluid. Jogi described the streets in Kolkata as rivers, flows of people and traffic that one needed to become caught in to move.

As a passenger, one is perhaps more sensitive to passage than points – the circuitous nature of movement, shifts in momentums, changes in direction and the potential of other possible passages that offer themselves up on the journey. Points are places of waiting and expectation of becoming mobile. As a passenger, one also became aware of the movement of art and the passages opened up through the pursuit of line, colour and sound.

I am reminded here of a scene in the film by Jean Cocteau titled *Blood of a Poet* when the poet plunges into a mirror on the wall.[6] The mirror does not break but becomes fluid and allows the poet to pass through its reflection into a surreal world of imagination –

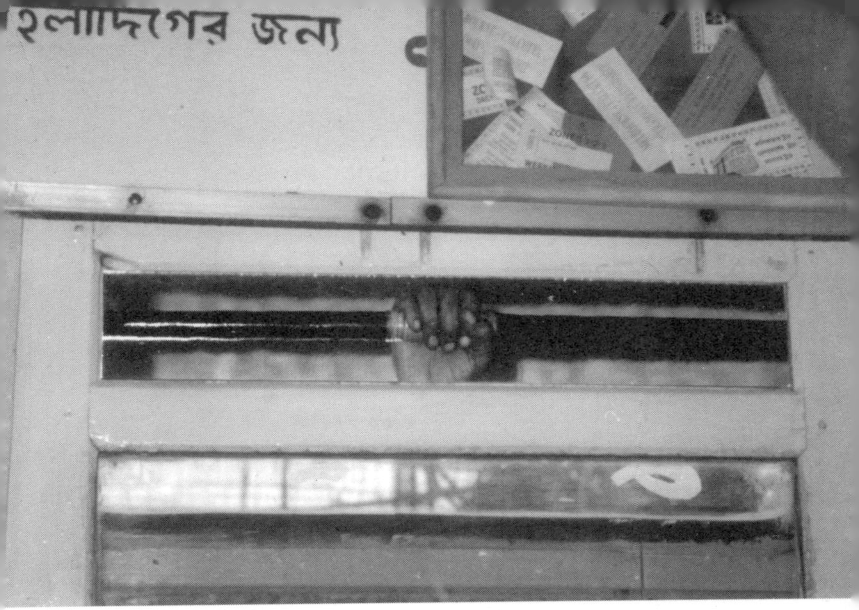


interestingly, in the film this was a corridor or passage. The art of *tramjatra* was like the mirror – it was encountered not as a reflection but as an entry into other lines of travel and paths. One was invited to become a passenger to be engulfed and swept up along at different momentums. To think of art as passage transforms the relation between viewer and art. Critical distances collapse – one may approach art as a window through which to look or be absorbed in its surfaces, composed of many lines of potential passages with which to connect and journey. Journey by art; journey by tram; passages of line, colour and sound.

Deleuze said 'art is never an end in itself... It is only an instrument for tracing lines of life'; he refers to it as 'a passage of life'. 'What it lays out are paths – it is itself a voyage.'[7]

My ticket of passage – 'What if a practice of critical selection, evaluation and re-presentation were to stimulate the potential of *tramjatra*?' – is still valid here in the context of this publication. I invite you to come along for a ride along a passage of *tramjatra*.

Jayashree Chakravarty's paintings composed of lines and colour swept you along wherever you entered; they did not demand deciphering so much as engagement and encouraged you to move. I have an image beside me of Jayashree painting a canvas at The Esplanade in Kolkata – her hand, holding a paint brush, gestures towards the canvas, marking it with black lines which in time became dense with line and colour expressing curious routes along a surface composed of both Kolkatan and Melbourne tramways. '"That place, this place, there and now and that's how you can go and return." She traces pathways. ... Imaginary tracks, places and destinations merge with the real, giving you an option in your journeys – when do you want to get off? When do you want to come on? Where do you want to go?'[8]

There were journeys which physically mapped points of *tramjatra*. *Smart Array* spread out across the City Circle tram route in Melbourne. Magnetic stickers bearing faces of tram workers leered out from tram poles. Incidental, discrete, ephemeral – picked up by gusts of winds and observant passer-bys. The displacement and reiteration of bright yellow tram prows had the effect of making visible *tramjatra* in the city of Melbourne. Prows, which are usually located at tram stops in the middle of the road with the purpose of sending cars off into flight rather than ploughing into people waiting, were displaced to footpaths, intersections and podiums. One became aware of the city as composed of lines and networks. *Curious Yellow* also opened up a space of passage – this time between above and below ground, between present and past. *Curious Yellow* is a 'W' class tram and as these trams do not have a front and a back, it is not evident which way it is travelling.

*Trambaby* also produced its own passages through distribution – in this instance, composed of the circulation of postcards and posters which told a story of a baby girl who was connected with *tramjatra*. Fifteen hundred postcards were handed out in a period of thirty minutes during the Kolkatan launch of *tramjatra*. 'This girl really got around the town.'[9] *Moving Message* also invited people to physically engage – not by picking up something and becoming a passage themselves but by entering thoughts as text into a long, rectangular, portable LED screen which was then transported around the city displaying in lights moving messages.

Passages of transformation were encountered in *Melbourne's Vault*. Re-built in Kolkata at 1:1 scale, the infamous Melbourne public artwork *Vault* was relocated albeit transformed. The passage of the sculpture from one city to another involved the transportation of images of the steel Melbourne *Vault* to Kolkata, its creation as a pandal made from fibre, and images of this Kolkatan vault, titled *Melbourne's Vault*, being taken back to Melbourne.

Making visible the thickness of passage as well as lines of travel was encountered in *Diamond Cutters* – hundreds of metres of pigment was spread at Howrah Bridge, the gateway to Kolkata. Between the tram tracks, the spaces were covered with pigments used for Holi festival. Colours of bright yellow, red, green and pink made the space between tracks present and thick. People and waves of traffic continued to spread the pigments and mark out other paths of movement and circulation. Here the passage is tidal and dense – tangible. Sound had a similar effect – the space of passages becomes full and as a passenger you are swept up, becoming buoyant. This was the affect and effect of the scroll paintings accompanied by song – imaginings of past and future conveyed through image and song, from one moment to another, one frame scrolling to the next.

A passage that went through the entire project was the film, *Kather Baxo*. Films as passages are also thick and animated with light, colour and sound. One becomes immersed in a film and is carried along with it, moving and moved by it. 'I remember sitting in a theatre in Melbourne, prior to our departure, watching excerpts from the film. I had not been to Kolkata before and I was struck by the images I saw projected onto the screen. It was full of information as well as dreamy images. The Maidan and the interiors of the tram, in particular, made a deep impression. As we sat there watching the film, each of us was imagining ourselves in Kolkata and its tramcars.'[10] These images and imaginings from that encounter continued to affect me throughout the project. The film was projected again at the Max Müeller Bhavan in Kolkata as part of a *tramjatra* get together, and then a public showing at The Esplanade tram terminus where passer-bys requested several encores. And in Melbourne, it was projected in the First Site Gallery as part of the *tramjatra* exhibition. Each encounter was different.

The sound in the film was haunting in a lingering way – invoking a call to take passage. I still hear it when I think of Kolkata: 'A strange melodic urban call – a sound of motion that beckons siren-like. ... It is as though the city has spoken to you – the tram's connection to the ground as it weaves its way through the streets of Kolkata gives voice to the city. And the sound is not one of lament, nor nostalgia but something which affects you in an intangible way – a song of the present redolent with the past.'[11]

This passage of text brings me to another passage, this time composed of lines of writing, in particular the daily column in *The Statesman* newspaper over the period of *tramjatra* in Kolkata and *The Passenger* broadsheet in Melbourne. These passages of text were not only extensions of the project like trajectories shooting off at junctions; they were intensions, in the sense of intensities produced within the journey, within *tramjatra*. The passages of text became vehicles for connecting people with the project; they conveyed the project to people and connected them to various passages of the project. Each passage became an invitation for others to come for a ride, to be passengers in the project through encounters of reading, imagining and imaging, to contribute their own ideas.

*The Statesman* is India's largest selling English newspaper, which has a daily readership of more than two million. The idea of a daily column was not pre-planned but emerged during the project due to a culmination of forces and evolved into a column written daily over a period of five weeks. This passage continued in Melbourne although in a different mode. A daily column in one of the Melbourne newspapers would not have been possible given the different forces – so we published a weekly broadsheet in a similar spirit. This was called *The Passenger*. We printed and distributed 1,000 copies a week over the duration of the project.

Writing the daily column for *The Statesman* and preparing text for *The Passenger* affected my life in immeasurable ways. In Kolkata, hours of each day were spent sitting in front of a computer at the

Touring Guest House – lines of text producing columns and mapping out passages at different velocities depending on all sorts of factors as the deadline of 3pm advanced. (A good example of passenger passivity and activity!) Or in the long basement corridor of First Site Gallery, where Jogi, Neal Haslem and myself wrote copy and pasted text to produce issues of *The Passenger* – often working overnight to meet the first newspaper print run in the morning.

These passages were also moving in other ways – I have vivid images of the interiors of *The Statesman* – seemingly endless corridors, small smoke-filled rooms, sitting opposite John Thomas, an editor, talking about big issues encased within an enormous neoclassical building with a circular exterior that made it both advance and recede into the otherwise congested streets of Kolkata. I enjoyed being in this space, lingering amongst journalists, breathing in an atmosphere full of history and particles from 129 years of printing yet engaged and intense with current issues. I hadn't thought of it at the time; it was only later that I remembered my grandfather was a journalist – an editor for *The Argus* in Melbourne. Like *The Statesman, The Argus* is also a neoclassical building with a colonialist past. My visits to *The Statesman* affected me – my becoming journalist produced a passage I continue to travel.

This passage, however, is coming to a point of arrival – or is it departure? It's impossible to tell when some trams don't have a front and a back.

1 Nicola Morelli, 'One night in India', appears in *The Statesman*, 2 March 2001; *The Passenger*, Melbourne: *tramjatra*, 16 November 2001; and *Artfan 9*, Autumn 1999, 36. This text was written in 1997 when the Melbourne–Calcutta Friendship tram was doing the routes of Melbourne. Formerly at the Politecnico di Milano and RMIT University, Morelli is now at the Institute of Architecture and Design, Aalbourg University, Denmark.

2 See Gilles Deleuze, 'To have done with judgement', in *Essays Critical and Clinical*, translated by D.W. Smith and M.A. Greco, Minneapolis: University of Minnesota Press, 1997.

3 Gilles Deleuze, 'What children say', in *Essays Critical and Clinical*, translated by D.W. Smith and M.A. Greco, Minneapolis: University of Minnesota Press, 1997, 63.

4 Michael Douglas, *tramjatra* press release, February 2001, Kolkata.

5 Michael Douglas, 'A Tracking Vehicle', unpublished Durable Visual Record of Masters of Arts project, RMIT University, Melbourne: 1997, 30.

6 Jean Cocteau, *La Sang d'un poete (Blood of a Poet)*, 1931.

7 Gilles Deleuze, 'What children say', in *Essays Critical and Clinical*, translated by D.W. Smith and M.A. Greco, Minneapolis: University of Minnesota Press, 1997, 63.

8 Jayashree Chakravarty, *The Passenger*, Melbourne: *tramjatra*, Friday 9 November 2001, 1.

9 Lisa Young, *The Passenger*, Melbourne: *tramjatra*, Friday 9 November 2001, 2.

10 Suzie Attiwill, 'A reflective journey', in *The Statesman*, 30 March 2001, 3.

11 Suzie Attiwill, 'A different sound, a different story', in *The Statesman*, 20 February 2001, 3.

DEPARTING

TRACKING

**NETWORKING**

SHEDDING

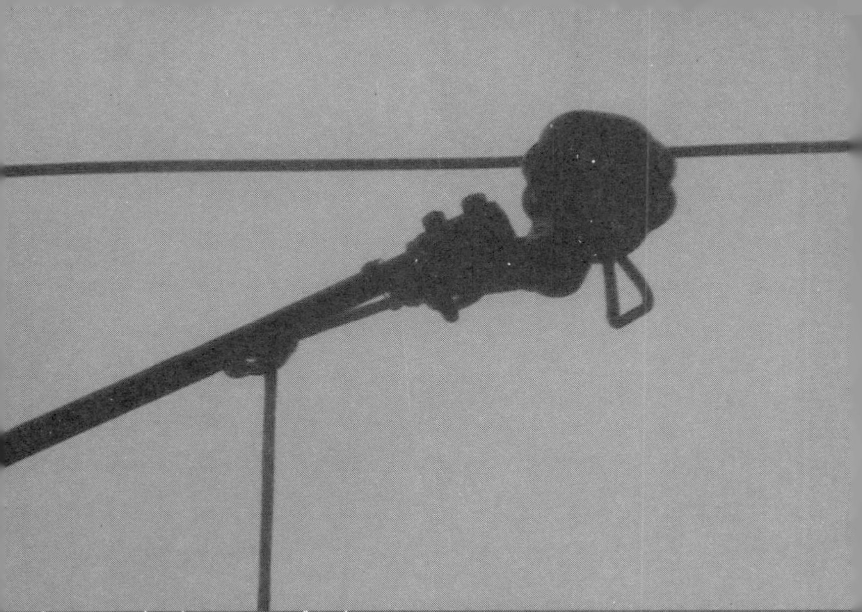

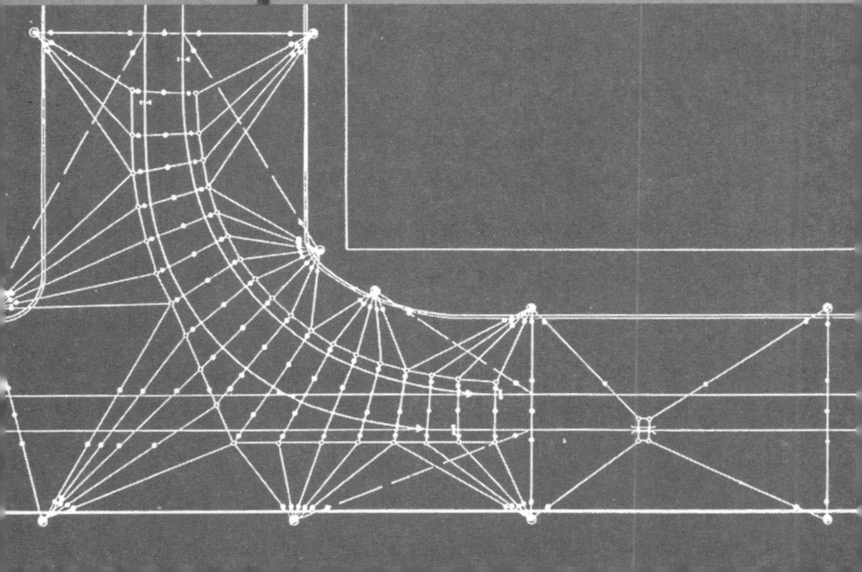

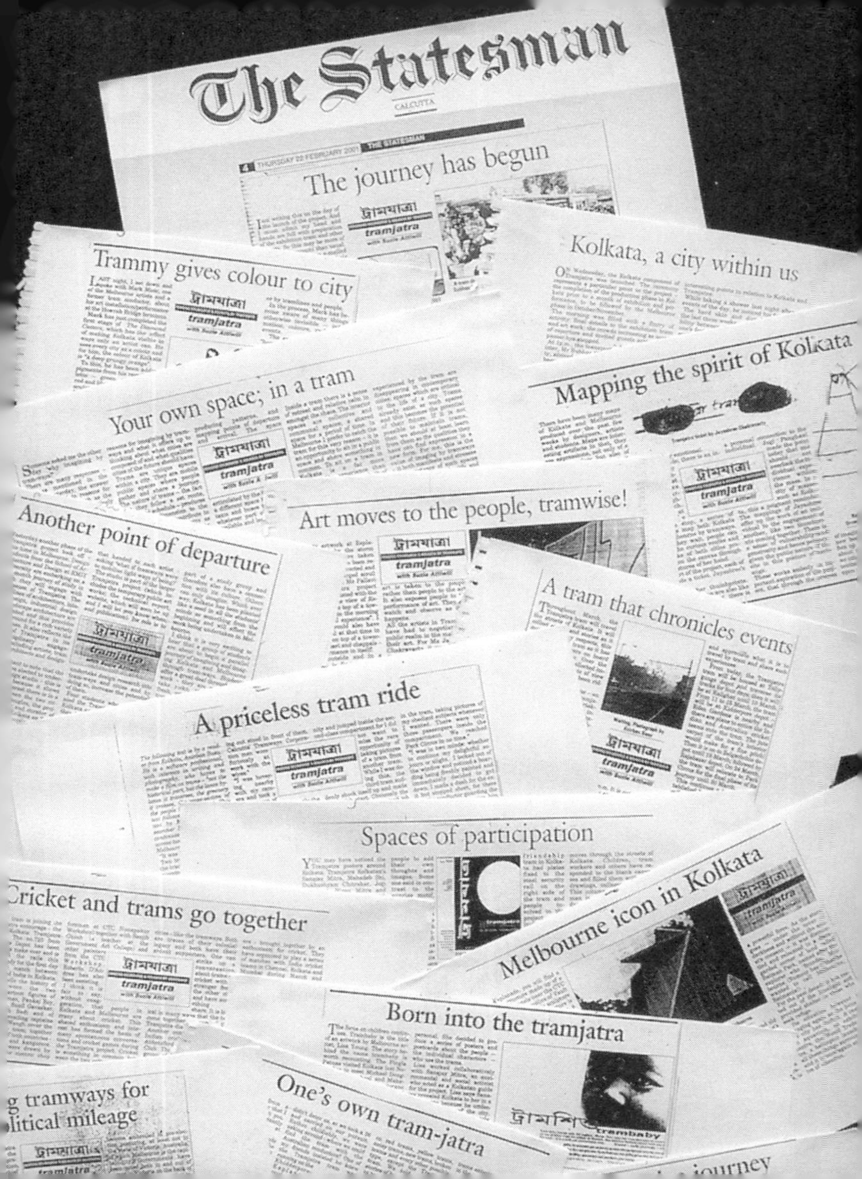
The Statesman
CALCUTTA
The journey has begun
ট্রামযাত্রা
tramjatra
Trammy gives colour to city
Kolkata, a city within us
Your own space; in a tram
Mapping the spirit of Kolkata
Art moves to the people, tramwise!
Another point of departure
A tram that chronicles events
A priceless tram ride
Spaces of participation
Cricket and trams go together
Melbourne icon in Kolkata
Born into the tramjatra
trambaby
One's own tram-jatra
g tramways for
litical mileage
journey

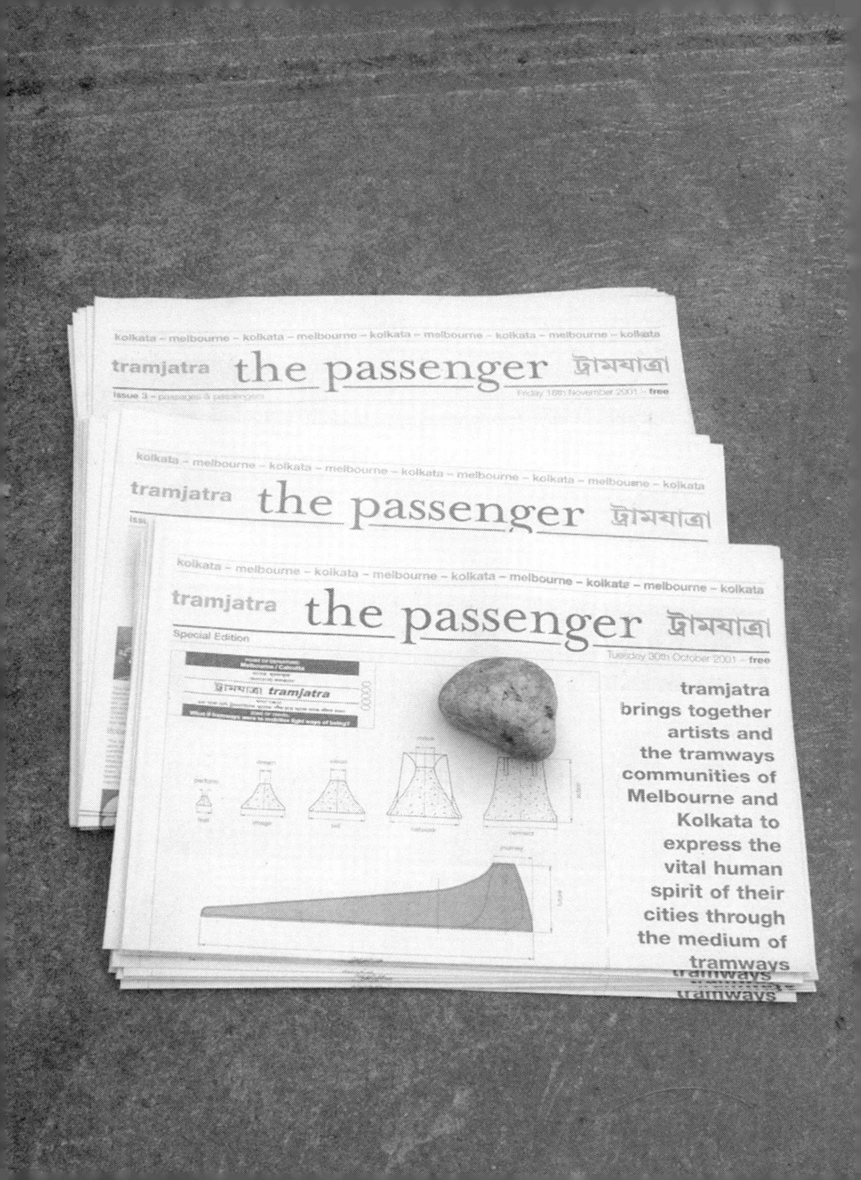

kolkata – melbourne – kolkata – melbourne – kolkata – melbourne – kolkata – melbourne – kolkata
tramjatra the passenger ট্রামযাত্রা
issue 3 – passages & passengers
Friday 16th November 2001 – free
kolkata – melbourne – kolkata – melbourne – kolkata – melbourne – kolkata – melbourne – kolkata
tramjatra the passenger ট্রামযাত্রা
kolkata – melbourne – kolkata – melbourne – kolkata – melbourne – kolkata – melbourne – kolkata
tramjatra the passenger ট্রামযাত্রা
Special Edition
Tuesday 30th October 2001 – free
ট্রামযাত্রা tramjatra
tramjatra brings together artists and the tramways communities of Melbourne and Kolkata to express the vital human spirit of their cities through the medium of tramways

**...a journey of a different kind – one that highlighted the soul of Kolkata...**

*Hindustan Times*, Kolkata: 14 March 2001, education supplement.

**ট্রাম বাঁচাতে হাত মেলাল কলকাতা আর মেলবোর্ন**

*Ananda Bazaar Patrika*, Kolkata: 19 February 2000, 6.

**Goodwill tram**

*Turning Point*, vol 5; no 3, Melbourne: Public Transport Corporation, 27 February 1997.

**Melbourne boost for city trams**

*The Statesman*, Kolkata: 3 February 2001, 1.

**Ratbag ambassador stays on the rails**

*The Age*, Melbourne: 22 September 1997, Metro 1.

**Kolkata, Melbourne in tram interface**

*The Economic Times*, Kolkata: 21 February 2001, 7.

**Tramjatra charms jaded city**

*The Times of India*, Kolkata: 22 February 2001, 1.

**ট্রামের তুল্য যান নেই আসুন, নতুন করে ভাবি**

*Ananda Bazaar Patrika*, Kolkata: 22 February 2001, 4.

**...euphoria generated by the tramjatra...**

*Times of India*, Kolkata: 11 March 2001, 10.

**...forced the two governments to sit up and take notice...**

*The Telegraph*, Kolkata: 23 January 2000, Metro 1.

**A connie's new carriage through India**

*The Age*, Melbourne: 23 February 2001, 9.

**The language of trams**

*The Melbourne Times*, Melbourne: 14 November 2001, 14.

**Kolkata will see one of its most novel cultural projects...**

*The Economic Times*, Kolkata: 21 February 2001, 7.

তিনি নিজেকে ট্রাম ভাবেন

*Ananda Bazaar Patrika*, Kolkata: 28 May 2000, 4.

**Tram enthusiasts...have campaigned to save the trams and they've succeeded – for now.**

*India*, Lonely Planet travel guide, 9th edition, Melbourne: Lonely Planet Publications, 2001,453.

**Tramjatra binds together two cities at opposite ends of the socio-economic table....Tram global, feel local.**

*The Age*, Melbourne: 3 November 2001, Saturday Extra 3.

**Going gaga over a city tramcar**

*Hindustan Times*, Kolkata: 21 February 2001, 4.

**A journey to salvage a dying culture**

*The Statesman*, Kolkata: 5 February 2001, 4.

**Right on track**

*The Economic Times*, Kolkata: 22 February 2001, 8.

**International friendship through trams**

*Metro News*, Melbourne: 15 March 2000, 10.

**From:** ranajay@vsnl.com
**To:** "Tramjatra_Kolkata" <tramjatra_kolkata@yahoogroups.com>
**Date:** 19/03/01 8:36 AM
**Subject:** [tramjatra_kolkata] Face Off in The Telegraph

---

Mayor vs. Minister in **The Telegraph** (Kolkata, 17 March 2001):

---

**FACE OFF/TRAMJATRA**

---

**High on heritage, short on use**

---

**Subrata Mukherjee**
Mayor of Calcutta

The latest drama of Tramjatra is nothing but a big joke. The transport minister is only interested in playing to the gallery. Does it make any sense to get some retired people down from Melbourne and creating a huge hoopla over how trams are dying in Calcutta? Really, it's just another gimmick by the transport minister to attract attention.

The 'yes-tram' brigade should just talk to residents on Chitpur Road or Harrison Road. We have received numerous complaints of noise pollution and associated health hazards from those who live in houses close to the tram tracks. And it's not just sound pollution. Go personally and check out the condition of roads where trams run. They are in real bad shape. The Tram Company doesn't even pay us for the damage caused by their vehicles, putting us under severe financial pressure to repair roads. It's common knowledge that roads comprise only six per cent of the city area with encroachment rampant in many localities. Under these conditions, the city just cannot afford trams on some of the streets. I must say that I, too, love trams and I would like to see revamped trams on some of the streets. But in their existing form, they belong to the museum alone.

---

**Subhas Chakraborty**
Transport Minister

The Tramjatra has proved a huge success. The aim was to create awareness about the condition of tramways in the city and muster support for this form of transportation. With so many people coming forward, from artistes to ordinary people, we have decided to make the Calcutta-Melbourne Tram Festival an annual event. How can you ignore heritage? How can you sacrifice something that is so beautiful on the altar of a warped idea of modernisation?
Trams have been, are, and will continue to be a symbol of Calcutta. I am aware that some people are opposed to trams. But I believe trams are a fantastic mode of transport, which is so eco-friendly. And it is in keeping with the character of the city and its people. I want to assure all tram-lovers that these cars, which are an integral part of the heritage of Calcutta, will not be phased out. We are formulation several plants to improve the infrastructure for tramways in the city. We want to extend the tram network and have already started modernisation of cars. in this context, an American company has conducted a survey and a Rs 500-crore pilot project will be launched from Esplanade to Thakurpukur.

---

Victoria, ... Technology,

AUSTRALIA.

Calcutta—30/5/2000.

— 1 —

Dear friend,

As per your advertisement in our Bengali Newspaper called "Ananda Bazar patrika" dated 28/5/2000, I came to know that you are not only a tram lover but doing everything for welfare of tram lovers of Melbourne and Calcutta. It is to say that I am a tram lover too and always like to travel in a tram to see beautiful places/View of Calcutta and like it very much.

I am very much interested to make real friendship with you and wish to write you regularly and like to be your real friend. I am very much interested about Australian people and their culture and like to know more about them, because am very much interested about your beautiful country Australia.

It is my intention to marry a beautiful Australian girl and to stay with her in Australia and work there.

I am an Indian, Hindu, Bengali young man and my date of birth is 23/1/54 and am unmarried. My complexion is fair and figure is slim. My height is 5'–3". I have black eyes with curly black hair. I am B.A. from Calcutta University (1979) with Bengali, English, History and political Science. I passed the poultry training course in 1986. I passed the short course on Museum studies in 1987 and also passed the film projectionist course in 1987. I have few knowledge of Indian Bengali cooking and am teaching few children as a private tutor. We have our own house at Calcutta and am living along with my mother and two younger brothers. My father died on 21/8/99. We have only a sister who get married and living just nearby of our house along with her husband and two sons. Herewith am enclosing my BIO-DATA/photograph for your real friendship purpus. Please write me details about yourself along with your photograph at an earliest by Air Mail. Please also write me about your beautiful city Melbourne and your beautiful country Australia too. Please write me details about yourself along with your photograph at an earliest by Air Mail and please be my real friend and I shall be thankful to you. In India there are no colour, race and religion. In India and Calcutta you will see "The Temple", "The Church" and "The Mosque" for pray. What's the weather like in Melbourne?

Enclo:— Contd ......../2. P.T.O. →

8

# passengers

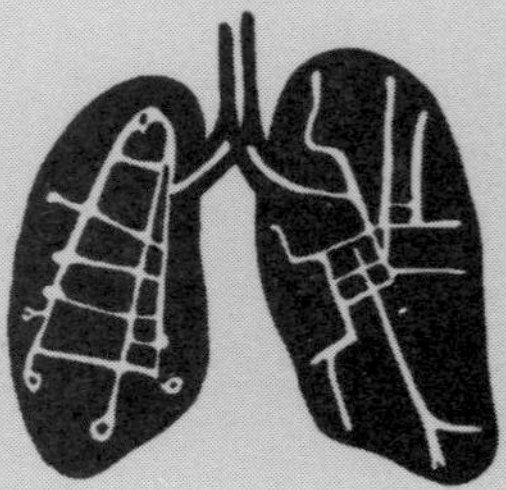

## unhurried

Man has always had a craving for speed. To legitimise his desire, he has hurriedly used the word 'fast', not even pausing to reflect that the term 'fast food' is an unqualified specimen of ridiculous coining in the English language. Thankfully, the coining has stopped short as far as the food for our mental faculties are concerned – no amount of hurry can invigorate our mental abilities, it needs its own pace and time.

And so does the tram. Trams, like trains, have always fascinated me. Perhaps because both create a pattern of images and a rhythm which is unique to both their forms of movement. There is one difference, however. Unlike trains, trams in India, or in Kolkata for that matter, present a picture of an era gone by.

The tram traveller in India is a quintessential Bengali, a dreamer and a poet. No wonder the tram has been able to survive the rude onslaught of being derailed from Kolkata on the sham excuse of ushering in speed. The tram is by no means lacking in redeeming features as a means of transport. Its unhurriedness is as legitimate as is required in the 'alaap' of a 'raga'.

I do not remember the exact date when the movement called *tramjatra* started. All I remember was my pleasant surprise in noticing an unassuming column in the middle pages of *The Statesman* inviting articles, images, thoughts, ideas and what-have-you on trams, and it was signed – Suzie Attiwill.

In this ironic human civilisation, where speedier modes of transport are attempting to make the world 'smaller' and secessionist forces are trying to divide the world into watertight compartments, *tramjatra* stands out as exemplary. It deals with one of the oldest and slowest modes of transport in attempting to build a bridge between two cities across two hemispheres.

*Tramjatra* is the beginning of a journey, perhaps of a dawn. Given its due time, it will transform the lives of those it touches. For some, it already has.

*Anirban Basu – software professional, Kolkata*

## tangled by tramways

I was lured by the signage in a hallway off Swanston Street – 'Imagining Melbourne & Kolkata by Tramways'. How could it be so personal?

In my imagination, as a Sydney girl, Melbourne was the land of trams set in a landscape of grey skies and dusty bluestone, associated with the knarled, tragic sensibilities of Tucker and the sleek bleakness of Bracks – those twentieth-century Melburnian painters. Curiously, I remember too the concrete expanse of RMIT Building 14 on Swanston Street – the engineering heartland of the metropolitan tech. Walking past with a Sydney friend many years ago, he pointed to this as the site where he had learnt his craft. It stuck in my mind – the incongruity of this wall and the sensitivity of my literary, arty friend – how possible?

I never imagined my own lifeworld would overlap with this space one day – right by the tramline, right inside RMIT. Nothing simple – probably not even accidental – some design unfolding, beguiling, ensnaring.

My first exposure to the world outside Sydney was via Kolkata and its trams – a kaleidoscope of colour and bursting sunshine on barren ground, festooned with glitter and crimson. Here: exposed to unimaginable, unfathomable wealth and poverty, yet, easy entry into local curiosity and communication – to an India that accepted the English speakers that we were, despite its own mixed and bloody experience of the English.

Trams – both in Melbourne and Calcutta, then, now – English in derivation but vernacular in realisation in time and space. Not just vessels of transport – not just here and there.

And right in the middle of Swanston Street, down in the cavern of the RMIT art gallery, it all came together again – surreal – out of time – enveloping – tears welling in my eyes at what was possible – to love and hate, to know and be ignorant, to desire and be repelled, to languish and be fulfilled, to be foreign and familiar – all tangled up, interwoven even – sensations, needs, actions – at RMIT and in trams – in Melbourne and Kolkata. Gathered in that space were the connies with their olive green shorts and brown leather bags, the wiry ebony-skinned storytellers and their scrolls, the theorists eyeing scraps of notes, the earnest academics clasping folders, bright-eyed students with video cams, the art dealers looking for a bargain, transported by memory and yearning, having arrived at another transitory 'spot' in time, in all its Wordsworthian splendour.

*Mary Kalantzis – Professor of Education, RMIT University, Melbourne*

So, we're collecting with you *tramjatra* VIPs at this house party in Fitzroy! You're the toast of the town, you Naxalitedar, in your Mao inspired coat, you bidi-smokerdar in your lovely dhoti-showing-leg outfit, and of course you my globe trotting Non Resident Indian, Bonsoir dar, as you hold that glass of chardonnay. And I – what do I call myself – let's settle on Tashdar, an Anglo Indian from Calcutta. There you stand my pre-Kolkata Calcutta brothers. Assembled. In the courtyard of this inner-city Melbourne house opposite a park. What do you think of the joint? Ha, ha, ha. You are too polite to say – 'Tashdar it bloody looks like the backstreets of Cal!'

'How so?' I would taunt, pretending not to know your Calcutta checklist of real estate where pissable side streets, grotty park, derelict looking bridge, pollution means you are in the back streets of Cal, Mother Theresa territory, the missionary position. Tick, tick, tick. But my friends, you are now Down Under, here the values are ulta pulta – inverted, grotty is chic, derelict – vintage, narrow streets – intimate. This place has sooo much character.

Bonsoir dar you are looking so estylish in your lungi and black shirt – you have the hot look. You could become a guru here y'know, just let the pigeon drip its markings onto your forehead and a fortune awaits you.

And here is the Orientalist telling Naxalitedar about Hinduism! Let him. He's enjoying himself so. Tad awkward though. Him knowing more about your religion than you do. And he's revelling in the telling, listen to him sheeting it in – the genealogy of the Hindu pantheon; the inner significance of the Vedanta; why Gandhi slept with the virgin; and wait for it...here it comes...Tantric Love – Sacred Sex, they all have to get to THAT! How to have a root and not give a hoot. Try not to let the resentment flame in your old revolutionary eyes Naxalitedar. You are the Oracle. Indulge the Western expert. String him along. Then make up a story – tell him that Ganesh married Parvati and sired the bull Nandi – and reel him in like hilsa fish on the end of a bamboo rod. Keep a straight face and speak firmly when you spin your tale and he'll believe you because you're the genuine article, ashol not nokal. Yes, now you have him on the run.

And what of you my bidismoker dar. Only you know what rapture lies in that rolled up tendu leaf. Inhale. Breathe in this house, this ulta pultadness. Exhale quickly! They want you to sing. They've gheraoed you. Look up at the cross-cultural dressers. This one near you wrapped in Indian silk looks like a Hare Krishna on leave, that one with the bangle bought his Indianess from the corner shop, and bidismoker dar, try not to ogle Honey Hips. C'mon give them all a tale or two for old time's sake. Tell them about *tramjatra* – the journey. Tell them what we both know.

*Keith Butler – writer, Melbourne*

## tram sport

Seldom have I been further from playing a cricket match than travelling through the back blocks of Kolkata on a tram. But I mean that only in a metaphysical way of course, because anyone who has been there knows that there is no place like Kolkata for a game of street cricket.

To an outsider, the Abottsford Anglers Cricket Club might have appeared to have journeyed to India to play cricket, and certainly that was part of the deal. In fact, one of the founding tenets of the club, formed on the banks of the Yarra in Melbourne two years to the day prior to our arrival in Kolkata, was to conduct a tour of India.

Yet for the Abottsford Anglers Cricket Club, formed around the philosophy of bringing like-minded souls together over willow and leather and a fine afternoon tea spread, it seemed only natural that the concept of togetherness would lead us to sharing an experience with people of Kolkata through our association with *tramjatra.* And if anything, for all of us it is not the cricket match that sticks in our minds from our visit to Kolkata, but the hospitality, sense of occasion and friendliness of the people we encountered.

Our arrival had been preceded by tales of a 10,000-strong crowd at the match between us and the Calcutta Tramways Company, yet nothing could have prepared us for the chauffeured tram ride to the rain-soaked ground on a tram painted with our club logo, an article in *The Statesman* newspaper and the presence of the Transport Minister to begin our match.

It was a surreal time.

The ground was so muddy a new pitch had to be laid on an adjoining ground. Union flags from both countries were flown above the clubhouse, balls were bowled, runs were scored, wickets fell, and a massive meal was had at the end of it all with a never-ending line of trophies distributed to both sides. It was a gala banquet.

The following day we toured the city on a 'children's tram' set up by *tramjatra*, punching tickets and sharing our experience with some of the city's school children. Later that year a return cricket game was staged in Melbourne between the Anglers and all the visiting Kolkatans and local *tramjatra* people, and a 'cricket tram' entered in Melbourne's Moomba Parade with *tramjatra* that spread the word of communities working together to help each other.

The Anglers lost that big cricket match of the season, but as it usually is with India, the journey through Kolkata was more exciting than any specific event.

*Lyall Johnson – journalist and Abottsford Anglers Cricket Club member, Melbourne*

## who owns the city?

With all the pursuit and protection of self-interest, who cares about the city of Kolkata? Who represents the city in its plurality? Little wonder that there seems to be a complete absence of any positive vision, since polarisation has come to be in the nature of things. This city can break from its colonial legacy and build itself anew. The current problems – whether of slums, or of choked canals and traffic-stalled streets – could become the key means for renewal. But for any of that to be realised, the question of civic ownership has to be confronted. Who owns the city?

Public transport is of utmost public importance to citizens. Everyone is affected. In Kolkata, public transport has been an issue on which massive protests, rioting and vandalism has taken place. However, the entire public discourse is distorted. A truly public perspective, one that harmonises different and conflicting interests, which is fair and just, based on thinking out the subject in all its ramifications – is conspicuous by its absence. Instead, we have perspectives that are essentially private, or partisan, which are foisted on the rest. And one also has a dichotomy between public discourse and ultimate practice – the former needing to be 'populist', and the latter simply acquiescing to the private interests of the well-off.

Is there a critical mass of people, rooted in the city, aware of its wealth and poverty, diligent and honest, who can further the public interest, whose personal interest is this public interest? Who can understand and communicate with diverse interests? Who have a clear vision of the future that is not a gimmicky formula, but like Debasish Bhattacharyya's valiant campaigning for sensible public transport policy in Kolkata, help to articulate public consciousness?

Through the issue of public transport it is possible to visualise a large-scale public participation in developing a truly city ethic, a restraint of narrow interests and cooperation with others to erect, avail of, benefit from and enjoy the public sphere. A bus company or a tram company, whether owned by the government or some private entrepreneur, is a public asset. Its sound economics is of utmost importance to the quality of the service it can provide. It is vital that a citizen think of this, and thus take ownership. This is also one of the meanings of Mahatma Gandhi's concept of *swaraj* (self-rule).

What struck me in particular about *tramjatra* was the earnest attempt to make the project an organic expression of our city, and to attempt social communication across socio-economic, cultural and other barriers. *Tramjatra* has to be seen in the context of the city of Kolkata's future, as a humane and healthy city, affording convenient public transport, with a citizenry and civil society that is aware about city matters and challenges, and is alive to its responsibilities to secure such ends.

A positive vision of Kolkata, involving tramway, the desire for this vision, the comprehension of the ramifications of such a vision, the capability to bring this about – all are sadly lacking. The city of Kolkata needs to be awakened from the torpor of apathy and cynicism it has fallen into, thanks to four decades of economic, political and social blight. The *tramjatra* project is bold, imaginative, visionary – and vital. It is about acting to build, protect and secure the public domain, civic society and city community against the assaults of private mafias, capital and the state.

*V. Ramaswamy – civic activist and business manager, Kolkata*

## the twin trammies

There were several ways of experiencing *tramjatra* in November of 2001 in Melbourne. You could attend any number of fixed events – performance evenings, forums and an exhibition – or you could happen upon artworks and activities scattered across the city, thereby finding yourself, quite by chance, a festival participant. I preferred the latter: what happened in the street, at tram stops and on trams.

Roving the tram stops and riding the rails at whim were *tramjatra's* 'twin trammies': Melbourne's own, Roberto D'Andrea, and a connie from Kolkata, Prabir Kumar Goswami. For a man with a name as bright as an exotic bird, Prabir was remarkably reserved. Behind a large round pair of unfashionably heavy glasses, his dark smiling eyes fixed themselves upon the world with a calm and steady gaze. If Prabir resembled any bird, it was an owl.

Roberto's a kookaburra: when he laughs, you laugh. Nine years ago, Roberto and I were tram conductors stationed at South Melbourne depot. Nine years later, he still sends me a stream of mail filled with tramway news, big envelopes that burst at the seams jammed with notes hurriedly scrawled in his distinctive, rolling script: 'rally next week – can you make it?'

Roberto introduced me to Prabir. We all took part in an early morning interview on ABC Radio to promote the Melbourne/Kolkata tramways partnership, the value of our respective tram networks, and the merits of a festival celebrating trams.

When questioned, Roberto leant forward and spoke at length in a voice that bubbled with unqualified excitement. By contrast, Prabir sat perfectly still and considered each question in the kind of prolonged silence that makes radio presenters extremely nervous. His replies, when they came, were slow and deliberate, placed before the public like the testimony of an expert witness during legal proceedings.

What both men undoubtedly shared was a deep and informed passion for the preservation and advancement of reliable, affordable and extensive tramway networks, as well as a great feel for the social and imaginative possibilities aboard each and every tram. In the best possible way, they took themselves seriously. I wished that more of us could find in trams the things they apprehended.

After the radio interview, I met them again only by chance – because I'd bump into them somewhere in the city, or at a tram stop, or gathered together at the back of my tram making tourists laugh. Each time, the same thing: Roberto the first to greet me and behind him, Prabir, composed and attentive.

I rode their tram several times without them ever knowing. One stop here. Two stops there. Whatever I required. That's when you saw them at their best – working the tram as connies once did. They could stand in a doorway issuing directions to a crowd of noisy passengers and never lose their balance though the tram heaved beneath them like surf. They shifted their weight from side-to-side and bent at the knees in one fluent move, an action repeated a thousand times over without any thought or strain.

When I last saw them together they were on a tram, up the front, one to the left and one to the right, peering into the driver's cabin, over his window and on to the tracks. They watched in silence as the tramlines rushed beneath the moving carriage, and everything about the expression on their respective faces said that here were two men who saw in those tracks a poetry both strange and inexhaustible.

*Paul Bateman – writer, Melbourne*

## moving time and space

On Bourke Street in Melbourne, as I look at the avenue from the wide window of the tram, two Australian horses suddenly seem to take the rein of the coach. Bizarre. But that's how the first Kolkata tram was pulled. Way back in 1873 when the city was the capital of British-ruled India.

Suddenly, here I am in one of its second-class coaches from Sealdah station to Dalhousie Square (now BBD Bag) via Bowbazar. Our ultimate destination – Armenian Ghat on the River Hooghly. The poor Australian horses, despite their strength, are unable to pull the coach. It's too heavy with so many passengers inside. The people give a hand. Push, push, they strain their muscles and the coach is on its way. I peep at the first-class coach. Only five passengers! Three Europeans, two Indians. But so what, we are on our way. People line the streets to look at us, dumbstruck by the novel sight, and wave cheerfully.

I shake my head. Why, I dozed off to the last century Kolkata. But here I am in modern Melbourne. The skyscrapers are there, so are the Victorian buildings and the beautiful central station. Can I see Kolkata's Victoria Memorial from here? Oh yes, if I close my eyes, I can see its majestic dome from the window of the Khidirpur-bound tram. I wake up with a start at the 'clang-clang'. Ah, so far away but so near! The tram bell back home in my Kolkata and here on the Melbourne street sounds so similar.

Sweet memories flood into my mind. My coming to Kolkata as a bride, the first sight of the city and the tram on the Howrah Bridge as I and family alight at the Howrah railway station. My first ride in the tram, making a beeline to the ladies' seat. Taking my daughter to school in the tram, taking around my guests in trams to 'see' Kolkata when they visit me (much like today's Metro, a must-be-experienced event for newcomers). In my slow introduction to the city, the tram is invariably woven into it.

Arriving in Melbourne, I want to explore the city. I follow the directions from the hotel receptionist and jump into a tram. Where to buy a ticket? They don't have conductors like we have in Kolkata. Guess what? There is this Indian student, who introduces me to the intricacies of the ticket vending machine but pays for my ticket. A good beginning indeed. Within a day or two I get the hang of the place, recognise which route to take for which destination, make use of the city circle tram to experience the hub of the city. I don't feel lonely though I am alone. The familiarity of the tram helps me to familiarise myself with the city, I make friends on the way and talk about my city with the same kind of coaches. Somebody exclaims, 'Of course, I've been to Kolkata too!'

*Ranjita Biswas – writer, Kolkata*

## connecting

I succumbed to the *tramjatra*. How many opportunities does one get to 'connect'! *Tramjatra* provided a connection of people, cities and cultures, but was not always about connecting: more often it was about exploring something or someone that I thought I knew too well. When we arrived at Melbourne airport – a first time for all of us, the men in uniform at the airport took us aside to politely check on us. What brings us here? Would we go back? He almost gagged when I said that fourteen million people wouldn't be able to hold me back from my city (a population only a little less than that of the country I am visiting!)

The first of surprises from my 'firingi' friend was his perception of spring. We were invited to enjoy spring. A spring when the air cut through our bones. Moyna wrapped her saree around tightly, Dukhoda lit one cigarette after the other and Mahadeb was bending double. But as the day grew older, the sun shone brighter and we felt warmer. And familiar tram tracks winked like signs in the sunlight saying, 'This is tram country.'

Melbourne is very much a tram city. A city that is less noisy, fairly efficient yet not very rushed. The tram bells could be heard from our guest-house. And a strange sound every time the traffic signal changed. I discovered later that the sound was to warn visually challenged pedestrians. I appreciate the sensibility of a city that takes care of its people.

We roamed through the city in a big group with Roberto leading. The entire tram community seemed to know him. And when we got on to a tram, he had similar ideas to ours when it came to buying tickets! I pushed all the right buttons in the ticket machine but did not put in the coin when it asked me to do so! Cheating could be a huge adrenalin kick.

When Moyna and Dukho performed on the streets, I would locate a bench and settle my bulk on it and watch – watch unashamedly the trams crawling, the brown-coloured heritage tram, the purple-coloured one with an advertisement of a woman taking a shower in champagne, people pouring out of the railway station all wrapped up in their own worlds, people playing on the big chess board on Swanston Street, the young guy of East Asian origin on the street playing violin.

The 'urban fabric' of the city is sewn together with tram tracks under a maze of overhead wires. Back home I see the fabric fraying. Moyna asked me why we couldn't have trams the way Melbourne has – we too have cars like them, we have buildings like them, then why not trams? In the last few years so many of our tram routes have been maimed to accommodate fly-overs. One gets the feeling that no one is interested in trams anymore. When I see the rickety trams in my city trying to crawl, I feel that it may be too late to do anything, but connecting with fourteen million fellow city dwellers instills confidence in me. If we cannot do it, then who will?

*Aparna Das – architect and planner, Kolkata*

## that purple patch

As a result of *tramjatra* one of the world's poorest and most overcrowded cities has had an area of vivid purple pigment applied to a grimy road surface between badly maintained intersecting tramlines. Its incongruity makes for a graphic photograph. And that makes for a good exhibition in a wealthy city and that leads to learned discussions about 'public art processes' and 'transculturalism'. When culture is discussed I reach for, unlike Goering, my remote.

In the meanwhile, has Kolkata's public transport infrastructure been improved as a result of this activity? Is it any faster? A major cause of complaint. Is it more reliable, more frequent, more comfortable? Is the service expanding rather than contracting? Do Kolkatans feel better about their trams now that they had a pink and yellow patch?

Originally, one of the reasons for Melbourne tram workers getting involved with the tramways of Kolkata was to celebrate its survival, for like Melbourne's, they are the last of their kind in their respective countries. Another was to support the continued existence of that service in Kolkata, which was, and still is, under attack from the bus and car lobbies. The infrastructure needs to be improved and can be through professional advice. And lastly, and importantly, we need to celebrate the tramway culture to be found in each city.

How could we also turn around that lack of esteem and respect for its trams and its tram workers with both cities suffering with rundown systems? Without popular support and demand for better services, government finance will not be forthcoming.

As a Melbourne conductor in the early 1990s, I decided to amuse the passengers and staff by writing and putting up in the trams short anonymous stories (often about themselves) in a poetry style, elucidating along the way as to why there were the problems they were experiencing. Trams have frequently been used in Melbourne in creative ways. Painted by artists, as a moving photographic gallery, for the staging of plays, for Mad On Trams Week where everyone from musicians to tapdancers were invited to strut their stuff. In any mass transport system creativity must appeal to and involve as many as possible, it should connect with them.

*Tramjatra*, which has subsumed the original project, is esoteric, Western and intellectual. Significantly, when it came to Melbourne in 2001 it was hosted by a university. Its academic participants were largely highly paid theoreticians. Whether *tramjatra* artists connected with the public was irrelevant for most of the Western artists created art highly charged with theory, to impress their peers, and to be discussed by the theoreticians. Melbourne has a population of three million. The small number who attended were by and large the usual gallery attendees. Nevertheless the project has been well documented, a book published, and careers advanced.

Meanwhile the vivid purple pigment will have faded and more bag-of-bones Kolkata trams will have jumped their tracks. So it goes – or in this case, so they don't go.

*Malcolm Just – poet, former tram conductor, and much else besides, Melbourne*

## I travel by tram

My joining the *tramjatra* team was by a chance circumstance. I was asked to help in formulating a theme for the scroll painters to portray which would encapsulate their use of trams. I reached the venue to find that the problem was cultural. The difficulty that the organisers were facing in explaining the subject to the patuas was the fact that the Australian artist – judging from the members of the team – either never had, or had given up, the use of a set of accepted metaphors and symbols which through shared traditions would act as an narrative vocabulary in the events/works that art presents. For them a work of art is singular and individual.

The patuas have an array of symbolic icons/images/subjects/themes based on a shared tradition woven out of mythology, folklore, etc–a sort of community mnemonic. One has to enter into this structure to be able to communicate. A bald statement of the theme or subject will not emote the necessary expressiveness. Of course for a member of the community there is no need to consciously enter the 'community mnemonic' – it is part of his heritage.

I have since stayed in connection with the team through Mick. My friendship with Mick has gone beyond the ambit of the *tramjatra* because within the august environs of academia he is a congenital subversive. Of course he sometimes speaks and elaborates on a subject like an academic but this is his ultimate disguise and the proof of his being a thoroughly true-blue subversive. This digression is necessary because it explains why I have continued to think of *tramjatra*. Moreover, I travel by tram whenever possible. The contingent of Indian NGOs and intellectuals who helped in various degrees were primarily users of taxi. I liked this a lot because it is a capsule picture of what India is all about – a mess which attracts foreigners because, I presume, that for them it is a unique experience.

Since the cultural factor of the users of trams – i.e., rural folk on a visit to Kolkata and of course Kolkata's poorer sections – was not made the basis of the programme, the project did not create a lasting impression on the minds and perceptions of the actual users of trams. To conclude that the project was not positive would be a canard. As long as it lasted it was vibrant. It brought together a number of different professionals and a non-descript like me. People with different profiles coming together and working on a common programme is a great need. In a world, not of service-oriented but of market-oriented globalisation, such a coming together of individuals from different climes and cultures working to a common programme is a ray of hope, part of the methodology of building a better blueprint for the future.

*S.R. Rajen – independent learner and poet, Kolkata*

## imaginary journeys, meaningful encounters

Writing shortly after the fall of the Berlin Wall, Salman Rushdie invited us to imagine new possibilities of communication and understanding in a world freed from the polarities and armed divisions of the Cold War. However, he was prescient enough to warn of potential new dangers and uncertainties that accompanied those seismic changes. Nothing more than Rushdie's own predicament at the time exemplified how miscommunication and misunderstanding can have catastrophic consequences.

We now inhabit a world dominated by intense fear and uncertainty, a world so paranoid it sanctions the incarceration of children behind razor wire. Surely, it can only be through education and communication that we can be elevated above the prevailing gloom and mistrust. As we, like Rushdie's characters, grapple with the myriad forces that shape our world and identities, deeper understanding of these forces can only be achieved through engagement with others. Communication and dialogue need to be maximised – across cultures, religions and languages.

*Tramjatra* provides just such an opportunity. As a vehicle for cultural and artistic dialogue, *tramjatra* permits us to take real and imagined journeys of discovery – be it in the language of Moyna, Sama and Dukushyam's patua scrolls and songs; along the geographic features imagined by contemporary artist Jayashree Chakravarty; or through the assembled paraphernalia and rituals of travel recalled and deliriously enacted by conductors Roberto D'Andrea and Prabir Kumar Goswami.

To draw a connection between tram networks in Melbourne and Kolkata may seem fanciful, but that is precisely what Jayashree's topographical contours depict. These markings, linking disparate locations like South Melbourne Beach and Ballygunge, suggest a path which Lisa Young's submerging tram on Swanston Street enables us to traverse. It is a journey Roberto and Prabir, in their tramways uniforms, guide us along; a *jatra* enabled, recorded, documented and discussed by artists, designers, activists, theoreticians and film-makers. *Tramjatra* – in providing a vehicle for meaningful communication and understanding – has left a lasting impact on all who boarded, be it at real or imagined points of departure and arrival.

*Paul Molyneux – educator, Melbourne*

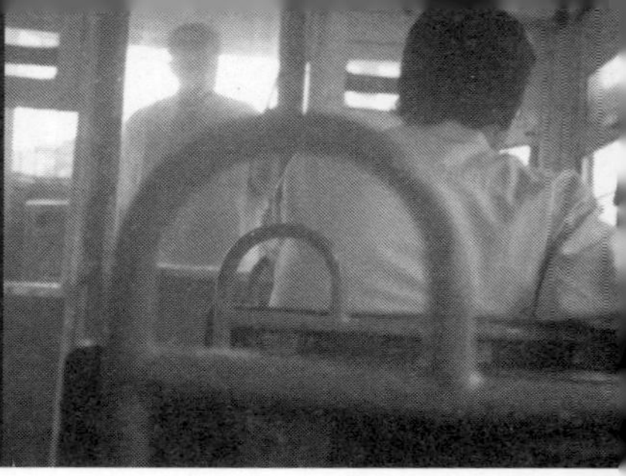

9

# transports of pleasure: memories of tramways in Kolkata and Melbourne

Dipesh Chakrabarty

Trams have their magic, the magic of slow, gentle movement amidst and against the whirlpool of faster traffic and harried pedestrians. That magic is common to the trams of Melbourne and those plying in Kolkata. But beyond that obvious similarity, there are big differences. Difference of appearance. And other differences as well.

Trams in Kolkata do not any longer look as if they are the object of anybody's affection but they used to, once – in the 1950s, for instance, when I was a middle-class child in a city that still basked in the glories of the Empire. The Calcutta Tram Company was still a British-owned corporation. Trams expressed some of the social distinctions of colonial Calcutta. For middle-class people such as my parents who could not afford cars and for whom taxis could only be an occasional pleasure but who nevertheless had middle-class pretensions to civility, trams spoke of subtle distinctions of gentility and status and also of the undemocracy that usually went with such feelings. Each tram consisted of two articulated carriages, respectively called the first and second class. The first-class cars had cushioned seats. And – very important in summer – they had ceiling fans. If you were lucky enough to get a seat near those fans, they helped you fight off not only the heat but also the smell of sweat that summer invariably produces in public transport in Kolkata. Now, that was a real privilege.

In the second carriage, you sat on wooden seats and enjoyed no luxury of fans. The difference in fares was small but the distinctions embodied in the two parts of the car were very important. I still can hear conductors in the first-class carriage telling off passengers who looked poor or working-class, for attempting to go first-class. 'Go to the car at the back,' the conductor would yell, 'this is first-class!' We middle-class people, on the other hand, would avoid travelling in the second-class car. When we did that sometimes – for pressures of time or for other reasons – we would be desperate to avoid the glances of people we knew. How quickly a child imbibes ideas of status and class. Riding in a tram was a practical lesson in class practices for my child-self.

Given this social homogeneity in the first-class carriage of Kolkata trams and the regularity of travel for some passengers, trams quickly became something like neighbourhoods on wheels. People knew each other and talked. The gentle and smooth pace of the car allowed for verbal socialisation. 'When did you return from overseas?' I would hear an elderly man – asserting oneself in public was still only a male pleasure – ask of somebody younger, the questioner's voice elevated to an angle that made it travel easily over the heads of others. Or, 'Is your mother still ill?' The replies would come in short, somewhat uncommunicative sentences as the person questioned often felt a little embarrassed discussing their personal lives in terms that were, literally, loud and clear. But the audience listening in was not embarrassed in the slightest. Our ears would prick up, and we would listen with all the attention one pays a novel or a radio-play (for sometimes, if the tram was crowded, you could not even see the speakers). The only frustration – or challenge, if you will – was that

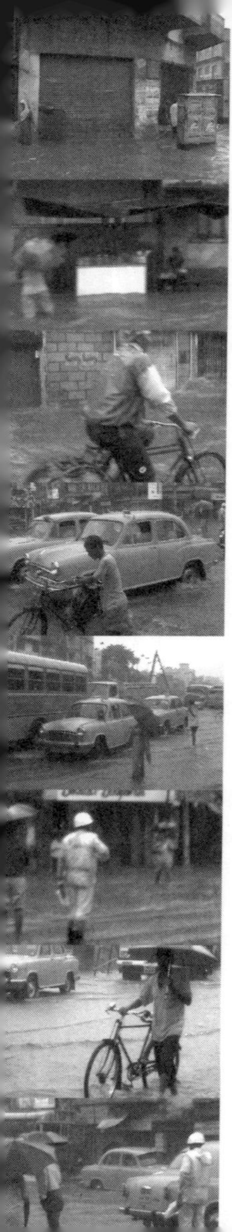

we, the silent listeners, would often have to fill in the blanks of the narrative with our own imagination. Little fragments of social stories – that's what these rides amounted to. And the trams with their slow pace, social homogeneity and smooth progress over iron-tracks provided the leisure for re-creating the social.

My particularly favourite spot in the car consisted of the seats nearest to the driver, at the very front of the carriage where the body of the tram tapered off to form a 'nose' as it were. There were two of these seats separated from each other by an aisle. Each could seat two. Some special privileges went with sitting there. You looked out of the car and not inside toward fellow passengers who would be mostly behind you. This immediately gave you a temporary right to privacy. And secondly, given the shape of Kolkata trams, these seats had the wind blow straight on to your face, a rare luxury in the hot season or even in the months that were mild. When I was in college, I would try and position myself in this part of the car and get absorbed in a book. Since that happened in the radical 1960s when Kolkata produced one of the most vigorous (and later violent) Maoist student movements of the last century, it would not be a surprise if I told you what books I read in the privacy of those front seats. The titles I remember are Emile Burns' *The ABC of Communism*, and Maurice Conforth's three volumes on Marxist philosophy, both authors perhaps hack writers for the British Communist Party.

But there was also a secret pleasure of sitting on those front seats that almost looked into the driver's part of the car (separated by a door). I was not even aware of this pleasure until now when I sat down to recollect some of my memories of Kolkata trams. This pleasure, imbibed long before I developed any sense of privacy or socialism, had to do with the sound and smell of hot iron and steel. If you sat close to the driver's cabin, you could even smell the heat that the engine generated. The smell was different from what an automobile engine produces. The sound of iron wheels turning on rails that acquired a shine through their constant encounter was like a shorthand mnemonic for the mysteries of industrialisation.

Melbourne trams, for me, were different. I rode them in the 1980s when I taught at the University of Melbourne and when I did not have a car. My classes were often scheduled for hours late in the afternoon so that 'mature age' students studying part-time could attend the university after they had put in their day's work. In winter, it would be dark by the time classes finished. I would make the trek from the Old Arts Building to Royal Parade past the Royal Melbourne Hospital to wait at a lonely and cold tram stop for my tram to take me to Brunswick where I lived. Still middle-class – indeed one of the pleasures I rediscovered in being a junior academic in Australia was that of being middle-class again, and happily so – but bereft of the densely social sense of neighbourhood in Kolkata, my rides in Melbourne trams would be a very different experience. Far more comfortable than the Kolkata trams, they would carry the 'multicultural' crowds of new Australia. No class distinctions here. No first- and second-classes. Middle-class men and women rubbed shoulders with their working-class compatriots. No sign here of the crowds or the heat or even the sociality of Kolkata traffic. Instead, a sense of privacy would cast its spell through the entire length of the car. People would bury their faces in newspapers – *The Age* or evening tabloids. No male voice would ring out, asking: 'Is your mother still ill?' If I heard voices, they would be low, and on the way to Brunswick, often in southern European languages that I did not understand. 'What holds this Babel together?' I would often ask myself. 'Is it just the fact that we are all immigrants to a land that provides opportunities?' 'Would we hold together if Australia did not hold out any promises? Was it the common search for the good life that made us into a community?' The questions returned but I never knew the answers.

Yet there is no doubt that Melburnians love their trams. Why else would there be a film like *Malcolm*, much of which was about the love of trams? When I saw that film, I felt sorry that nobody in Kolkata had thought about making films on trams. Trams figure in Bengali films but not as their true subject. I am not sure that people of Kolkata love their trams any more. The cars look uncared for. The tracks are badly maintained. Seeing a derailed tramcar is such a common sight in the city these days. Perceived as obstructions to other forms of transport in a city utterly cramped for space, trams have often been the target of utilitarian criticisms from politicians in Kolkata. The older sense of being middle-class that sustained the pleasures of tram travel has been replaced by an aggressive sense of democracy in public transport. Gone, along with the colonial company that managed the tramways of Kolkata, are the colonial distinctions of first- and second-classes. Both the carriages now have wooden seats. They are both equally crowded. The real distinction now is that of money: between those who can afford cars and those who cannot. The distinction does not say anything about cultures of transport.

It is uncertain that trams of Kolkata will survive. Maybe they will, on environmentalist grounds. Or maybe they will, as museums of memories of the olden days. Maybe we will learn something from Melbourne. It all depends on how Kolkata and West Bengal do in the years to come. If the city picks up economically, and its population takes pride in the city, trams may well come to represent what is distinctive about the place and its history. After all, history survives only when we feel that we have a future.

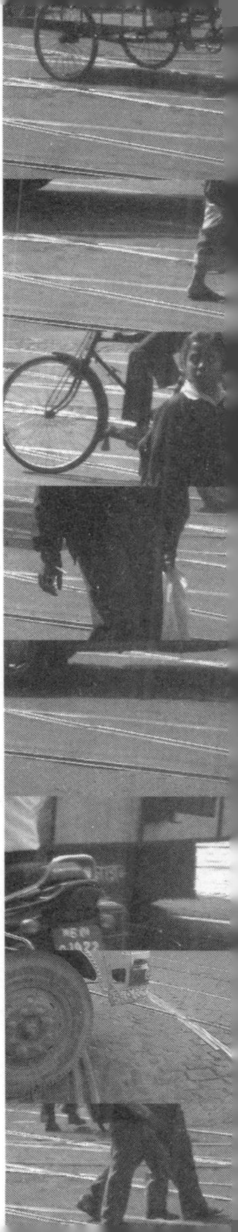

10

# engaging contradiction

Catherine Murphy

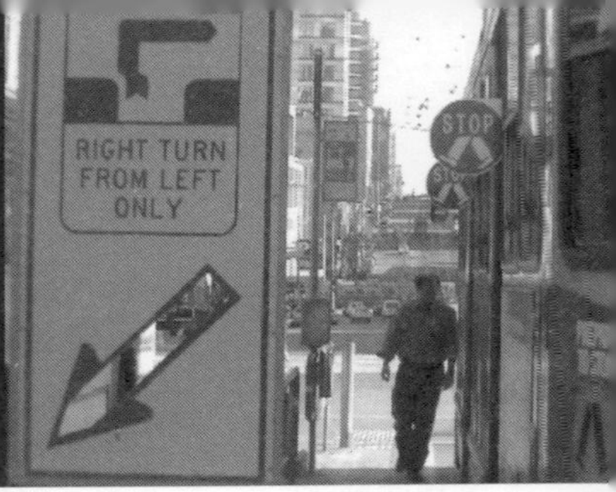


*Tramjatra* is a multi-layered ongoing international project, the view of which can be determined according to where you are standing: mine is the vantage point of public art in Melbourne, Australia. Since the late 1970s there has been a proliferation of 'public art' in 'public spaces', some of which has offered an alternative practice from the traditional gallery-based arts practice by directly engaging audiences. Much of this practice has come to be known as site-specific art: an art that addresses the particular qualities of locations, as well as larger concerns about social, historical, cultural and economic forces.

*Tramjatra* is one such site-specific project that has spread itself over several years in two cities in two countries, each with very different civic cultures, public realms and ways of doing and being. Its processes and products are often ephemeral. Its intentions range from the poetic to the activist. It is a public art project that is about networking, imagining, connecting and layering. Artists, designers and activists have engaged with others to produce work that facilitates a dialogue about urban space and site, public and audience – all as they pertain to tramways.

Urban critic Rosalyn Deutsche claims that cities are characterised by contradictions of 'uneven development', which interests of power seek to repress. She proposes that a role for public art is to appropriate the city and to act as a vehicle for illuminating the contradictions of the city. If official public art makes an aesthetic contribution to the dominant logic of capital driving redevelopment in the city, public art as an interventionist spatial praxis approaches this city in the cautious manner of the cultural critic described by Walter Benjamin. 'Confronted with "cultural treasures" – "documents of civilisation" – Benjamin's critic unveils the barbarism underlying their creation by brushing their history "against the grain".'[1]

The *tramjatra* project has only been possible with the official support of state government transport authorities in the states of West Bengal, India and Victoria, Australia. The project has gained official legitimacy around discourses of public art, most notably through gaining the institutional support of Australian government arts funding agencies. Increasingly this discourse values work that engages the context, conditions and people that make public art possible. This essay considers how *tramjatra* relates to or contributes to these discourses. Such a project reveals that contradiction underpins an engaged contemporary practice of public art, for the production of art in the public realm often does involve uncomfortable alliances which can lead to complexities and contradictions having to be addressed as part of the work. It should be said at the outset that this kind of public art discourse, located as it is in a Western context, has its limitations. I assume that the public realm and the social and institutional infrastructure that support the city of Kolkata are very different to those operating here.

**Public Art**

American critic Patricia Phillips offers this as a way of considering public art:

> Art generally performs; it does something, albeit in different ways to different people. Any consideration of public art must first acknowledge that art is an active agent rather than an amenity or diversion, that its circumstances and context are inevitably complex and deeply conflicted, and that viewers' experiences of it are always influenced by both personal and socially constructed preconceptions.[2]

Public art has for many years now been used to describe any form of art that occurs in the public realm. Public art can range from the long-term and long-lasting to the spontaneous and ephemeral, from the officially sanctioned to the informal and renegade. It is often more concerned with its processes than its aesthetic qualities; it often claims a political and/or social agenda; and it is often presented as something different from, even oppositional to, art in galleries. Public art practice has claimed that it can be more ambitious and less constrained than gallery-based work. As a result, public art has often been viewed as a different kind of art that is not critiqued in the same way and through the same avenues as other art. So rather than examine public art as part of art discourse, public art debate has taken place around broader issues of site, public, audience and community.

Site-specificity has been the practice that has most differentiated public art from art produced in relation to gallery settings. Site-specific work is produced in response to particular qualities of its location, such as its history or its materiality. Australian critic John Barrett-Lennard observes:

> ...while relatively recent, site-specific art can be connected with early twentieth century avant-garde movements, which attempted to radically reconfigure the possibilities of art practice and the viewer's connection to art and life. Frequently couched in terms of working with the everyday or in public, there has been an attempt to engage areas seen as excluded from traditional institutional settings, to step literally and figuratively beyond to incorporate a wider set of variables, and to develop a strong critique of social and cultural borders.[3]

Public art has also involved an interrogation of the concept 'public'. Public artworks are presented by their promoters as being there for the 'public' irrespective of age, gender, ethnicity or class. Critics of public art have questioned the very idea that there is any such thing as 'public'. Deutsche argues that rather than being a real category, the term 'public', like the city itself, 'is an ideological artefact, a contested and fragmented terrain'.[4] Given the nature of cities with their great diversity of peoples, is it possible for 'public' to have any meaning, let alone denote one voice or one identity? The city of the early twenty-first century is inevitably made of multiple 'publics' with multiple interests: an engaged, dynamic public art acknowledges this complexity.

Another area often discussed within public art discourse is the nature of 'public space'. Public artwork is sited within the everyday spaces of its audiences, areas of the normal and routine, rather than in the specialised spaces within which most 'cultural' activity takes place. Public space is that in which people most freely come into contact with one another; it is the site of connection between public art and the 'public'.

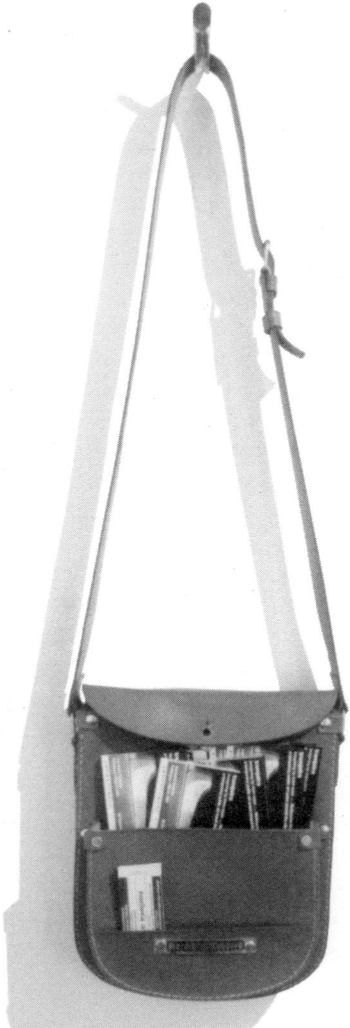

Discourses around public art have analysed the cultural, economic and political nature of space itself and the subsequent implications for the production of public art. Often not public at all, public space is frequently privately owned and heavily controlled. Indeed, the public's role in so-called public space is increasingly one of consumer and spectator; it is no longer a place for encounters that are unregulated. Even our trams in Melbourne, known collectively as 'public transport', are no longer publicly owned (although at the time of writing one of the 'private' tram companies in Melbourne is under financial collapse and has handed the trams back to the state to operate). Much public art produced is there just to entertain the crowds. This is art used as Hans Haacke's 'social grease' for tourism, crowd control, and high-income housing.[5] Public art discourse is interested in those 'spaces' where art can challenge and engage audiences in a way that is beyond simple entertainment.

The response and reception of an audience to public art is also of interest in the debates around public art. Proponents of public artworks have claimed a new and larger audience, as well as a less mediated relationship with that audience, than that of art in the gallery. However, the relationship of the viewer to the work is complex and varied. Some artists seek to involve a specific audience and at the same time hope to effect change in the social order; others appeal to a universal formalism that claims to transcend historical reference and its inherent conflicts.[6]

*Tramjatra* is a project that through its structure attempts to engage with these complexities. It has sought to create an open-ended space for the exploration and generation of ideas – it is concerned with what might be provoked (and even change) when an 'audience' encounter and experience art in their everyday lives that relates specifically to tramways. The project's products – tickets, temporary sculptures and installations, newspapers, forums, decorated trams, traditional Indian scroll paintings, cricket games – are less important than the processes that surround and create them, and the dialogue, dynamic and even chaos created by the process. *Tramjatra* is a networked project in which connections are developed between things and events over space and over time: there can be no one prescriptive outcome from such activity.

**Engaging**

*Tramjatra* belongs to models of public art practice that are concerned with engagement with an audience by focusing on some aspect of everyday life. This form or expression of public art tends to have an emphasis on specific 'communities' whose identities are in part formed by some particular concern or common interest. Seeking to intervene culturally in 'public space', artists in *tramjatra* engaged the 'community' of tram travellers and tramways workers.

This kind of contemporary activist art has its roots in the 1960s and 1970s when artists were interested in moving beyond the constraints of the traditional gallery setting. From this period, a body of performative work emerged that directly engaged audiences and their spaces. Some of this work was politically driven and inspired by the anti-Vietnam war movement and drew on the European traditions of fluxus and situationist performance. Other work was of more collaborative nature and associated with the feminist movement.[7]

By the 1970s and 1980s much of the work produced outside of galleries had turned to engaging audiences in the spaces and routines of their daily lives. The focus was on disadvantaged communities and those considered alienated from 'high art'. Community arts activities, as they were then known, were activist and interventionist, driven by social and political concerns. The emphasis was often on the process of collaboration rather than on the quality of the art produced. The artists, often describing themselves as 'community artists' to differentiate their practice from 'elite' gallery-based artists, produced work that focused on a particular community setting, be it a housing commission estate, a school, or a railway yard, usually in collaboration with a community group. Other artists were engaged in broader political issues such as AIDS, reconciliation with Aboriginal people and saving the environment, while still engaging the principles of collaborative practice.

In the 1990s, when such process-oriented public art activity became more prevalent in the United States, Suzanne Lacy coined the term 'new genre public art' to define community-based projects that are socially responsive:

> Dealing with some of the most profound issues of our time – toxic waste, race relations, homelessness, ageing, gang warfare and cultural identity – a group of visual artists has developed distinct models for an art whose public strategies of engagement are an important part of its aesthetic language....We might describe this as 'new genre public art', to distinguish it in both form and intention from what has been called 'public art' – a term used for the past twenty years to describe sculpture and

> installations sited in public places. Unlike much of what has heretofore been called public art, new genre public art – visual art that uses both traditional and non-traditional media to communicate and interact with a broad and diversified audience about issues directly relevant to their lives – is based on engagement.[8]

In the 1980s and 1990s a number of alternative artist-run spaces were established which supported arts practices hitherto neglected by mainstream galleries and arts institutions including performance, video, installation and political or activist work. These spaces and the work they produce, often in public space, are usually different from community arts projects in that they are more likely to present the work of individual artists who produce work in response to context and site.

*Tramjatra* built on this latter model of public art. It asked a range of artists from both Australia and India to engage with their audiences through the production of their own artwork. While artists did choose a collaborative mode of practice, this was not required. The artworks attempted engagement on two levels: the individual or personal experience, and the collective experience. They produced a range of artworks that sought to engage the public imagination about its tramways and hoped to provoke a sense of the consequence of individual desires and actions within a shared culture.

One of the ways in which *tramjatra* engaged its audience was through utilising the existing infrastructure of the tramways and also of the broader city. For instance, the thematic use of the tram prow, the bright yellow safety barrier unique to Melbourne's mid-street tram stops, was one important way of the viewer instantly locating the project as being associated with the trams because of their everyday familiarity. However, by locating these prows in unexpected places away from but close by tram stops in locations such as the steps of the Treasury building, the viewer was challenged to re-engage with this everyday object within a new context. Similarly, by publishing three editions of a newspaper, titled *The Passenger*, the project fed into a tried and true tram activity: reading the paper. But this newspaper was a special issue about *tramjatra*. And of course the project has consistently used tickets to facilitate an exchange between project participant and potential project 'passenger': again an everyday object utilised to attract the attention of the project audience and to get people to engage with and imagine their tramways in new and unexpected ways.

**Contradiction**

Like many public art projects which are attempting a critical dialogue, *tramjatra* cannot avoid getting caught up in the contradictions and complexities that arise when producing an 'art' project in public space.

*Tramjatra* has its legacy in smaller scale activities that were resourced by two key drivers of the project, artists Mick Douglas and Roberto D'Andrea. This early work enabled the project to be positioned as a public art activity and meant that in its later stages it was able to attract considerable funding from Australian government arts and transport programmes, giving the project further shape and a certain legitimation and official standing. The receipt of such funding inevitably gives rise to tensions.

On the one hand *tramjatra* was a project with its own activist and interventionist agenda, while on the other hand it was a project that received official endorsement from government bodies in Australia and India, the very institutions to whom such intervention might be a direct challenge. Does such official cultural sanctioning of the project actually restrict and contain the project? Or can such a project exceed the limits of official sanction and operate critically?

Such dilemmas are not uncommon in public art projects. Public art receives substantial support from the state as well as from private sector investment, and has been an integral component of widespread urban development. Public art is now understood as an element of urban renewal programmes, 'functioning as an emblem of culture and as a manifestation of economic wealth, a sign of the power of its patron'.[9] There are now many 'per cent for art' programmes in city governments whereby a percentage of every urban development project's budget, (say one per cent) is commissioned as part of the overall new building, parkland, apartment block etc.

The majority of projects that receive such state funding are not seeking to act critically. Rather, the integration of public art into much urban development has created what Deutsche describes as 'new' public art.[10] What distinguishes the 'new' public art is its functionality and usefulness. Such art is often a seat, a playground, a sign or some other object with a purpose beyond its artistic value, which makes it more socially accountable and acceptable than previous forms of art for art's sake. This kind of useful public art represents the majority of funded public art activity in Australia and around the Western world.

However, this 'new' art does not preclude other kinds of public art activities that provoke and challenge their audiences. Again, all over the Western world governments fund this kind of activity as well, albeit to a much lesser extent, often under arts programmes. The difference is that even though critical public art might receive funding from city governments, it is rarely initiated or managed by them. On the whole these projects are driven by individuals, who are often attached to artist-run spaces or universities, whose passion for some issue drives the project, in exactly the way of *tramjatra*. The official funding doesn't enable the project or account for what transpires – it is a contributor to an activity that is already occurring and that then enables it to expand. Herein lies an important distinction between funded activity that is driven by capital or the state, and funded activity, which is driven by artists or groups with their own agendas. Nevertheless, there are many compromises for activist projects once there is an official alliance between them and the state. How these are handled will be evident in the project.

Indeed, it could be argued that much activist public art actually sets out to engage with the contradictions that arise from working with the material of the city. As Rosalyn Deutsche says:

> As a practice within the built environment, public art participates in the production of meanings, uses and forms for the city. In this capacity, it can help secure consent to redevelopment and to the restructuring that make up the historical form of late capitalist urbanisation. But like other institutions that mediate perceptions of the city's economic and political operations – architecture, urban planning,

> urban design – it can also question and resist those operations, revealing the suppressed contradictions within urban processes. Since these contradictions stamp the image of the city with a basic instability, public art can be, in Althusserian terms, a 'site', as well as a 'stake' of urban struggle.[11]

Public art, by being placed in 'public' space, by necessity must position itself in relation to questions about who is controlling space and for what purpose. By extension, it must consider exactly what its role is in any particular situation, who is funding it and why, and what is expected from the alliances it forges. It can do this, funded or not, by recognising and engaging with the complexity of the issues that projects like *tramjatra* are addressing – for instance the very future of the tramways in Kolkata and the social role of tram conductors in Melbourne – and then attempting to structure the project to work with these complexities. If this results in tensions of contradiction being revealed, lots of open-ended questions, difficulties and a bit of chaos, amongst many people being drawn to be involved, then this is an example of an engaging public art practice at work.

1 Rosalyn Deutsche, 'Uneven development: Public art in New York City', in *Out of Site: A Social Criticism of Architecture*, (ed D. Ghirardo), Bay Press, Seattle, Washington, 1991, 187.

2 Patricia Phillips, 'Dynamic exchange: public art at this time', in *Public Art Review*, vol 11, no 1, Fall/Winter, 1999, 4-9.

3 Barrett Lennard, 'Reflections, inversions and the specific', in *Insite: Craig Walsh*, IMA Publishing, Brisbane, 2000, 9.

4 Rosalyn Deutsche, 'Uneven development: Public art in New York City', in *Out of Site: A Social Criticism of Architecture*, (ed D. Ghirardo), Bay Press, Seattle, Washington, 1991, 167.

5 Maureen Sherlock, 'Of bovines, buskers and beauties: Chicago's populist public art', in *Public Art Review*, vol 14, no 1, Fall/Winter, 2002, 16-21.

6 Patricia Phillips, 'Dynamic exchange: public art at this time', in *Public Art Review*, vol 11, no 1, Fall/Winter, 1999, 4-9.

7 Grant Kester, 'Beyond the White Cube: Activist art and the legacy of the 1960s', in *Public Art Review*, vol 14, no 2, Spring/Summer 2003, 4-11.

8 Suzanne Lacy, 'Cultural pilgrimages and metaphoric journeys', in *Mapping the Terrain: New Genre Public Art* (ed S. Lacy), Seattle, Washington: Bay Press, 19.

9 Harriet Senie and Sally Webster (eds), 'Introduction', in *Critical Issues in Public Art: Content, Context and Controversy*, New York: Harper Collins Publishers, 1992, xiv.

10 Rosalyn Deutsche, 'Uneven development: Public art in New York City', in *Out of Site: A Social Criticism of Architecture*, (ed D. Ghirardo), Bay Press, Seattle, Washington, 1991, 172.

11 Ibid, 164.

11

# made for a hybrid viewer: tramjatra

Gayatri Chakravorty Spivak

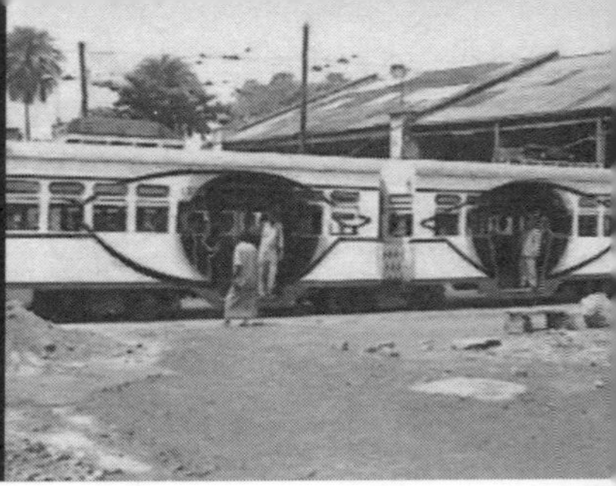

If you look at all the media material and paperwork surrounding Michael Douglas's video *tramjātrā*, you will see what a tremendous effort was there to bring Kolkata and Melbourne together. But suppose the video were to be seen by itself? I am a language person, a translator. I have tried to supplement the freestanding video with some observations from that perspective.

Among the many interesting things in the media material, there is a letter from Paromita Roy, who, with her two friends, was unable to find the actual *tramjatra* tram. 'Our search for the *tramjatra* tram that day might have been in vain,' she writes, 'but our own little "tram-jatra" definitely was not... I wish *tramjatra* does as much for the future of trams in this city as our little tram-jatra did for us that day.'[1] Take what follows in that spirit. I point at what I did not find in hopes for the future.

I saw the video twice, in altogether different settings. Once on the island of Rhodes, at an international conference, at one workshop among many, with a small all-white group, mostly Australians who knew Mike, with Tom Nairn taking notes in the corner. I said nothing. I remember Nikos Papastergiadis calling the folks in Calcutta 'Indians', and receiving a slight shock. To me they were some Calcuttans, some migrant labour, some middle-class culturalists, a bunch of office-goers – heterogeneous. I knew this was 'normal', the lonely reaction of the located among the internationally sympathetic. The point then is not to complain, and I didn't.

A few months later, I was revising some work on Harlem, work on lost inscriptions. I wrote this footnote:

> A case in point would be John Hutnyk's brilliant book *The Rumour of Calcutta: Tourism, Charity and the Poverty of Representation* (London: Zed Books, 1996), that talks a lot about writing. But the inscriptions of Kolkata remain illegible to him. Michael Douglas's marvellous video *tramjatra* (presented at a Conference on New Directions in the Humanities, University of the Aegean, Greece, July 5, 2003) could not accommodate the complex irony of the Bengali, Indian, and Calcuttan material captured by his technical equipment.

I put together my old friend John Hutnyk and my new friend Michael Douglas, Melburnian lovers of Calcutta.

In Rhodes, I had been unable to speak, because the time and the place were not right. I told Michael as I departed that we might have a conversation about his video some day. He graciously invited me to participate in this volume. And that is what brought about the second viewing of the video, in the format of a DVD sent by him.

It was Thanksgiving Day in my nephew's house in Roanoke, Virginia. His mother died in December, 2002. My mother – his father's mother – died in May 2003. It was important that the family assemble and Thanksgiving seemed the appropriate long weekend, although our connection to the spirit of Thanksgiving was rather tenuous. The video became informative for the next generation of Bengali Americans. The whites were their spouses. My siblings – the older located generation – were upstairs. I noticed new things in the video. But the main thing was the possible

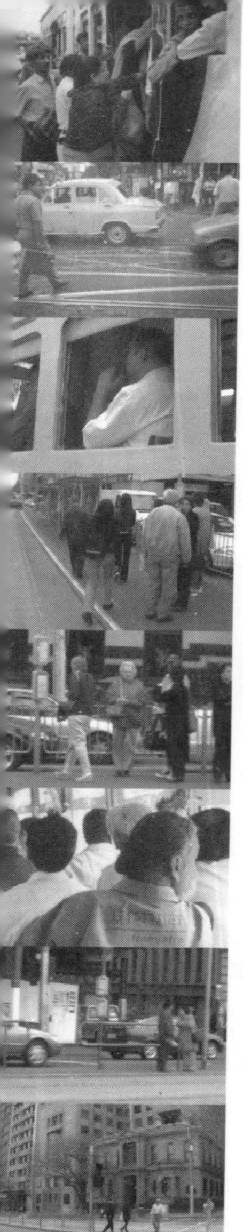

inclusion of a located Calcuttan as an implied viewer, and the considerable enrichment of the video if one considered the inscriptions as English/original Bengali/ translation.

The title, for example. In Bengali, *jãtrã* is a common noun, in English a proper name – a mark, not a signifier – untranslated because Bengali is not the original. 'Tram' is a word thoroughly lexicalised into Bengali. It is a Bengali word as *jãtrã* is not English.

*Jãtrã* is of course 'trip'. But it is also specifically associated with regional rural fairs on the occasion of the celestial chariot, the grand original being in Puri: *Rathajãtrã*. To associate the Calcutta tramways with the celestial chariot and the nostalgic cultural capital of rural Bengal was a fine touch. For the allusion to work in the circulatory orbit of the video, we need first generation metropolitan migrants – like Dipesh and me. Or the located middle-class – which brings me to the other meaning of *jãtrã* – the derivation of which is known to Bengalists but not to me – travelling pre-colonial theatre groups. (Maybe it was the travelling part that gave us *jãtrã*?)

The video begins with a pleasant middle-class female voice singing a narrative opening in a fair reproduction of a jatra-type performance, accompanied by the *ektara*, generic folk-instrument: 'Listen to the story of the Calcutta tram...' etc. This also is a good touch, since the affectionate middle-class appropriation of the jatra-form is so well known that for most viewers this will generally qualify as a 'folk opening', a jatra opening, like Dylan intoning 'Listen to the story of the Hurricane.' It is inevitable that such nuances are lost on a general international audience. (Comparative Literature works against these inevitabilities.)

As the voiceover went on: 'a hundred and fifty years ago...', one of my nieces asked, in Bengali, 'Really, a 150 years...?' I hit 'pause,' turned around from the computer, uttered superfast 'ghorar trum', before turning back and hitting 'play' again, as the voice went on, in jatra mode, 'pulled by horses...'. My interruption meant 'horses' tram', with the Bengali lexicalised version of the English 'tram'.

(The ritual conclusion of this song, in slightly antique language, calling the video 'tramkatha', somewhat like 'tram-matter' as in 'the matter of Britain', peters out before the actual end. Editing unsympathetic to the Bengali frame, alas; as is the translation of the Bengali description of the travels of the Trambaby (a wonderful idea in itself): the school moved from Sealdah to Ballygunge, as from Brooklyn to Manhattan, and the easy step into the tram omitted altogether.)

I treasure this interstitial diasporic moment in Roanoke, Virginia. My niece had flown in from Chicago and I from New York. I do not particularly want to 'theorise' the moment. Writing this in Bangkok airport on my way to China, it reminds me that I had learnt of the horse-drawn trams from my great-aunts and a great-uncle. It reminds me that a couple of years ago my sister, who lives and works in New Delhi and therefore is no longer a part either of the diasporic or the located Calcutta crowd, had wanted to ride the tram with me (and we did ride, from Dalhousie Square almost to Dhakuria) on a quick flyaway visit, because who knew how long the trams would last? *Tramjatra* indeed! The stories I could tell... .

What these two viewings showed me was that the most fun out of *'tramjatra'* will probably be had by the by-now pretty common audience of first-generation diasporic Bengalis in the metropole. Is the Melbourne part as thick? I can't tell; but Dipesh, or Aparna Das can. I can get the New York jokes in *Godzilla*.

By contrast to the structurally ignored jatra-song, the translation-Bengali is charmingly awkward. I cannot really share it with you, since they are all translations of English. I ask the felicitous viewer why, again and again, 'tramjatrar safar' (tram-travel's journey)? How is the 're-evaluation of the threads of the social fabric' 'jato shomaj-bandha shuto jachai kara?' 'Shomaj-bandha shuto' in a language that gave us "bandhanhîn granthi' some decades ago? 'Collection of routes' is 'jatrar pather jogphal?' I'm not asking for 'better translations'. Oh dear, there has been so much effort that I hate to say it: I'm asking for textual evidence of intellectual participation – may be some 'translations' going the other way? (In the event, Trambaby dashed my hopes some.)

Sometimes a spark is lit by this very incongruence. Where the English has the somewhat tired 'repetition/difference' the Bengali, by someone who hasn't shared the repetition-difference pomo stuff of the last few decades, produces 'phire phire asha /taphate jawa', so inspired in its literalism that I can re-translate this 'original': 'Coming back and back again/Going away, apart.'

But the brightest spark flashes up in response to 'long live tram travel!' Here the translation overflows the original in other ways, to mix metaphors. The title is wrenched from its proper name as mark, into signifiership. All unbeknownst to the only-English viewer, 'tram travel' is translated into the Bengali word 'tramjatra'. The first translation of the entire phrase is 'tramjatra dirghajibi hok', quite appropriate. But then the verb is thrown off, the English–Bengali hybrid tramjatra is forgotten, and a much older hybrid – connected to the Islamic world by way of so remote a connection to India's Islamic past that the word is thoroughly internalised as 'Indian' – usurps its place – 'tram jindabad' in Bengali, 'zindabad' in every other language, for the Calcuttan inevitably linked to that noble cry, anachronistic now, alas!, 'inkilab zindabad' – 'long live the revolution!' Here the pairing is 'Melbourne-Kolikata', by way of Calcutta-village's precolonial name, beyond the Calcutta-Kolkata divide, which the video, amusingly, straddles.

So, Michael Douglas jindabad. Make more hybrid videos, Mike, working more and more toward a genuinely bifurcated viewer. It seems appropriate that I will e-mail this to you tomorrow, from Kolikata.

1 *The Passenger*, 16 November 2001, 2.

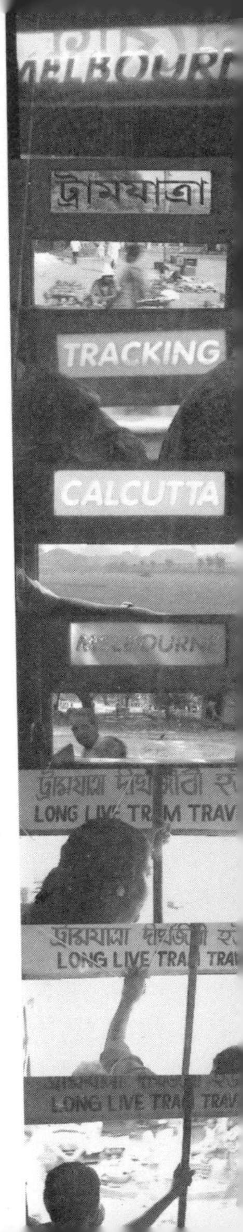

12

# ticket and travel

Bruce C. Wearne

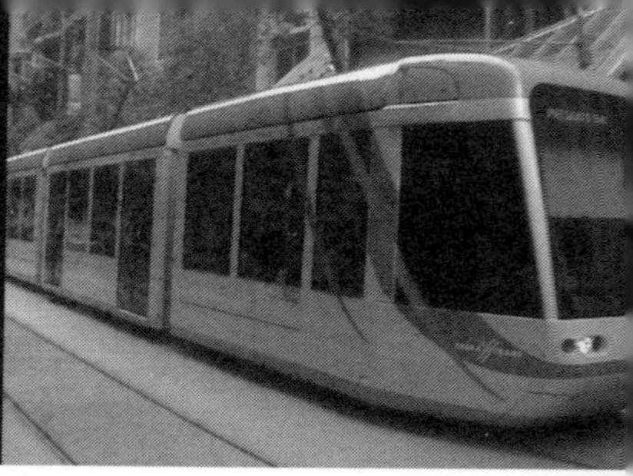

*SETTING OUT*

A ticket's price is only one aspect of a journey's value. Neither a tram journey nor those who work on trams are merely means to an end. Trams invite people to be 'travellers', yet now we are treated as merely 'customers' or 'commuters'. In twenty *stop points* I suggest an alternative horizon for urban planning that responds to the phasing out of Melbourne's tram conductors.

*FIRST STOP*

**Trams are social**

In our complex society there are complex networks of social travel.

*SECOND STOP*

**Trams are treasured**

Public transport in Melbourne cannot avoid its much-treasured tram network. An extensive track system winds its way through the metropolis and reminds us how Melbourne fits together.

*THIRD STOP*

**Trams are historical**

Trams are a part of the emergence of cities and their transport systems, a form of electrical rail transport for roads, with us since

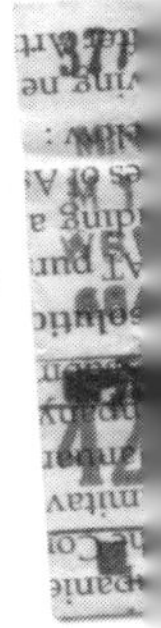

the second half of the nineteenth century. Trams are cousins to trains, an 'intermediate' form of transport that emerged in response to industrial demands for faster and easier worker movement.

*FOURTH STOP*

**Trams are risk management**

Safety has ever been important on trams – the red flag waver walking before the loco is part of our collective urban memory. Formerly the bell was rung as a signal from conductor to driver, a part of teamwork, managing risk. Even without conductors risk is managed with utmost care.

*FIFTH STOP*

**Trams are leisure**

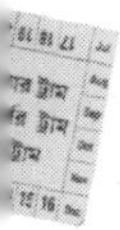

Trams are also leisurely transport and serve on the non-working weekend to ferry sporting crowds to football, cricket, the races... . They are a popular form of public transport. Trams are not just a response to leisure; they form facets of our leisured lives.

*SIXTH STOP*

**Tram travel and tickets symbolise our view of time**

Routes and timetables of buses, trains and trams map patterns of urban life. Taxis and private vehicles are also part of the system. Formerly, a ticket indicated whether you were on a tram, train or bus. Nowadays, tram tickets tell you your location in a geographic sense, and a commuter can travel in and across all three modes within the time period specified on the ticket.

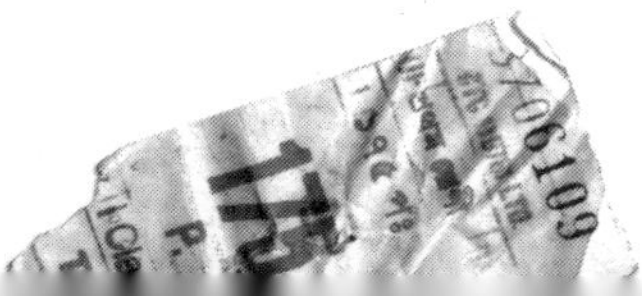

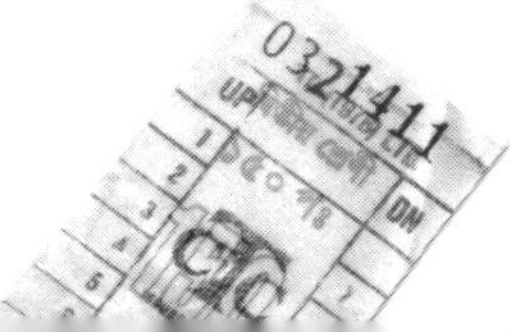

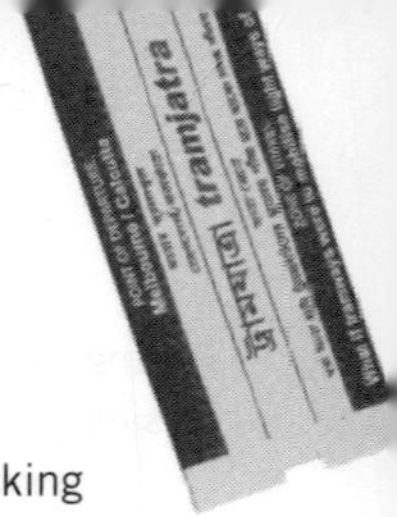


*SEVENTH STOP*

**Tickets are eloquent in other ways**

Tickets tell us other things about society. Buying and checking an electronic ticket is a highly regulated activity. The ticket is a mundane and routine symbol of the rich fabric of urban travel.

*EIGHTH STOP*

**Tickets reveal the system of public transport**

Tickets purchased from machines mesh the authorisation for travel on train, tram and bus into one electronic strip with data that allows movement through the system.

*NINTH STOP*

**Tickets and ticket-selling have their own history**

For 100 years conductors helped tram-travellers travel. Their work was co-ordinated with drivers and for some time Connies sold tickets and acted as inspectors. The tram ride is never a human-less process – and trams are important for many destinations other than work or play.

*TENTH STOP*

**Public transport bundles things together**

When machines were devised which could bundle separate tickets together into one electronic strip, public transport could be integrated into one system. Now the ticket symbolises an *integrated* system, which solves some problems but creates new ones. The former system had its own form of efficiency. The Connie was safety officer, 'personal care attendant', compliance officer and bell ringer. These days drivers have a different role.

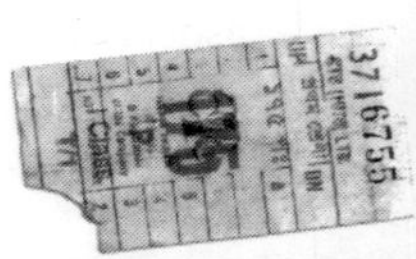

Roving ticket inspectors check tickets, and questions of safety remain.

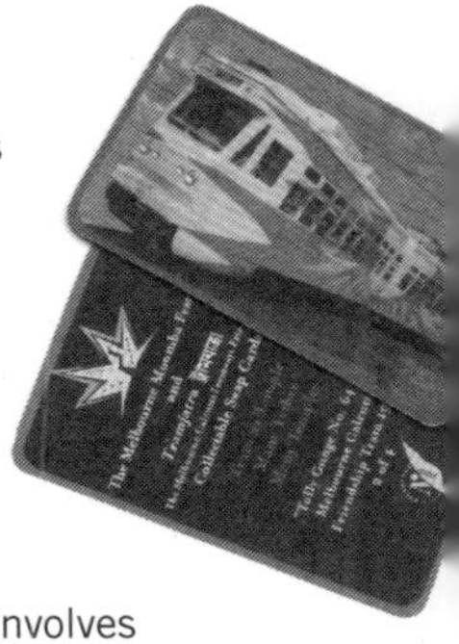

*ELEVENTH STOP*

**Tickets have always required mechanical production**

Tram tickets, and all tickets, are refined artefacts. They are exhibits of a process of mechanical reproduction, a cause and consequence of the mesh of our social fabric. Tickets and ticket selling always involves machines at some point. They are numbered.

*TWELFTH STOP*

**Justice and economy are integral to efficiency**

Justice – giving to each her/his due, and economy – wise distribution of scarce resources, are norms of our humanness that cannot be priced. Any transport system needs to be run in a way that embodies both.

*THIRTEENTH STOP*

**Tickets remind us that unpriceable and nonpriceable aspects are always attached to travel**

The unpriceable aspects of tram travel were focused on the Connie before the implementation of the present integrated system. The Connie, giving public form to travel justice and economy, made friendliness and 'trust' part of travel. Unfriendliness is also unpriceable and if roving inspectors are often experienced as unfriendly, then policy needs to recognise the fact and find ways to form travel friendliness as a normative aspect of the structure for travel.

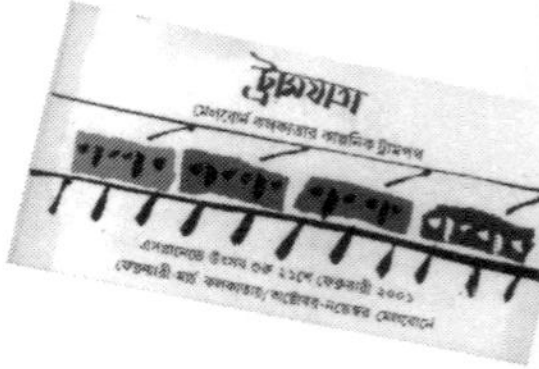

*FOURTEENTH STOP*

**Technological innovation requires renewal in communal co-responsibility**

Of course facilitating friendliness, communal co-responsibility, is a norm for everyone. We might say it is the outer defining boundary of the work of public transport employees, and that is also why the Connie role emerged. For urban travel to be a pleasant experience many elements need to come together. A friendly ethos can only be formed over time – it is not automatic.

*FIFTEENTH STOP*

**Technicism as an ideology destroys social relations and distorts history**

If an electronic ticketing system is formed with the assumption that a cash payment is the essential link between traveller and tram, then it is the transport policy itself which is creating tensions. The policy should be fostering public transport friendliness, in the context of justice and economy. 'Trust' roles, like that of tram conductors, must be re-conceptualised and the full character of social trust identified.

*SIXTEENTH STOP*

**Apart from dispensing tickets a mechanised system also makes its societal contribution**

The machine retains people's money but a ticket owner has many reasons for travel. No one will commute solely to possess a ticket. Commuters are also parents, schoolchildren, friends, shoppers, visitors, vagrants, businesswomen, elderly, tourists...with many

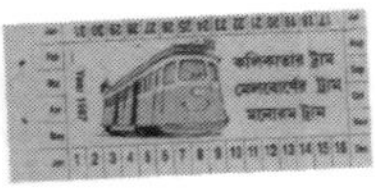

things to do. The Connie had an educative function in reminding people they were not just abstract commuters. Connies helped form an ethic of mutual responsibility across the entire transport system, and now new ways have to be found to ascribe respect to tram travellers as humans with 'bundles of roles'.

### *SEVENTEENTH STOP*

**Miscalculation of the true cost has social consequences**

To assume the cash nexus as the lynchpin of the transport system replaces justice and economy with the calculation of an abstract mechanical efficiency. Statistical data is needed for appropriate management of rolling stock and staff. But tabulating measurable performance indicators is but one facet of any review of service delivery. A transport policy's view of the social aspect of travel should not reduce it to abstract choices about physical movement.

### *EIGHTEENTH STOP*

**Respect for the distinctive integrity of all forms of societal interaction is a good basis for a just and economic ticket system**

Social policy needs to build respect for human interdependence. Travellers are never mere users – they board trams because they are going somewhere: home, school, shopping, the country, to catch a connection, to visit friends, or just going for a ride to get away.

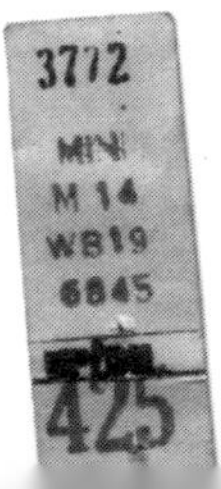


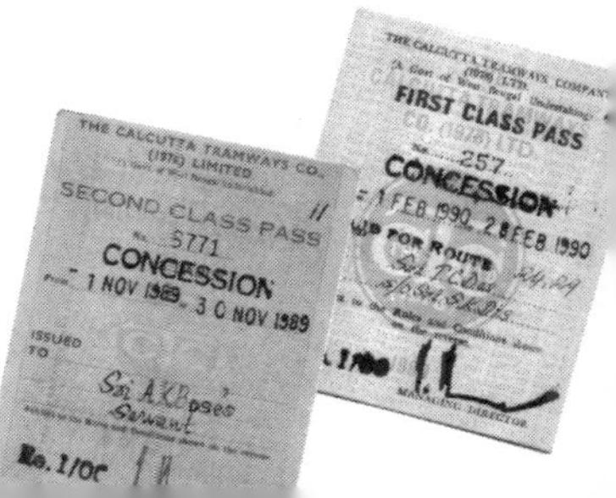

*NINETEENTH STOP*

**Tram travel contributes to urban living by bundling us together in moving spaces that move us around**

In an interdependent social fabric public transport systems enrich our lives by moving us from place to place and thereby contribute to work, commerce, sport, education, leisure, family, courtship and much more. Commuters are always 'going places' and trams are an important 'moving public place'.

*TWENTIETH STOP*

**Public movement is political, economic, aesthetic and purposive**

Public movement gives evidence of the way societal power is used to shape the life of the citizenry; gives expression to how we make use of personal and collective resources in terms of norms for stewardly use of resources; demonstrates the formation of an aesthetic fabric and life-style; and gives expression to how people view purposive behaviour and how they understand themselves as moving.

*TERMINUS*

Social interaction on a tram starts as a contractual agreement. The legal and financial aspects of a ticket purchase constitute the 'cash nexus' of public transport in a rich fabric of communal co-responsibility in which we care for our neighbours. Trams give multi-faceted support to us as we move around our variegated responsibilities in a complex differentiated society. The independence and interdependence of tram travel in public transport is a matter for ongoing reflection and action.

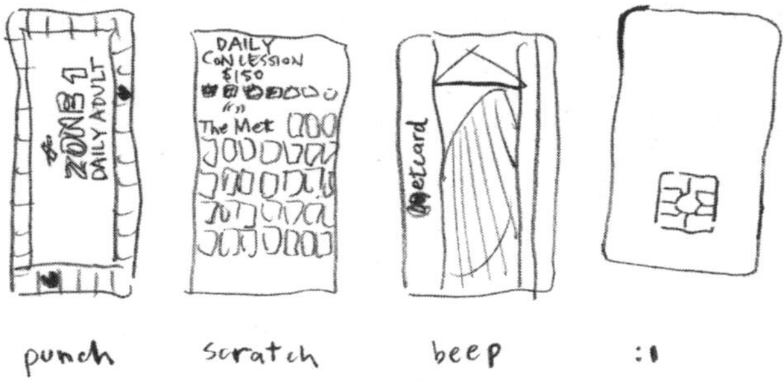
ZONE 1
DAILY ADULT
DAILY
CONCESSION
$150
The Met
metcard
punch
scratch
beep
:|

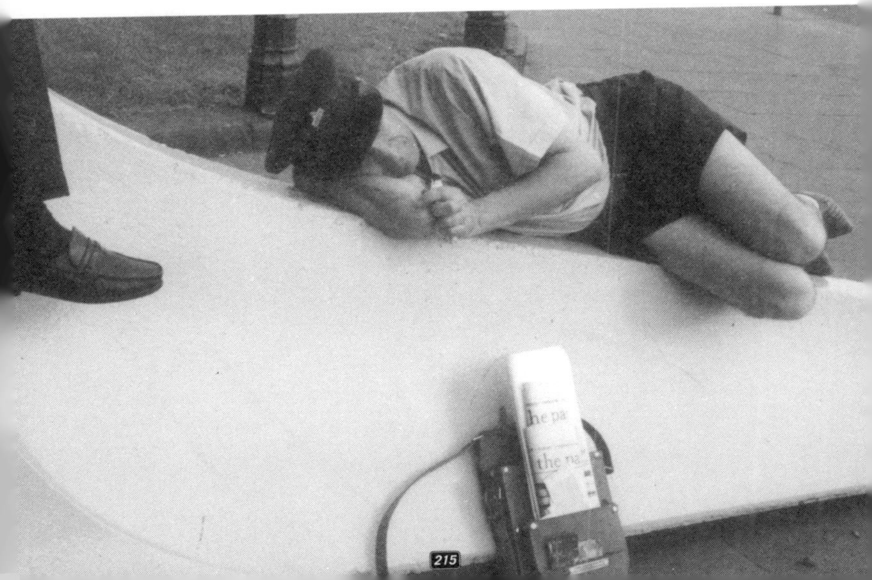

13

# pedagogic possibilities of *tramjatra*

Fazal Rizvi

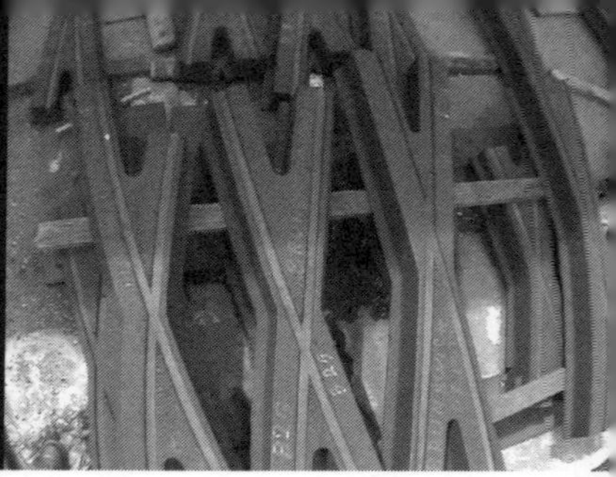

The idea of 'internationalisation of the curriculum' has become ubiquitous in Australian higher education, a part of the slogan system of the modern corporatised universities. One does not have to look far to find it in mission statements of most, if not all, Australian universities. In a way that has begun to sound like a mantra, Australian universities now insist that it is not enough to have substantially grown the number of international students on their campuses, partly of course as a way of expanding and diversifying their financial base, but that higher education curriculum must now be renewed, becoming more responsive to the compelling requirements of globalisation. A global university, trumpets a *Universitas 21* document, must now be characterised by its international content, its engagement with the global circuits of knowledge and communication. What is now needed is a greater emphasis on the global character of the university, its role and functions as well as its reach. In the global knowledge economy, the most basic purposes and operational structures of higher education need to be re-thought and re-articulated.

In search of a new paradigm defining the global character of the university, an Australian government report admonished its public universities, more than ten years ago, for 'being too narrowly commercial with insufficient recognition of student needs and the benefits of international education'. The report asserted that 'international education is an increasingly important part of Australia's international relations. It uniquely spans the cultural, economic and interpersonal dimensions of international relations'. It assists 'cultural understanding of all parties'; it encourages 'an international outlook' among students and staff alike. The report demanded a new approach to curriculum development 'which responds to the diverse and sophisticated nature of the global environment'. Internationalised curriculum, it maintained, must be based on the values of innovation, flexibility, client-centredness and enterprise culture on the one hand and intercultural understanding and sensitivity on the other.[1]

This general sentiment is of course not unique to Australia. It is broadly in line with the exhortations of international organisations such as the Organisation of Economic Cooperation and Development (OECD). The OECD defines internationalisation of the curriculum as an attempt to introduce an 'international orientation in content, aimed at preparing students for performing (professionally/socially) in an international and multicultural context, and designed for domestic students as well as foreign students'. Such an international orientation to the curriculum, the OECD argues, is necessary partly because of the requirements of the global labour market but also because of the social and cultural developments that are heading towards 'a multicultural and globally-minded society'. Here the OECD's economic instrumentalism converges with its support for a corporatist view of multiculturalism. Its rhetoric of internationalisation is underpinned by two discourses: of economic necessity and of cultural exchange and intercultural understanding. An ethical impulse is thus enjoined to globalisation's corporate interests.

So much for the rhetoric, however. How is the idea of internationalisation of the curriculum translated into practice? Over the past decade, this has emerged as one of the major challenges for Australian universities, and none of the universities appear entirely satisfied with their efforts. Most curriculum experiments have either been superficial or have lacked institutional support to ensure their longevity. It was in the context, in 2000, of a struggle to develop an appropriate policy framework for RMIT University's commitment to internationalise its curriculum that I, as the University's then Pro Vice-Chancellor for International Affairs, first came across *tramjatra*. And although *tramjatra* was never conceived as a curriculum renewal project, I was immediately struck by its pedagogic possibilities. It seemed to me to be a good example of the kind of project that could address some of the enduring problems associated with efforts to internationalise curricula in Australian universities. In what follows, I would like to discuss how.

Most universities in Australia conceive of the idea of internationalisation in a very narrow sense, referring largely to initiatives designed to meet the specific needs of international students, whose contribution to the financial bottom line of the universities is now enormously significant. Internationalisation often means providing support services to international students, helping them to quickly become used to their new learning environment. Now while such assistance is clearly necessary for those students who need it, this assimilationist view overlooks the complex politics of cultural exchange. Its focus is on individuals rather than on intercultural relationships inherent in the processes of teaching and learning. Its instrumentalism assumes internationalisation to be relevant to international students only, and not to the domestic students as well.

Yet another popular understanding of internationalisation addresses this criticism and involves highlighting curricular experiences offered to *all* students, local and international alike. These experiences are designed to enhance student understanding of international issues, and thus broaden their career or life options within the global economy. This conception of internationalisation demands experiences more inclusive of the diverse cultural traditions that are now represented on campuses. Such a curriculum can be achieved, so it is imagined, through efforts to teach a foreign language or through courses designed to help students learn about 'other' cultures. Area studies programmes are once again in vogue. These studies often involve study tours and educational exchange programmes. Indeed, the number of students engaged in study abroad programmes is often treated as a major performance criterion against which the internationalisation efforts of universities

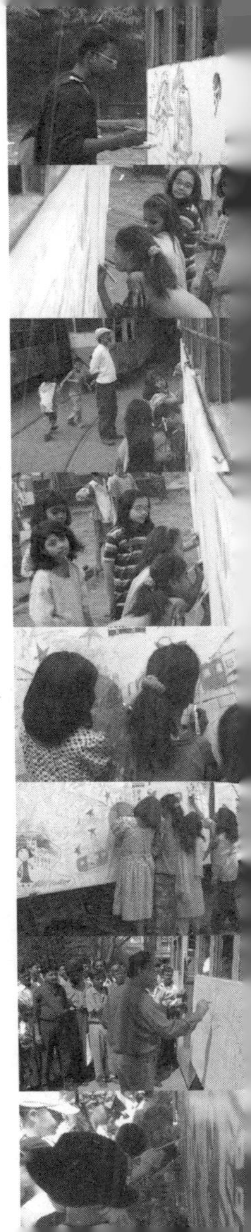

are measured and compared by governments, as well as by the institutions themselves.

Study abroad programmes are generally defined as those learning experiences that students have outside the boundaries of their own country, for which credit is given at the home university. Permutations of study abroad programmes are many and varied, and include such arrangements as international exchange between two or more universities, undertaken on a reciprocal basis, with tuition fees mutually waived; international industry or clinical placements or internships; international study tours specifically for credit; joint degree or diploma programmes; research at an overseas university for an award at home, and other similar collaborations. Most universities in Australia have set numerical targets for international study experience at 10 per cent of all commencing students, paralleling targets set by universities in Europe, already achieved by many under the ERASMUS programme of the European Union (EU).

Administratively, study abroad programmes represent a pragmatic, quick and achievable way of internationalising the curriculum. They do not require any significant change to the existing curriculum, and can always be 'added on' as educational options provided to the students within a programme. Because of their high visibility, universities can claim success, even without any demonstrable evidence that study abroad programmes help students develop a range of graduate attributes, including an understanding of a different culture that has enriched their education and challenged their cultural assumptions.

Universities often argue that study abroad programmes help in promoting a more cosmopolitan outlook among students. Here the arguments for internationalisation are broadly similar to those supporting various notions of corporate multiculturalism within the national arena. Recognition of and respect for cultural diversity underlies both notions. The fashionable language of 'productive diversity' applies, so it is believed, even more so to the global context than it does to the domestic policy arena. Within this liberal discourse of internationalisation, multiculturalism effectively 'goes global', with promotion of a combination of local and global values, such as openness, tolerance and cosmopolitanism.

Whether these values are in fact realised through study abroad programmes is of course an open question. The research on the outcomes of study abroad programmes is at best limited. Much of it relates to the questions of access to these programmes and to the administrative arrangements involved in their implementation. Very little of it examines the assumptions underlying study abroad programmes. Much of it assumes that study abroad programmes are intrinsically good, and that travel and global mobility will necessarily produce a cosmopolitan outlook in everyone alike, regardless of their gender, race and socio-economic background. There is also very little examination of the curriculum architecture of the broader programme within which study abroad experiences are embedded. Nor is there any assessment of the conditions necessary for the success of such experiences.

My own experience of study programmes, both as an administrator and as an educational theorist, suggests that students who go on study abroad programmes often derive a great deal of personal enjoyment and benefit from them. This is hardly surprising since many of these students come from affluent families and have already

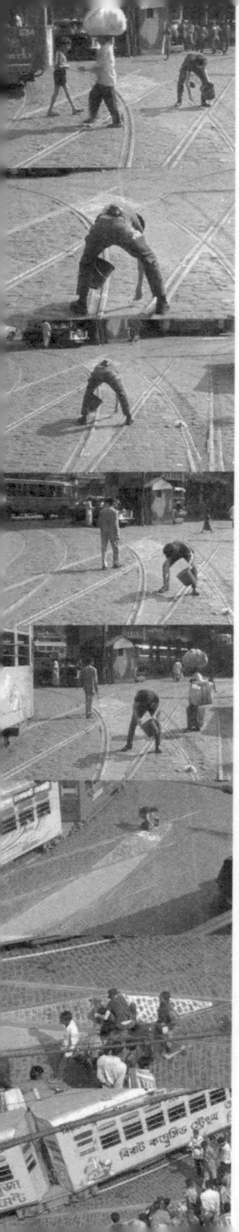

travelled internationally and are predisposed towards intercultural experiences, especially when it is presented to them as a consumable commodity, consistent with their desire for cultural voyeurism. The students are also led to believe that the international experience is advantageous to them in the global labour market, which increasingly celebrates the value of what the human resource management literature refers to as 'intercultural competence'. More positively, many students feel that the insights developed during the study abroad programme enable them to acquire a deeper interest in the country they visit, and to become more adaptable, confident, open and tolerant, qualities considered essential for international business.

Yet, other students come back from study abroad programmes disillusioned. Some even have their cultural stereotypes and prejudices confirmed and perhaps even extended. Clearly, the outcomes of study abroad programmes are as varied as the students themselves. One of the consistent problems with the study programmes is a lack of any systematic curriculum thinking in their design and evaluation. As a result, students are often poorly prepared for their educational experiences abroad and most universities have not yet developed ways of fully accommodating into the curriculum the intercultural insights and questions the students bring back home. Not surprisingly, therefore, many students complain that while they are encouraged to go abroad, their experiences are accorded little pedagogic value upon their return. Most of their teachers simply don't want to know, and have not considered the ways in which study abroad programmes could be pedagogically productive. The programmes are often viewed as 'add-on' experiences, treated as if they were 'extra-curricular'.

Beyond these legitimate student concerns, I want to argue that there are more profound issues surrounding study abroad programmes. These issues concern not only questions of access and educational experience but, more broadly, debates about the development of transnational networks and the global politics of cultural knowledge and communication. Here the questions of who goes on study abroad programmes, and where, are crucial. The available data suggests that more than 80 per cent of Australian students participating in study abroad programmes go to a European or North American country. A very small number go to Asia or Africa, largely because Australian universities have failed to develop effective sustainable exchange arrangements with universities within the Third World. Students, it seems, prefer to remain in their cultural 'comfort zone', and universities in turn do little to challenge them into exploring broader issues of global inequalities. Despite much talk about global interconnectivity and interdependence, contact thus remains within globally differentiated cultural communities, the West versus the Rest. In so far as transnational mobility is considered as a major characteristic of the current phase of globalisation, it is remarkable how the movement of Australian students through study abroad programmes has a pattern that reproduces asymmetrical power relations within the world community.

*Tramjatra* is an exception to this, and, from my viewpoint, challenges the comfortable pattern of Australian 'educational tourism' to Europe and North America. In seeking to establish a cultural dialogue between Melbourne and Kolkata, *tramjatra* enables participants to explore similarities and differences between an affluent city at the core of global capitalism and a city at its periphery. But more significantly, it focuses on the nature and scope of cultural and political relations between the two cities, both historical and contemporary. It enables participants in both cities to interpret and work with the complex politics of globalisation, and the patterns of global inequalities it produces, from positions located at different ends of the circuits of world capitalism.

Although, as I have already noted, *tramjatra* was never designed as a study abroad programme, it did experiment with pedagogic possibilities by establishing contact between RMIT Architecture + Design students and students at Jadavpur University in Kolkata. A small number of RMIT students visited Kolkata, worked with students from Jadavpur, joined with Kolkatan and Melburnian activists in numerous forums, and collaborated with artists in using the trams, tram shelters and depots as canvas to paints images depicting figurative links between Kolkata and Melbourne. Students also undertook mapping investigations of Kolkata tram streetscapes, designed billboards promoting the project, and returned to Melbourne to develop design propositions to increase the value of tramways to the two cities. A reciprocal visit from Jadavpur University was planned but did not eventuate because of the lack of funds. But even with its limitations, *tramjatra* indicated the enormous potential it had as a study abroad programme. It enabled students to work against the grain, so to speak, to generate grassroots relations, as an example of 'globalisation from below'. It helped students from both countries to explore their common colonial history, on the one hand, and contradictory processes of contemporary cultural globalisation, on the other.

One of the main limitations of most existing programmes of educational exchange is that they are confined to the classroom, with students undertaking a similar range of courses in another country, with appropriate credit transfer. What is distinctive about *tramjatra* is that it is embedded within a broader political project, designed to forge transcultural relations that are both complex and multi-dimensional. In this way, it encompasses a potential for both creativity and criticality that appear absent from most study abroad programmes. *Tramjatra* provided students with opportunities to work with local artisans and activists, to investigate the complex processes of global interdependence and to develop transnational networks from below to resist what often appears to be the juggernaut of global capitalism from above. It helped students to understand how localities are historically constituted and are formed politically, under constant pressures for change.

The *tramjatra* project has now been in existence for more than eight years, and has a clearly defined activist agenda. The project involves collaboration between tramway workers, artists, students and activists in Melbourne and Kolkata, established at a time when Kolkata tramways faced the threat of closure and Melbourne tramways were being privatised and restructured. The introduction of electronic tickets in Melbourne threatened, and resulted in, the loss of tram conductors altogether. Communities whose very existence was defined around tramways felt betrayed and sought understandably to establish a political struggle to save the trams. *Tramjatra* emerged out of this struggle.

When Mick Douglas and the well-known Melbourne tram personality, an ex-conductor, Roberto D'Andrea, first visited Kolkata to explore possibilities of collaboration, they found a major network of political activities, all seeking to save Kolkata tramways from the threat of closure. The network included artists, environmentalists, engineers, tramways workers and the general public; all convinced that trams occupy an important and vital place in the constitution of the city, both physically and poetically. Trams do not pollute, and make sounds that many find totally captivating, almost hypnotic. Mick and Roberto found these enthusiasts keen to establish a transnational network that not only celebrated the role trams played in defining urban collective memory, but also shared political tactics to pressure their governments against both the closure of the tracks in Kolkata, and privatisation and restructuring in Melbourne.

*Tramjatra* has attached a great deal of importance to the metaphor of networks, of both people and the trams themselves. As Mick points out, networks are about ways of 'being interconnected in the life-world'. 'For rather than fostering totalising images or narratives, networks present us with their capacity to remain open-ended, always enabling us to enter because their economy does not contain or enclose. By focusing attention less upon form, networks can enable us to pursue movements which perform.'[2] Through creating new networks and consolidating existing ones, the *tramjatra* project has created a dialogue of creativity and imagination between two cities. It has involved a number of exchange visits and collaborative projects that have produced outcomes that were initially unimaginable. The threat to closure in Kolkata has dissipated, as many politicians now seem ready to embrace *tramjatra*; and while some tracks have closed, Kolkata is better positioned to invest in trams again.

2001 was a significant year for *tramjatra*, with major festivals conducted during February and March in Kolkata, followed by a similar festival held in Melbourne over October and November. In Kolkata, Roberto D'Andrea became a familiar figure on Kolkata trams, issuing tickets and invitation to events. His banter on the trams made many Bengalis give him the honorific title 'Pugla', meaning something like the Shakespearean fool. Such was the level of interest in Kolkata that Suzie Attiwill, one of the project's so-called 'critical passengers' and a lecturer who accompanied the RMIT students, was granted a daily column in the Kolkata's premier newspaper, *The Statesman*. She wrote some thirty short articles generating letters to the editor in response and encouraging other local writers to publish short articles and even poetry in celebration of trams. The West Bengal Minister of Transport became a fan of the project.

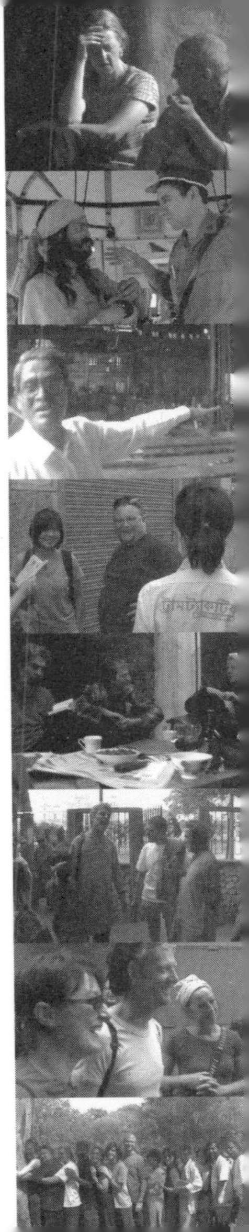

In October-November 2001, a delegation from Kolkata made a return trip to Melbourne to participate in a similar festival. There were a number of forums, exhibitions, bazaars and performances during the festival, in which artists and activists from both countries participated. Discussions centred on a whole range of subjects, from cricket to food, but always returned to the trams – the joys of riding them, the success and failures of *tramjatra*, the stories about tram journeys, the similarities and differences between the two systems, discussions of global economic restructuring and its differing consequences for trams in cities like Kolkata and Melbourne; and the politics of preserving the tramways systems.

Tramways systems in Kolkata and Melbourne have much in common. Both were first developed in the late nineteenth century by their British colonial rulers; both once served as capital cities of their respective new nations; both were once great centres of industrial production; both were once great sea ports; both are regarded as great cultural and sporting centres; both have a great intellectual and activist tradition; and both are the only cities in their countries to have retained tramways. In short, in both cities, tramways lie at the core of their imagination about their identity. But while Kolkata and Melbourne are linked to each other by their common colonial history, they relate to global capitalism in radically different ways. It is the broader and complex context of these similarities and differences that makes *tramjatra* so exciting, and an excellent project within which to embed activities designed to internationalise the curriculum.

Even this short description of *tramjatra* suggests a range of creative and critical pedagogic possibilities. A project such as this does not only have the potential to encourage students to reflect on how differing life experiences in Australia and India are structured but also explore the possibilities and the politics of transcultural dialogue. It enables educational engagement at levels of both formal and organic informal learning. Such informal learning necessarily encourages students to think outside their own disciplinary boundaries and their parochial cultural assumptions, to consider issues of global interconnectedness, and to establish intercultural dialogues about how particular communities are affected by globalisation.

The major pedagogic strength of the *tramjatra* project is that it enables Australian students to study the global–local interplay on the ground, in all of the untidy contingencies of Kolkata. Their transcultural dialogues help them to explore the criss-crossing of transnational circuits of communication and cross-cutting of local, translocal and transnational social practices. With their attention directed to the ways in which tramways define their localities, the students consider the contested politics of place making, the social constructions of power differentials and the making of individual, group, national and transnational identities, and their corresponding fields of difference.

Collectively the students are able to look at the practices of everyday life, and more importantly were able to stretch their analysis to encompass a transnational imaginary. Unlike the dominant versions of study abroad programmes that mostly relocate disciplinary studies at another site, *tramjatra* enables education to be viewed as a collective political action, based on practically grounded narratives and historically situated transnational dialogues. The students are able to locate themselves within a transnational network, with a clear resistance agenda. They are

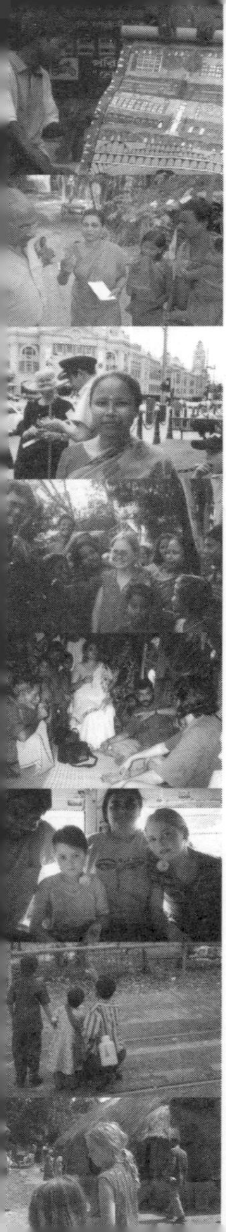

able to give meaning to their international education through a developing network of communication, and imagine alter-native constructions of how the world might work.

For more than a decade, Arjun Appadurai has argued that 'globalization is not simply the name of a new epoch in the history of capital or in the biography of the nation-state. It marks a new role for the imagination of social life'. One of the major goals of internationalisation of curriculum should, in my view, be the development of the global imagination that Appadurai speaks of – a recognition that we all have 'elaborate interests and capabilities in constructing world pictures whose very interaction affects global processes'. If this is so then internationalisation demands de-parochialisation of the processes of learning and teaching, highlighting the importance of 'grassroots' global networks opposed to the dominant corporate narratives of globalisation.[3]

In his recent book, *The Ethnographic Imagination*, Paul Willis has also highlighted the importance of imagination in education. He emphasises:

> ...The ethnographic as conditioning, grounding and setting the range of imaginative meanings within social thought. Ethnography provides the empirical and conceptual discipline. Ethnography is the

> eye of the needle through which the threads of imagination must pass. Imagination is thereby forced to try to see the world in a grain of sand...Experience and the everyday are the bread and butter of ethnography, but they are also the grounds whereupon and the stake for how grander theories must test and justify themselves. They should not be self-referenced imaginings but grounded imaginings.[4]

Although Willis does not specifically discuss transcultural contexts, and he is writing about ethnographic method, his remarks are helpful in reconsidering a more robust conception of the idea of internationalisation of curriculum. For transcultural contexts demand ethnographic understandings of the micropolitics of cultural representation, of the ways in which cultural others are represented and may be re-imagined through transcultural dialogues and collective action. International educational exchange can thus involve *transcultural imagination*.

Within the global context, we need to resist two contrasting approaches to the study of the transcultural that appear to dominate the literature on international education. On the one hand, the transcultural is viewed as an epiphenomenon of the universalising power of late capitalism. On the other hand, the transcultural is assumed to relate simply to local processes, with their distinctive form, disconnected from the logic of transnational capital. Neither of these views is satisfactory. We need to recognise instead that transcultural practices are constituted by the inter-relations with and groundedness within historically specific circuits of power relations. Cultural exchange is an ever-changing product of human practices rather than a reflection of deeper economic imperatives.

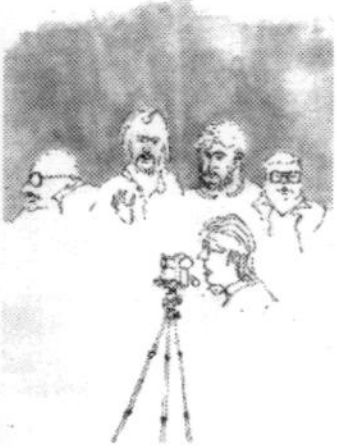

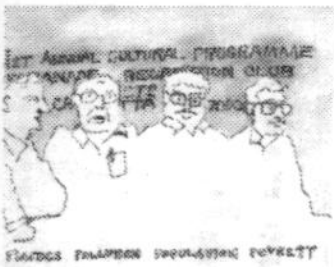


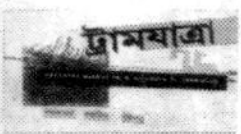


To me then, internationalisation of curriculum is best viewed as an attempt to help students come to terms with their situatedness in the world – situatedness of their knowledge and cultural practices as well as their unique positionality in relation to social networks, political institutions and social relations of race, ethnicity and gender as well as class. This understanding is best achieved collectively in transcultural collaborations, in seeking to understand local problems comparatively, and in relation to global processes. The task of transcultural imagination is thus to examine the materiality of our collective and interlinked circumstances in order to imagine how things might be otherwise and to devise strategies to work towards the alternatives so imagined. The pedagogic potential of *tramjatra* is best encapsulated in the opportunities it provided all participants in the project, students and non-students alike, to do this, through networked learning, both formal and informal.

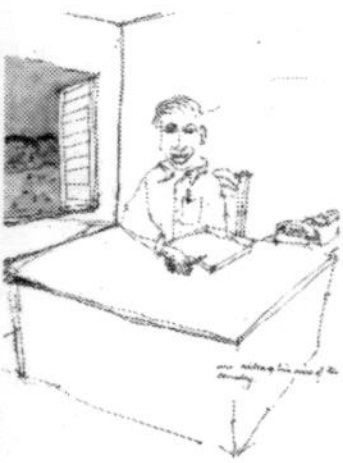

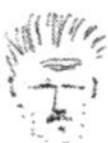

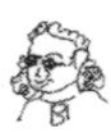

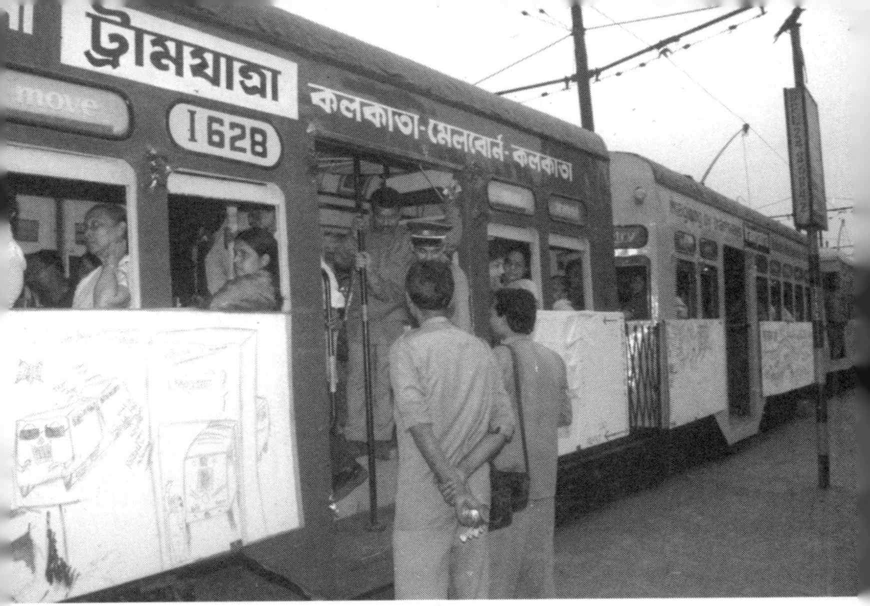


1 Kim Beazley, *International Education in Australia through the 1990s*, Ministerial Statement, Canberra: Australian Government Publishing Service (AGPS), 1992.

2 Michael Douglas, 'Tracking a tram-way of knowing: Poetic search & speculative design', *Design plus Research: Proceedings of the Politechnico di Milano Conference May 1 -20 2000,* Eds. S. Pizzocaro, A. Arruda, D. De Moraes, Politechnico di Milano, 139-145.

3 Arjun Appadurai, 'Grassroots globalization and the research imagination', in A. Appadurai (ed.), *Globalization*, Durham and London: Duke University Press, 2001, 14.

4 Paul Willis, *The Ethnographic Imagination*, London: Polity Press, 2000, viii.

14

# speculations

Tramways and their infrastructure are so embedded in the cities they inhabit that we can mistakenly come to disregard them for being ordinary. But no mode of transport is ever simply a conveyance from one point to another. Tramways facilitate particular types of street-based social experience whilst contributing their extraordinary character of lines, textures, rhythms and sounds to the urban landscape. The extra dimension of this mode of conveyance – the culture of tramways and tram travel – is little built upon in comparison to the cultures of the car and the train that abound with myths. How might we better understand and increase the value of the relation between tramways and their city? What is the cultural potential of entwining ways of the tram and themes of urban culture? What tools of representation and analysis might assist understanding the experience of passage in tram travel? The following speculations explore these questions.

*# work by students of the School of Architecture + Design at RMIT University*

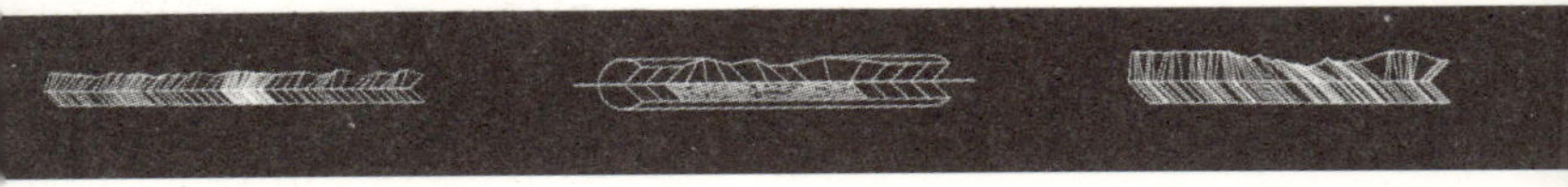

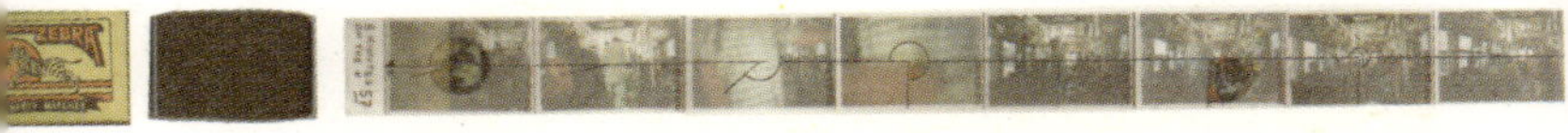

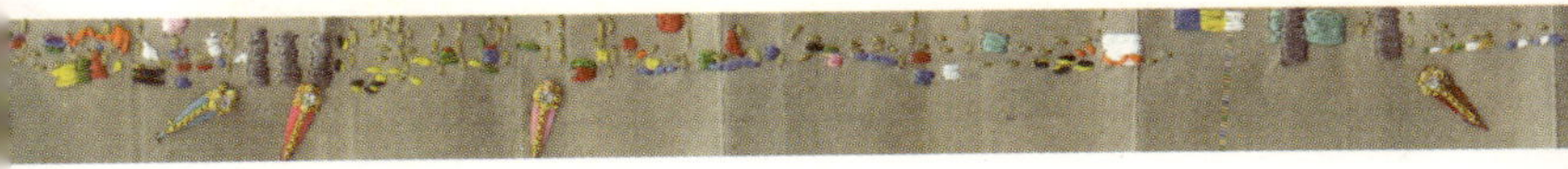

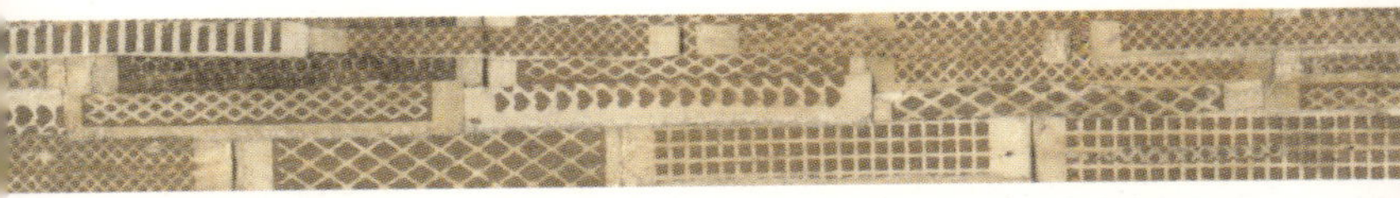

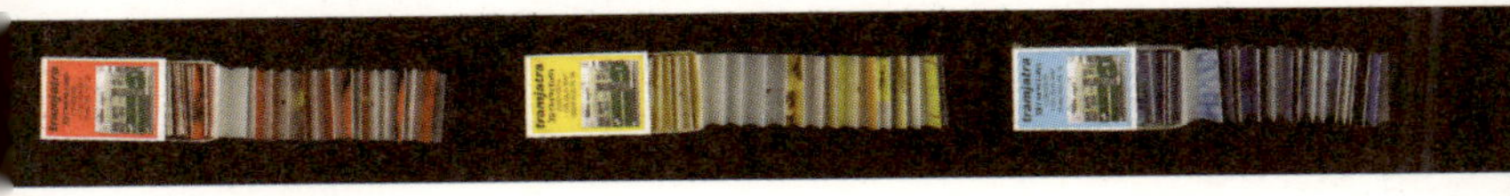

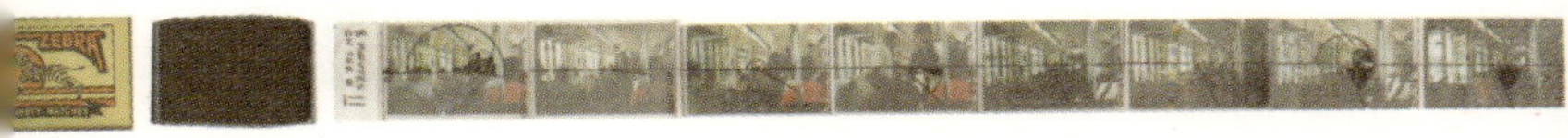

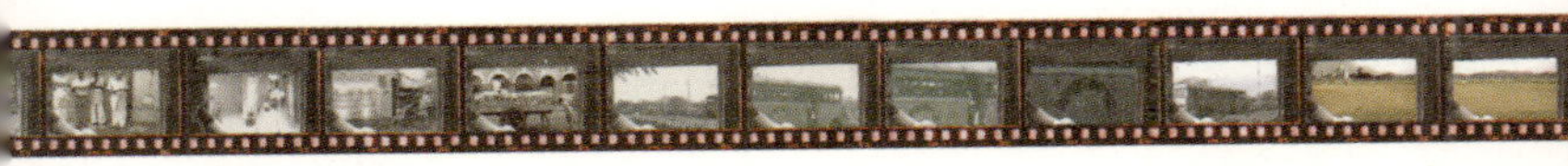

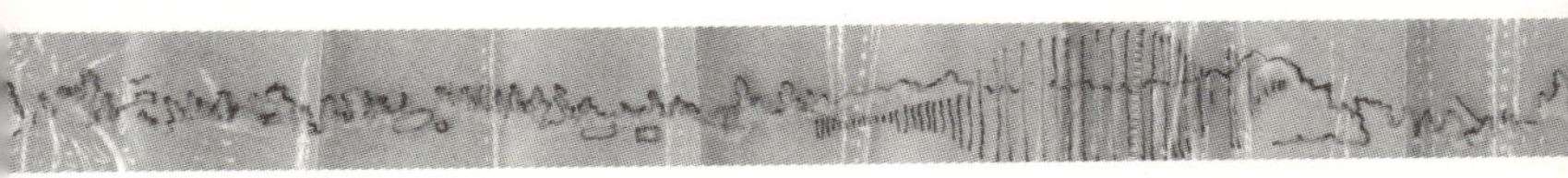

#

## Weeping Wall

Julian Canterbury #

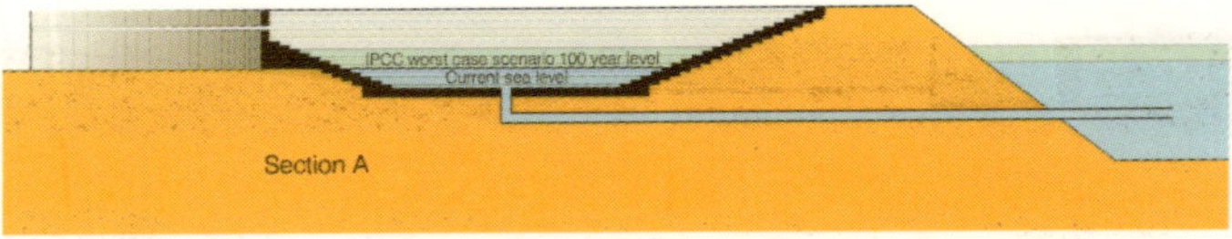


According to the Intergovernmental Panel on Climate Change (IPCC) sea levels have risen between 100-200mm in the past 100 years, and will rise between 100-1000mm in the twenty-first century.

It may seem that a city such as Kolkata is both a more polluted and polluting city than, for instance, Melbourne. Yet the average Australian produces eighteen times more carbon dioxide (a colourless and odourless greenhouse gas) than the average Indian.

Comparisons are complex. Whilst pollution such as airborne particles are largely a local problem, global warming is not, nor are rising sea levels caused by melting polar ice and seawater expansion at higher temperature. Densely populated low-lying delta land areas like much of Bengal would be severely affected.

The fixed track upon which tramways are based provides a common sense of firm ground in a city. By placing a section of tram track at sea level in both Kolkata and Melbourne, a common datum gives a shared

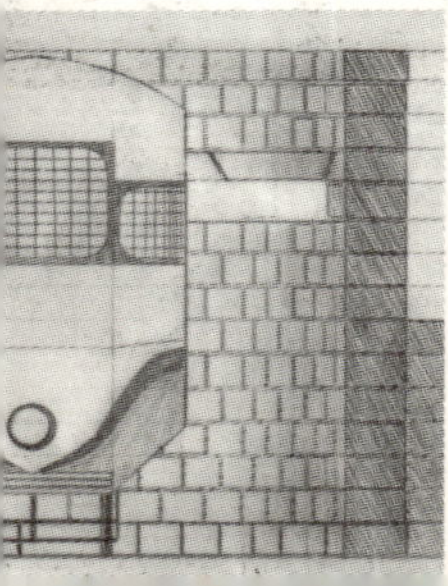

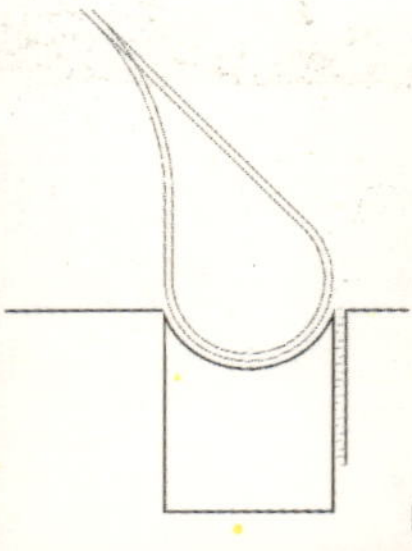

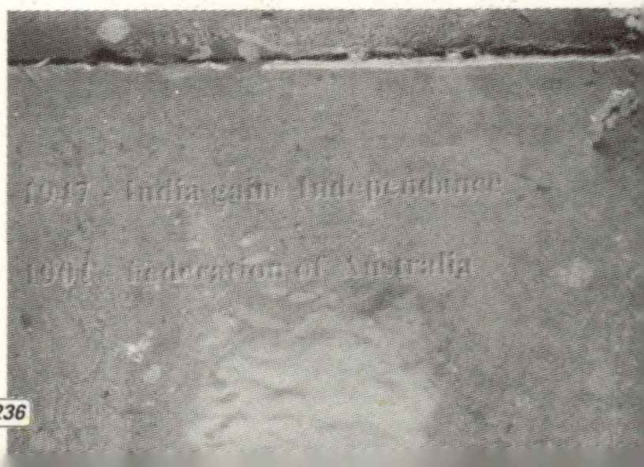

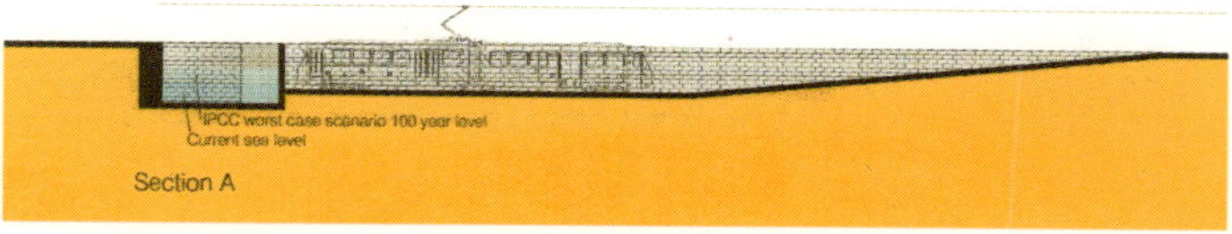


measure between the cities across the globe. The trams riding this sea-level tram track deliver the city dweller to the Weeping Wall at the River Hooghly and at Port Phillip Bay.

The sea level of 100 years ago, of today, and of that predicted for the end of the twenty-first century, are marked on the face of each Weeping Wall, along with other historical moments that have marked a local change in greenhouse gas emissions, global warming and rising sea levels. The wall conveys the impact of rising sea level in a directly experienced way. Whilst daily water levels vary against the wall markings according to seasonal rain and tides, a patina created by the continual seepage of water through cracks in the drystone wall conveys the larger pattern of levels. The higher the water level, the greater the seepage. If oceans continue to rise so the walls in Kolkata and Melbourne will join in weeping.

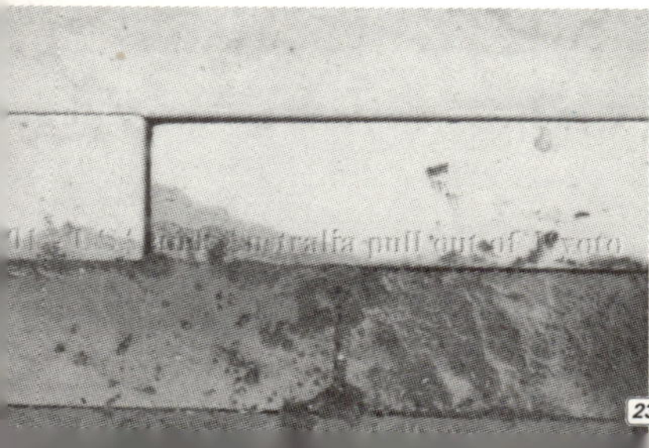

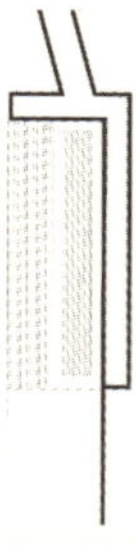

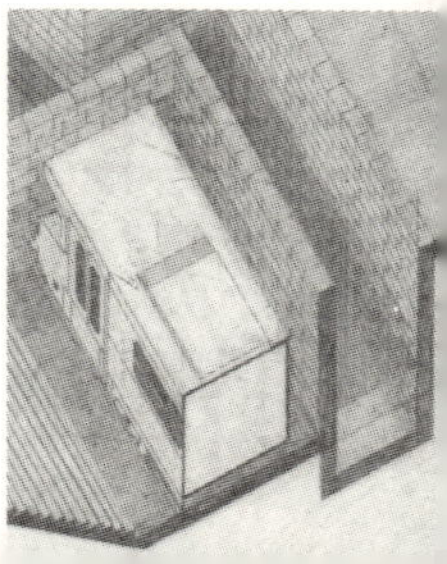

## Urban Activity-level Responsive Architecture

Rory Hyde #

The number of heart beats per minute indicate the level of activity experienced by a human body. Similarly, the number of tram-ticket validations per minute on the entire Melbourne tramways system indicates the level of activity experienced by the tramways, and by extension, the level of activity of the city.

A uniquely located, small, triangular site of land is formed at the northern end of the Melbourne central activities district where the Melbourne city grid meets the larger north-south road pattern of greater Melbourne at a thirty-degree angle on its main north-south central axis (Swanston Street, corner of Victoria Street). Tram tracks diverge and converge at this site where a small tramways operational control building has long stood still. This site, one that reads as a pivotal wedge cutting into the order of the city, could be alive to the dynamism of the city with an architecture that physically moves, altering its spaces, programme and performance in immediate response to the real-time condition of Melbourne's tramways in the same way that a heart is responsive to a living body.

In the body, the heart responds to intensified activity by pumping faster and increasing its own intensity. Similarly, this architecture responds to the increased intensity of the tramways by intensifying experience of its spaces, first through manipulating positions of its walls that act as screens for projecting images onto, and second through increasing the rate of change of the images projected. As city activity increases, as measured through tram-ticket validations, the fixed-dimension screen-walls move on tracks to bring about an increasingly intense proximity, whilst real-time images of the city's life in streets and in trams are projected at speeds increasing to sixty images per minute. The architectural structure of shifting screen-walls and projected images undergoes daily expansion and contraction, relaxing and intensifying as a trampulse to the life of the city.

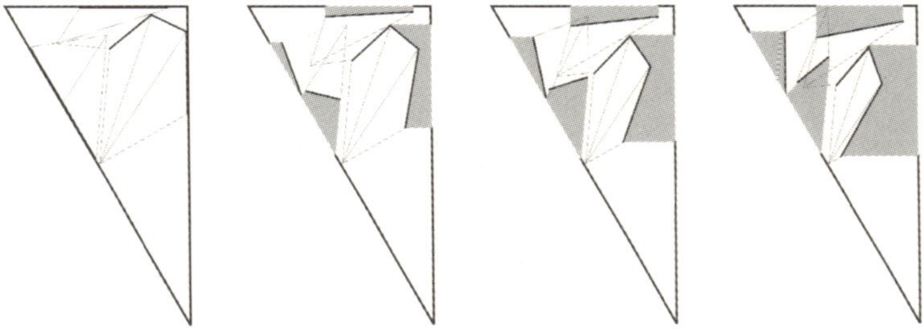

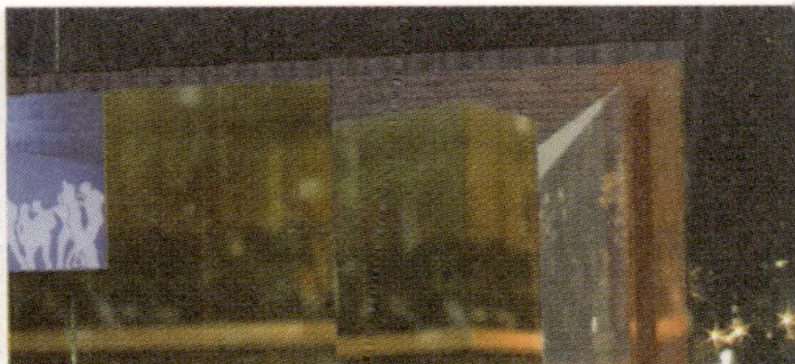

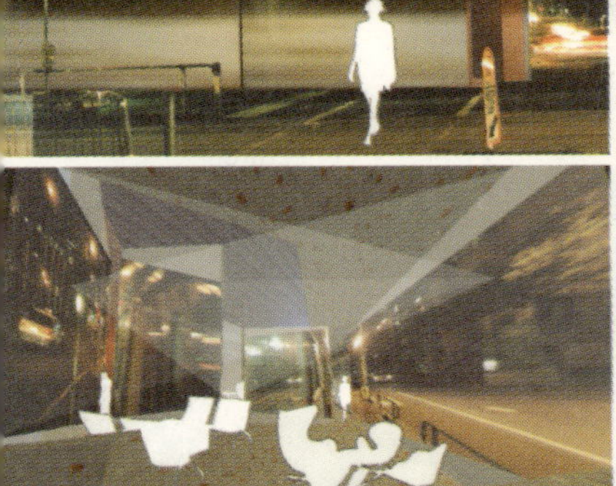

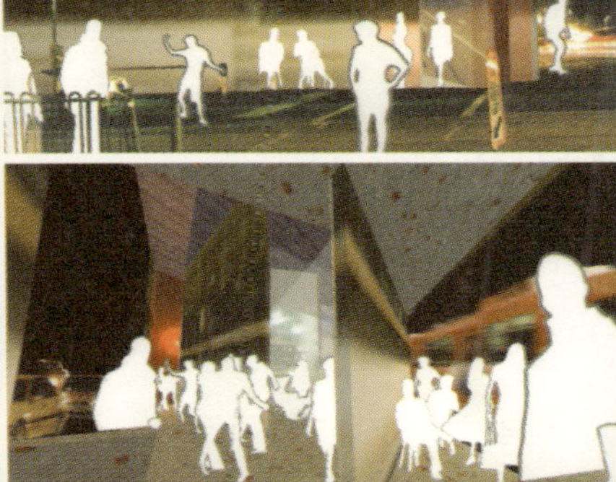

Lisa de Jong, Yuen Ping Tai, Annette Warner, Sophie Zelder #

The infrastructure that shapes the possibilities of urban living easily becomes normalised into the accepted life patterns of city dwellers, for better or worse. The more subtle effects that infrastructure has upon our ecological, social, economic, cultural and psychological landscapes are little understood. If tramways punctuate our experience of sky and horizon in the city through the overhead canopy of wiring linework, could the effects of this be poetically enhanced as if to intensify heights of the imagination? What might happen if the singing of steel wheel on steel track and the other particular sounds of tramways motion are identified and 'tuned' for their role in orchestrating the collective city that resounds in our experience and memory? Could new labour service roles improve intractable traffic congestion problems, for instance by providing the flexibility of a time-of-day-adjusted tram prioritisation strategy?

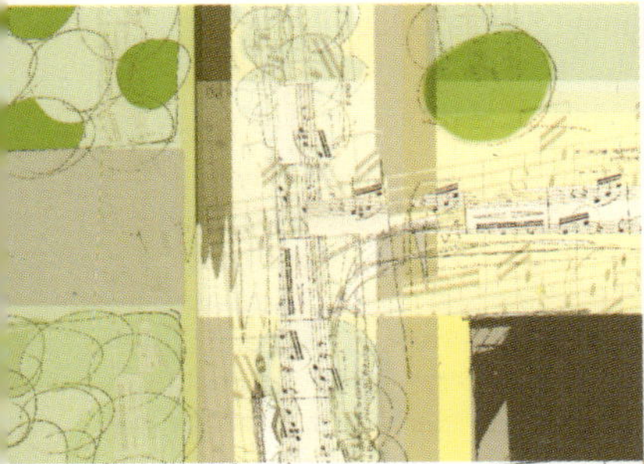
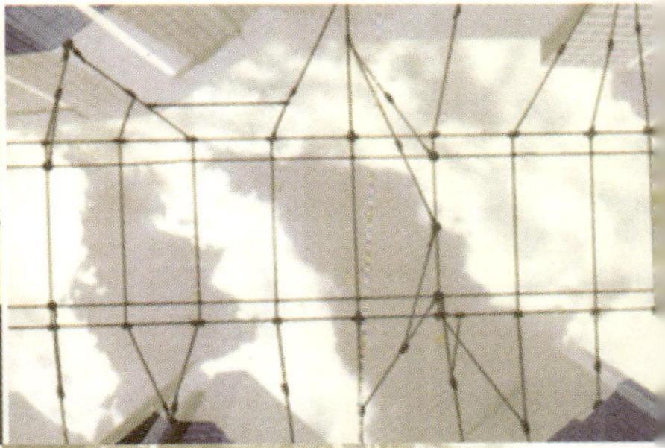
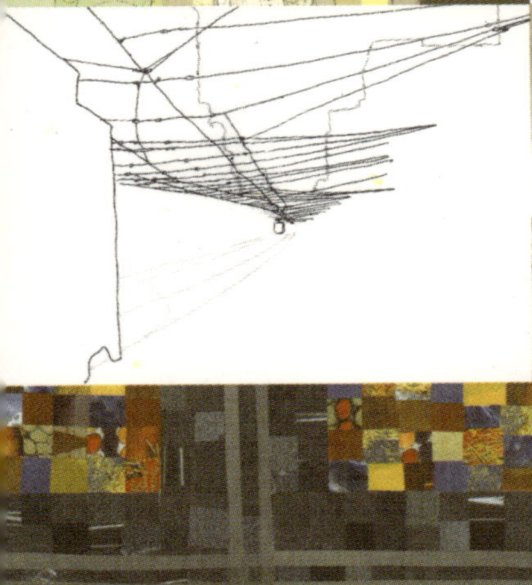
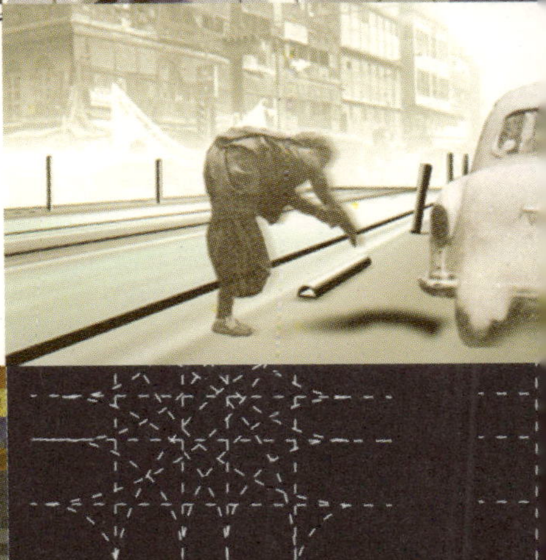
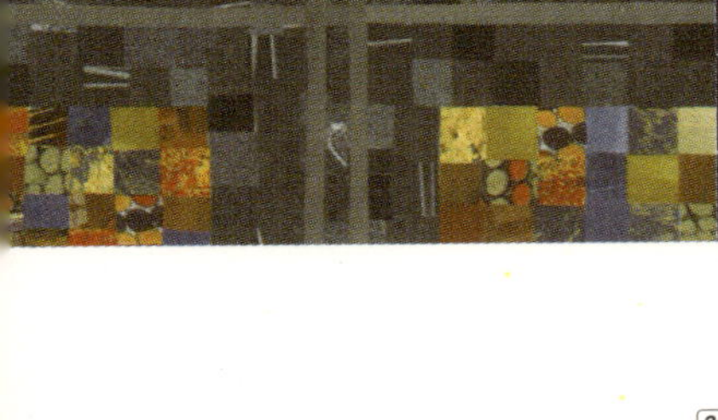

## Users Change the System

Geoff Binder #

When you travel in a car you choose which radio station to listen to. By using the tramways system in Melbourne or Kolkata, passengers could choose to invest in their preferred way to change the tramways system.

Each time a passenger travels on a tram, they choose a project of benefit to the tramways. A small levy on the purchase price of each ticket is credited to the project of the passenger's choice. In Kolkata, a 25 paise levy on an annual patronage of 73 million would generate Rs 18,250,000 (A$730,000) per year. In Melbourne, a 5 cent levy on an annual patronage of 127 million would generate A$1,270,000 (Rs 31,750,000). In Melbourne individual tram routes would generate between A$200,000 and $500,000 per year while in Kolkata this figure would be between Rs 200,000 and Rs 4,600,000. Passengers choose their project at the point of ticket validation on a Melbourne tram, or by selecting a colour-coded project ticket from the conductor on a Kolkata tram.

Passengers can purchase the usual single-trip style of tickets or purchase long-life multi-travel ticket in advance at reduced cost – not only cost-effective to passengers but also a capital-raising strategy to leverage investment in the tramways system. For example, purchase a ten-year ticket valid for the school years of a child, or a lifetime ticket for passengers over fifty years of age, and invest a larger proportion of levy to a preferred project.

Projects would include a distinct visual feature that symbolises the passenger-driven change to the system. For example, renewal of a section of track would be embedded in a green cast block concrete, allowing passengers to clearly identify a change in the system for which they can take some pride.

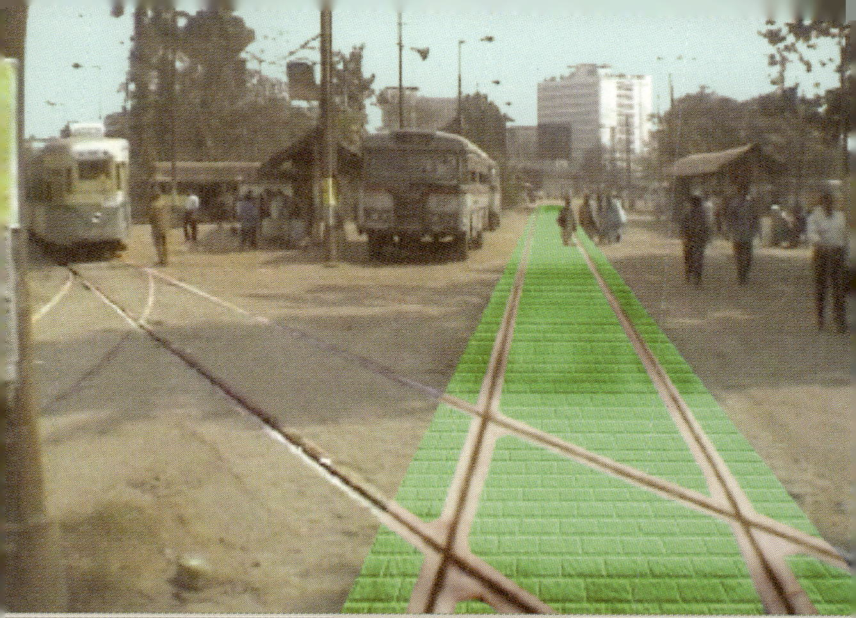

**calculations_Tram_Revenues.xls**

| A | B | C | D | E | F |
|---|---|---|---|---|---|
| **MELBOURNE** | | | | | |
| TOTAL WHOLE SYSTEM | Passengers | 5 cents | 1 cent | | |
| Daily | 347,945 | $17,397.26 | $3,479.45 | | |
| Weekly | 2,442,308 | $122,115.38 | $24,423.08 | | |
| Monthly | 10,583,333 | $529,166.67 | $105,833.33 | | |
| Annually | 127,000,000 | $6,350,000.00 | $1,270,000.00 | | |
| | | | | | |
| 5 cent per ticket | Daily | Weekly | Monthly | Annually | |
| Route: | $1,011.36 | $7,098.99 | $30,762.30 | $369,147.66 | |
| 11 | $577.22 | $4,051.62 | $17,557.02 | $210,684.27 | |
| 12 | $725.22 | $5,090.50 | $22,058.82 | $264,705.88 | |
| 48 | $542.68 | $3,809.22 | $16,506.60 | $198,079.23 | |
| 70 | $942.29 | $6,614.18 | $28,661.46 | $343,937.58 | |
| 75 | $1,450.44 | $10,181.00 | $44,117.65 | $529,411.76 | |
| 86 | $1,519.51 | $10,665.80 | $46,218.49 | $554,621.85 | |
| 96 | $1,450.44 | $10,181.00 | $44,117.65 | $529,411.76 | |
| 109 | $8,219.18 | $57,692.31 | $250,000.00 | $3,000,000.00 | |
| TOTALS | | | | | |
| | | | | | |
| **KOLKATA** | | | | | |
| TOTAL WHOLE SYSTEM | Passengers | 25 Paise in AUS$ | 5 Paise in AUS$ | | |
| Daily | 200,000 | $2,127.66 | $425.53 | | |
| Weekly | 1,400,000 | $14,893.62 | $2,978.72 | | |
| Monthly | 6,083,333 | $64,716.31 | $12,943.26 | | |
| Annually | 73,000,000 | $776,595.74 | $155,319.15 | | |
| | | | | | |
| In Dollars AUS @ 25 Paise per ticket | Daily | Weekly | Monthly | Annually | |
| AJC Bose/APC Rd | $231.48 | $1,620.34 | $7,040.76 | $84,489.11 | |
| Rabindra Sarini | $192.90 | $1,350.28 | $5,867.30 | $70,407.59 | |
| Esplanade | $212.19 | $1,485.31 | $6,454.03 | $77,448.35 | |
| Khidirpur | $212.19 | $1,485.31 | $6,454.03 | $77,448.35 | |
| [illegible] Sarani | $212.19 | $1,485.31 | $6,454.03 | $77,448.35 | |

## Grooving

Mick Douglas with RMIT Industrial Design students #

Woven lines of steel animate the surface of the city streets. Half the steel's profile sits slightly proud of the street surface as scar tissue standing amongst flesh; the remainder of the steel profile indenting a shallow groove set below the street's asphalt, concrete or cobbled skin. This punctuation of the street is felt under the heel of pedestrians and by the bicyclist whose free-moving wheels must resist falling prey to the certainty of the track's groove; it is noted by the motorist experiencing the sensation of rubber tyres gliding on the hardened scar of the track's steel; it is seen by the eye in the street as it glints under the reflections of light capturing its contour. Most fundamentally, the wheel of the tram is intended to reside en track, flowing within the groove so as to locate direction.

If only these tracks could reveal something of the passages that have transpired upon them. Just as a needle amplifies the grooves of a vinyl record to reproduce recorded sound, could we fashion devices and performances to bring imaginative life to these grooves of the street?

*'Grooving' was performed at Melbourne's Moomba festival in 2000.*

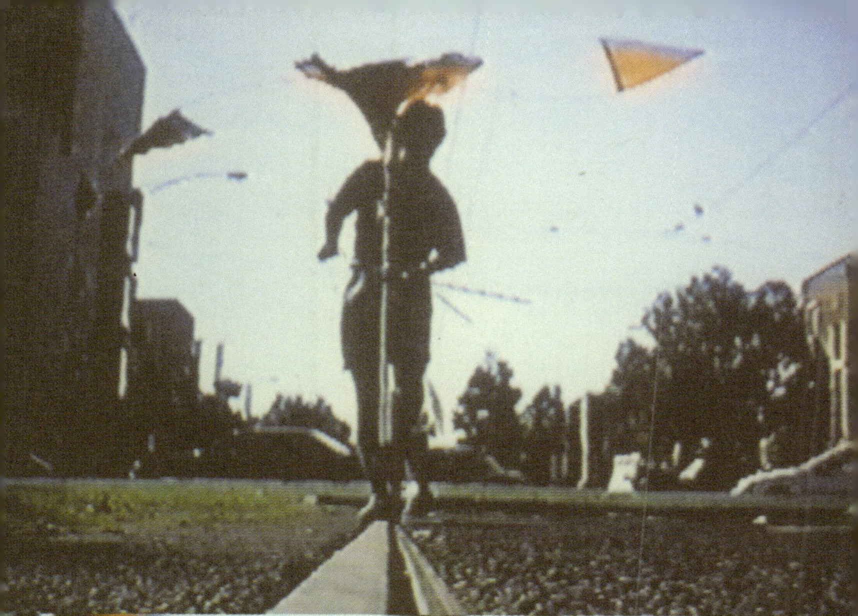

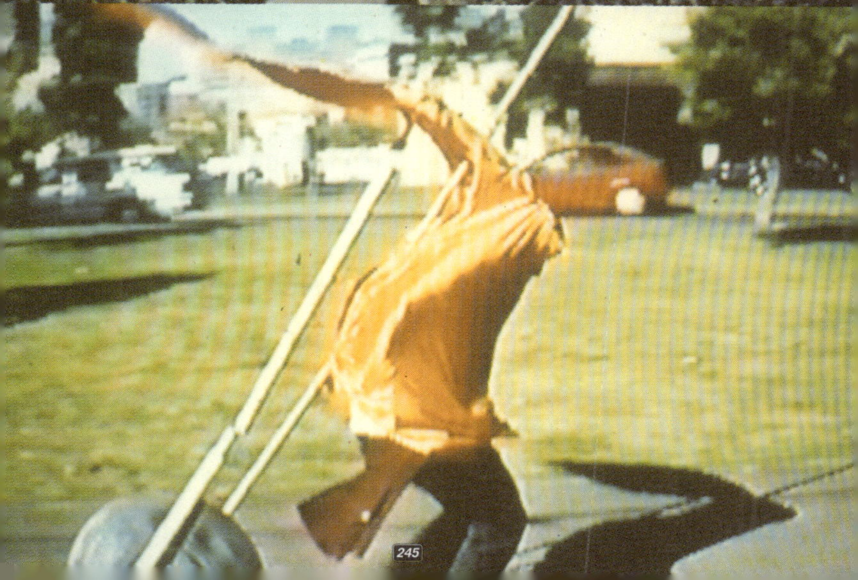

**Devil**
Mark Misic

I am watching 'Rock-Bunny' paint his devils and beasts that dance around trams suspended in a ladder of songs. These devils amaze me with their horned big heads, flaming tongues and long, thin bodies of arms and legs in grey and green. Does the boy see these things or is it the stories through the generations that make them appear? Do devils play with trams, as much as they play with the desires of people? Where on earth do these pictures come from?

I really like watching him paint. He is very fluid and at ease with himself in making pictures. But he is no different to boys back home of the same age. Monsters appear everywhere, and why shouldn't they? Why should devils be vanquished? Maybe they desire to befriend, to be found. A picture made by a young boy brings them into the world, frees them to be seen. Rock-Bunny transforms their desire to frighten and make havoc into a bit of amicable nonsense.

How about it...let's make devils the guardian of the tramways? Imagine that. Wow! We could make a coat of arms that might feature two devils eating a tram, or spinning it on their fingers. Or we could have a tram inside the devil's guts, as a metaphor for an agnostic notion of life, as a journey through the gut of the devil.

But why not make friends and honour these imagined boogiemen of the system? Are trams part of a learning that is about good and bad? Is a tram a good thing? Albert Tucker, an Australian artist, saw them as part of his pantheon of evil things. Trams to him haunted the dark and ran people down. But maybe old Bertie was making a comment about the flatness of Australia's imagination at the time. Australia till today has a very flat mythological imagination. How do we discuss the devils in our culture and how do we make friends with them? How do we play with them as a kid does?

Rock-Bunny's images of funny green meanies hanging onto the outside of the tram remind me of myself. I once was a green-clad conductor on Melbourne's trams. Was I also once a devil? Maybe, but I definitely was a loutish and truant conductor. That conductor I remember, that silly younger me, used to hang on to the outside of W-class trams, walk along the side board, and re-enter between the doors while the tram was hurling along towards loony St Kilda Beach. Passengers' faces would protest concern about the sanity of the conductor. But somehow I never had any fear, or thought for a second that maybe I was possessed by a show-off 'Dare Devil'. Maybe art is about a bit of possession and I say, Rock-Bunny follow your devils.

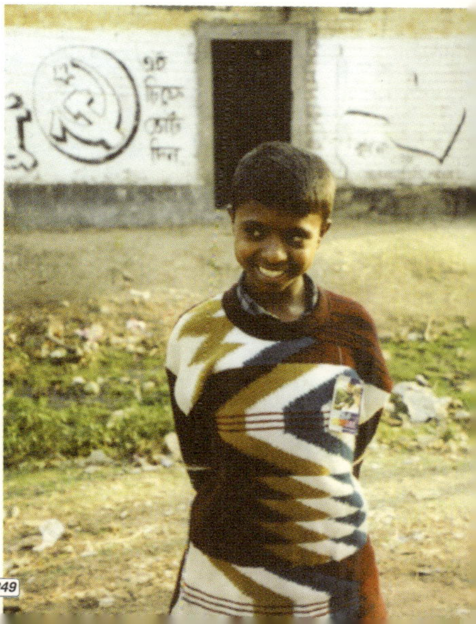

*Rabbany 'Rock-Bunny' Chitrakar is the youngest son in the patua family of Dukhushyam Chitrakar.*

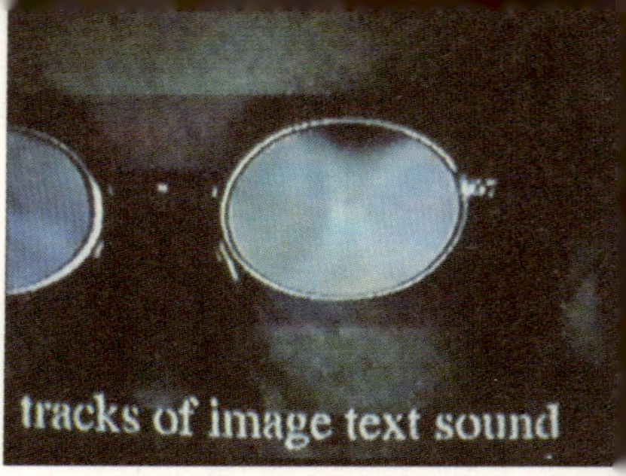


## Performance Code for a Tracking Vehicle

Mick Douglas

0.1 The Tracking Vehicle randomly circulates about the metropolitan tram tracks of Melbourne twenty-four hours a day, conforming to tram speeds and regulations. This is not a passenger vehicle: it is a vehicle that has no purpose other than to track.

0.2 The vehicle consists of an architecture of electronic hardware, physically dominated by large double-sided light-emitting Screens, and a structural architecture, visually derived from iconic elements of the (sub)urban landscape. The Screens of images and text span the length of the vehicle, parallel to the tram tracks, directing their pixelated light into the enclosure of the streetscape. Sound Cones are located on each side of the vehicle, projecting sound into the spatial volume of the city.

0.3 A chance-factor-variable code programmed in the vehicle's on-board computer intelligence system determines the vehicle's Random Path of travel. Every four hours the vehicle briefly overrides its Random Path and veers into the nearest tramways depot for the Changing Of The Driver. As the departing driver steps down from the cabin, the name of the new driver is drawn from a dynamic database of available depot drivers and scans across the vehicle's text screen in green light. It flashes yellow, flashes green, flashes yellow, scans across the screen...and the new driver locks the cabin door from the inside.

0.4 The Tracking Vehicle acts as an independent repository for the cultural life of Melbourne – a living museum accumulating a dynamic Digital Memory Bank of recorded images, text and sounds generated for particular sections of streetscape. The on-board computer intelligence system processes data from a variety of sensors enabling the vehicle to undertake its travel with a reflexive awareness of its location, immediate streetscape and its own performance. The vehicle's intelligence system is programmed to bring forth particular Tracks of images, text and sounds in specific relation to the streetscape through which the vehicle travels, such that the emitted images, text and sound behave in coded relationships of synchrony with the location of the vehicle and the speed of its movement. Unlike the cinematic form of film, the change and movement of images, text and sound is not restricted to one linear sequence, but is able to traverse multiple trajectories through its repository of digital Tracks of coded correspondence to sections of streetscape. The vehicle's intelligence system selects, processes and emits these tracks through the real-time processing of Performance Codes.

0.5 As the vehicle undertakes its Random Path of travel, text scrolls along the screen in direct proportion to the vehicle's movement, as though the passing vehicle brings into being words of illusionary spatial body that are statically suspended in the street air.

0.6 Images emitted by the vehicle's Screens undergo transformations of scale, type and speed of movement relative to the vehicle's travel speed and location. The speed of moving image constantly shifts in an inverse relationship to the vehicle's travel speed. At slow travel speeds, the emitted images move quickly – when the vehicle travels quickly the images move slowly. Images freeze on Screen as the vehicle passes through an intersection of streets – one image frame carried across the perpendicular street with ritualistic appearance, establishing a collection of ephemeral vistas attached to particular viewpoints within the city. As the vehicle traverses the city, images are stretched around street corners with a visualised exaggeration of concentric force, and shifted in scale in response to the width of the adjacent street and the depth of its built facades.

0.7 The vehicle's Sound Cones distribute sound laterally into the city, punctuating adjacent architectural volumes with resonance. Acoustic traces of past inhabitancy and artful sound interventions tune architectural volumes like instruments, folding sound back into the street. Laneways abruptly echo, utterances are recalled and stories muttered at tram stops and intersections as the vehicle wraps the city with reverberating nuances blurring the distinction between individual body and collective city.

0.8 The Tracking Vehicle acquires digital Tracks of imagery, text and sound corresponding to particular streetscapes through two parallel processes of generation. On one side is a Process Track which collaboratively generates image, text and sound through a reliance upon re-constructing the significance of particular places and streetscapes through community consultation and archival research. The other Process Track enables the speculative expression of artists commissioned to produce Tracks in correspondence with particular streetscapes. The Process Tracks remain parallel, over time generating multiple Tracks for each section of streetscape from which the vehicle may select, process and emit.

0.9 The Tracking Vehicle interacts with the interior space of the city – the city as it is inhabited, remembered and inscribed. The vehicle articulates a language of space-time, a digital form of expression in dynamic interaction with the city. Its unpredictable movement and ever-changing accumulation and emission of tracks relay a montage of historical events, collective memories, narratives and fantasies as though representing the unconscious of the city's dwellers, promoting experiences of the city not readily accessed in everyday life. An encounter with the vehicle is an unpredictable moment, never grasped in totality, only remembered in its absence. The vehicle's Tracks of imagery, text and sound acquire a residual significance through their repeated emission at particular places, building a form of ephemeral social architecture – an architecture of memory and imagination.

*(First published in 1995 for the exhibition TRACKING at Linden Gallery, Melbourne)*

DEPARTING

TRACKING

NETWORKING

# SHEDDING

# The
# Calcutta Tramways Company (1978) Ltd.

( A GOVT. OF WEST BENGAL UNDERTAKING )

**File No.**________________

**Name**____________________________________

**Subject** __________________________________

**Serial Nos.**________________ **To**_______________

**From (Months)**_____________ **To**_______________

**Year**_____________**19**

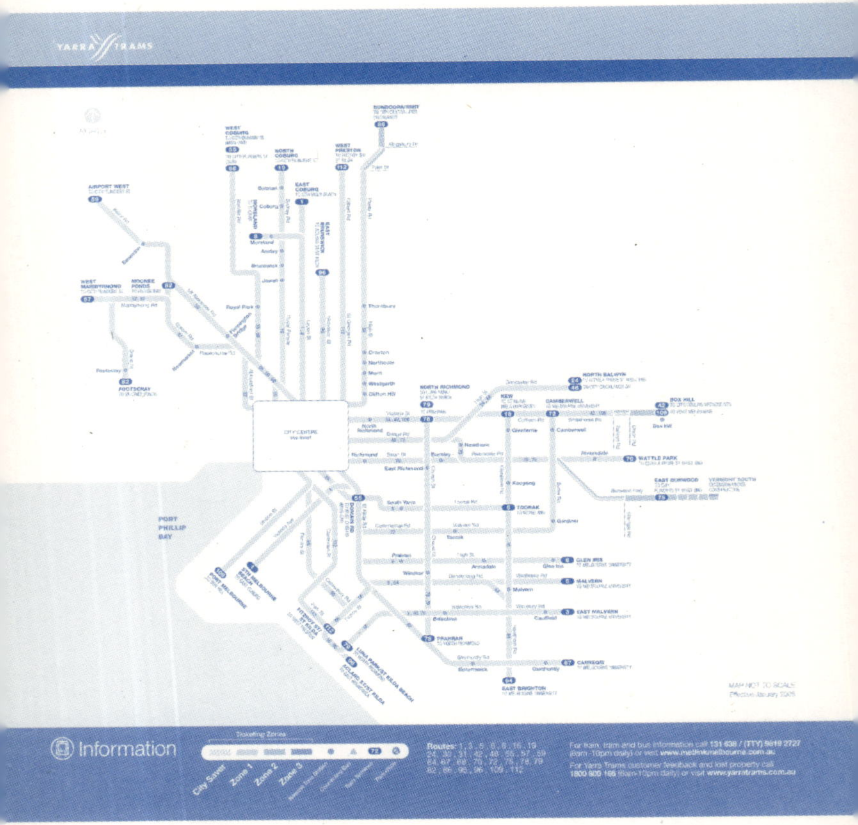
YARRA TRAMS
CITY CENTRE
PORT PHILLIP BAY
EAST BRIGHTON
MAP NOT TO SCALE
Information
Ticketing Zones
City Saver
Zone 1
Zone 2
Zone 3
For Yarra Trams customer feedback and lost property call
1800 800 166 (6am-10pm daily) or visit www.yarratrams.com.au

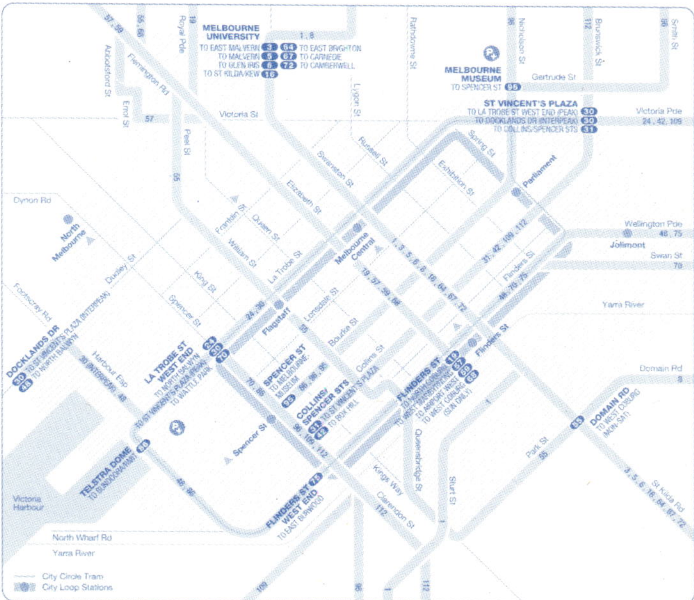
MELBOURNE UNIVERSITY
TO EAST MALVERN 3 64 TO EAST BRIGHTON
TO MALVERN 5 67 TO CARNEGIE
TO GLEN IRIS 6 72 TO CAMBERWELL
TO ST KILDA/KEW 16
MELBOURNE MUSEUM
TO SPENCER ST 95
ST VINCENT'S PLAZA
TO LA TROBE ST WEST END (PEAK) 30
TO DOCKLANDS DR (INTERPEAK) 30
TO COLLINS/SPENCER STS 31
Royal Pde
Abbotsford St
Flemington Rd
Errol St
Victoria St
Peel St
Lygon St
Rathdowne St
Nicholson St
Brunswick St
Smith St
Gertrude St
Victoria Pde
24, 42, 109
Russell St
Swanston St
Spring St
Exhibition St
Parliament
Elizabeth St
Dynon Rd
North Melbourne
Franklin St
Queen St
William St
Melbourne Central
Wellington Pde
48, 75
Jolimont
Swan St
70
Dudley St
King St
La Trobe St
Footscray Rd
Spencer St
Flagstaff
Lonsdale St
Bourke St
Flinders St
Yarra River
DOCKLANDS DR
LA TROBE ST WEST END
SPENCER ST
COLLINS/ SPENCER STS
Collins St
FLINDERS ST
Harbour Esp
Domain Rd
DOMAIN RD
Park St
TELSTRA DOME
Spencer St
Kings Way
Queensbridge St
Sturt St
St Kilda Rd
Victoria Harbour
FLINDERS ST WEST END
Clarendon St
North Wharf Rd
Yarra River
City Circle Tram
City Loop Stations

# CALCUTTA TRAMWAYS SYSTEM

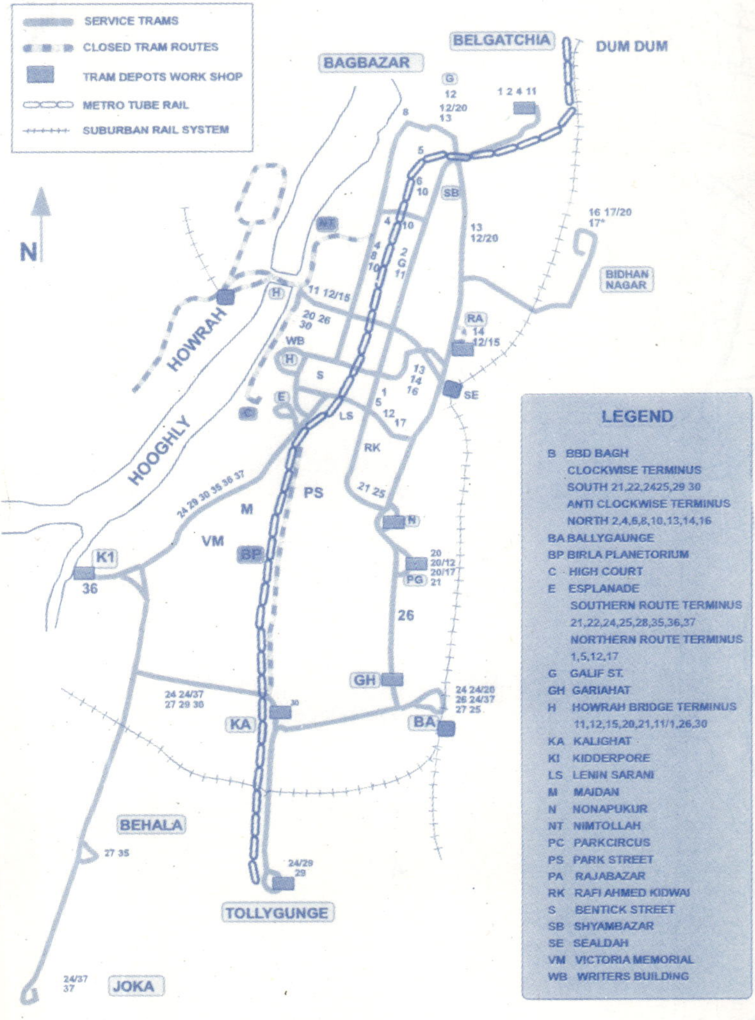

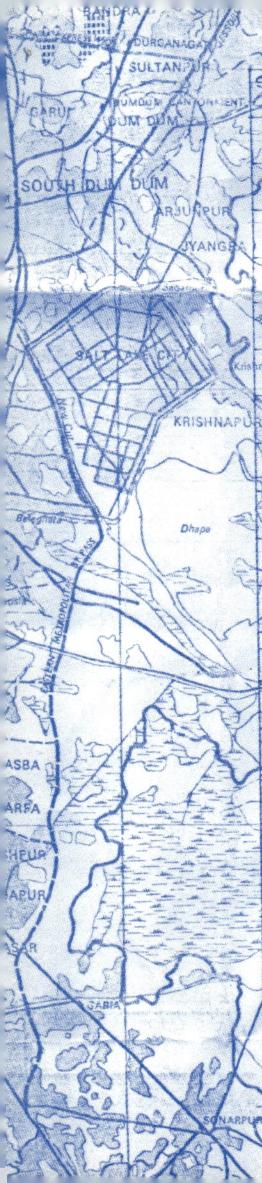


| Sl. No. | LOCATION | LATITUDE. | LONGITUDE. |
|---|---|---|---|
| 1. | BEHALA TERMINUS | 22°29′33″N | 88°19′10″E |
| 2 | TOLLYGUNGE DEPOT | 22°29′43″N | 88°20′56″E. |
| 3 | KALIGHAT DEPOT | 22°31′08″N | 88°21′00″E |
| 4 | BALLYGUNGE TERMINUS | 22°31′14″N | 88°22′24″E |
| 5 | GARIAHAT DEPOT | 22°31′24″N | 88°21′59″E |
| 6 | KHIDDERPORE DEPOT | 22°32′23″N | 88°19′31″E |
| 7 | PARK CIRCUS DEPT. | 22°32′29″N | 88°22′14″E |
| 8 | BIRLA PLANETARIUM TERMINUS | 22°32′53″N | 88°20′53″E. |
| 9 | NONAPUKUR WORKSHOP | 22°32′53″N | 88°21′56″E |
| 10 | ESPLANADE CONTROL | 22°33′44″N | 88°21′03″E. |
| 11 | HIGH COURT TERMINUS | 22°34′01″N | 88°20′42″E |
| 12 | OVERHEAD DEPOT | 22°33′57″N | 88°21′21″E |
| 13 | HEAD OFFICE | 22°34′11″N | 88°21′10″E |
| 14 | HOWRAH TERMINUS | 22°35′00″N | 88°20′42″E |
| 15 | RAJABAZAR DEPOT | 22°34′20″N | 88°21′31″E |
| 16 | ULTADANGA TERMINUS | 22°35′29″N | 88°23′46″E. |
| 17 | SHAYAMBAZAR TERMINUS | 22°35′49″N. | 88°22′25″E |
| 18 | GALIFEST. TERMINUS | 22°36′05″N | 88°22′21″E |
| 19 | BAGBAZAR TERMINUS | 22°36′11″N | 88°22′03″E. |
| 20 | BELGACHIA DEPOT | 22°36′21″N | 88°23′03″E. |
| 21 | JOKA TERMINUS | 22°26′34″N | 88°17′42″E. |

FOREIGNER

ফিরিঙ্গি

FIRINGI

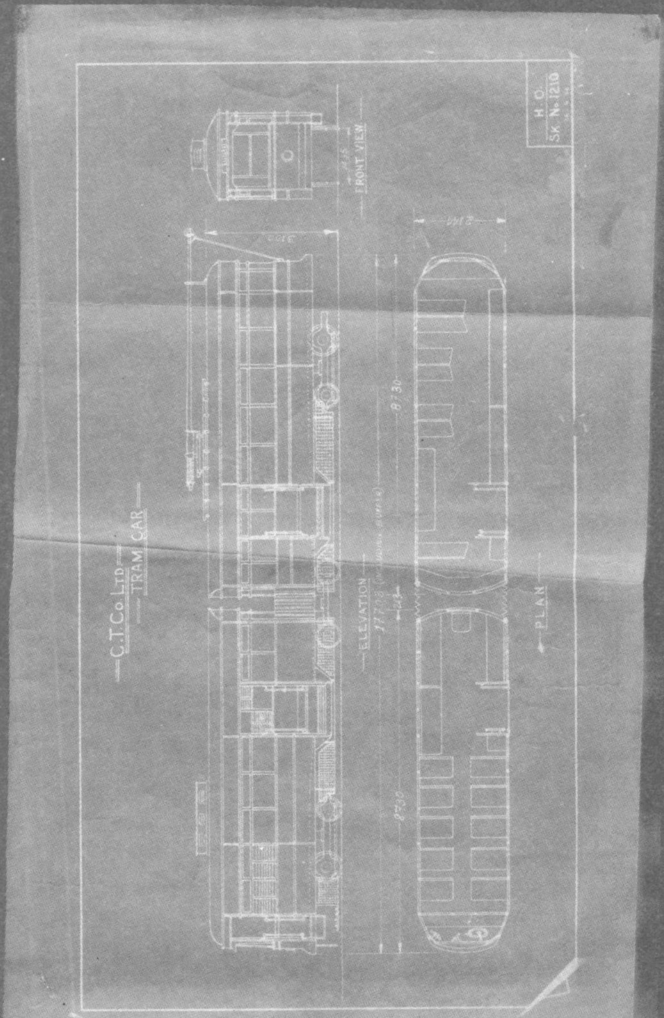
C.T.Co. LTD
TRAM CAR
ELEVATION
PLAN
FRONT VIEW
H.O.
SK. No. 1210

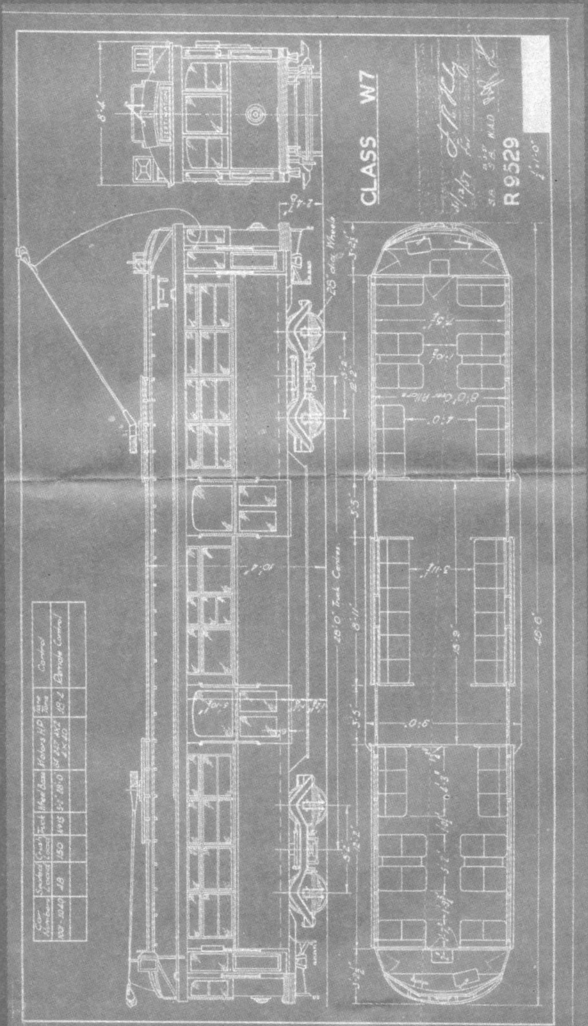
CLASS W7
R9529

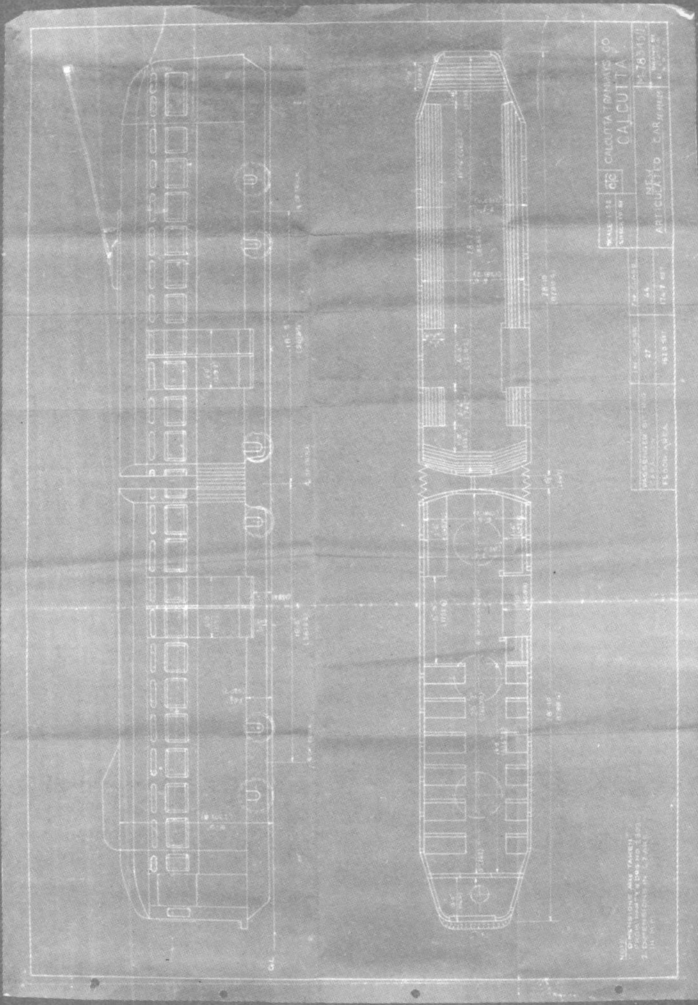
CALCUTTA TRAMWAYS CO.
CALCUTTA

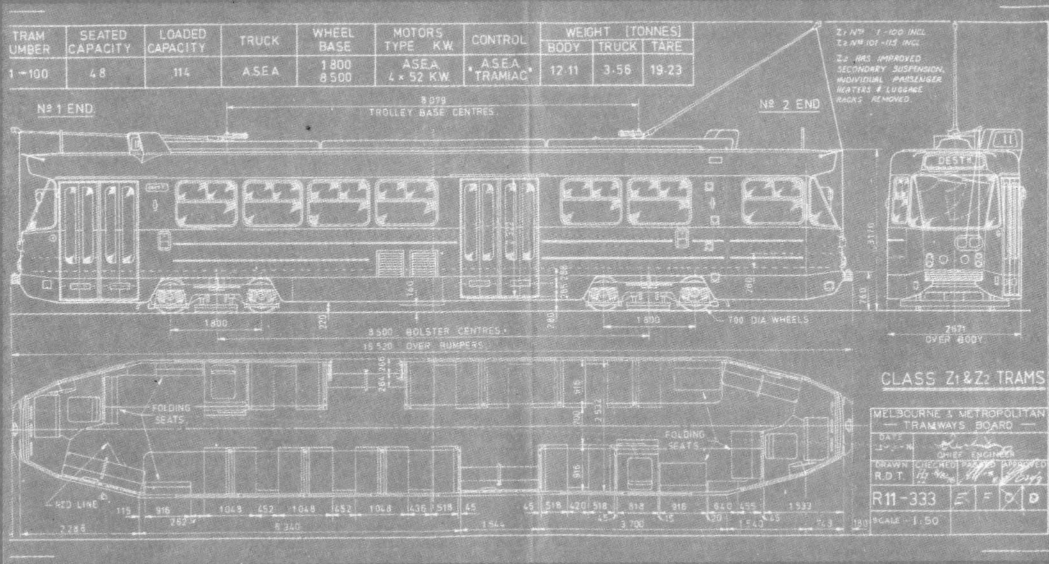
TRAM UMBER
SEATED CAPACITY
LOADED CAPACITY
TRUCK
WHEEL BASE
MOTORS TYPE K.W.
CONTROL
WEIGHT [TONNES]
BODY
TRUCK
TARE
1 – 100
48
114
ASEA
1800 8500
ASEA 4 × 52 K.W.
ASEA TRAMIAC
12·11
3·56
19·23
Z1 Nº 1 - 100 INCL
Z2 Nº 101 - 115 INCL
Z2 HAS IMPROVED SECONDARY SUSPENSION, INDIVIDUAL PASSENGER HEATERS & LUGGAGE RACKS REMOVED.
Nº 1 END.
Nº 2 END
8079 TROLLEY BASE CENTRES
DESTN
700 DIA WHEELS
8500 BOLSTER CENTRES
15 520 OVER BUMPERS
2671 OVER BODY
FOLDING SEATS
RED LINE
CLASS Z1 & Z2 TRAMS
MELBOURNE & METROPOLITAN — TRAMWAYS BOARD —
CHIEF ENGINEER
DRAWN R.D.T.
CHECKED
APPROVED
R11-333
SCALE - 1:50

# INSULATED

On some intersections where tram tracks of two roadways cross each other, the contact

trolley wires where they cross.

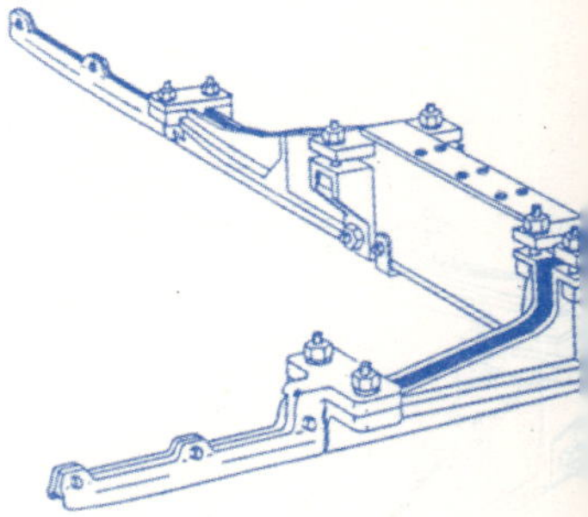

**17. CIVILITY.**

When dealing with passengers a Conductor is expected to be **civil, courteous** and **obliging.** All passenger enquiries must be answered to the best of his ability and he must always be prepared to show passengers his badge number, when called upon to do so. **Conductors must at all times avoid altercations with passengers.**

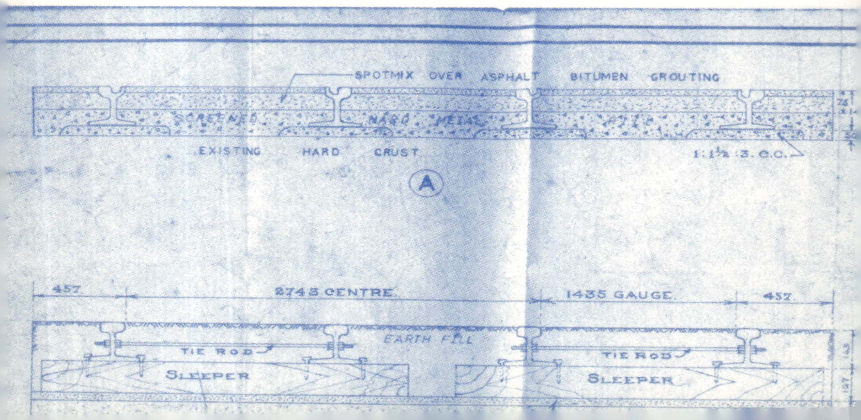

# CROSSINGS

trolley wires also cross each other. An insulated crossing is connected to the contact As shown in figure 18

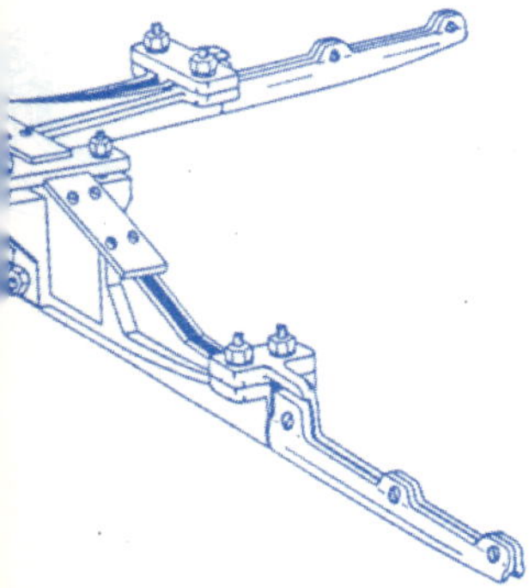

- Long socks must be worn with shorts and pulled up.
- Socks must be black or bottle green in colour to match the uniform.
- Non-uniform badges are not to be worn unless as per Rule 26.

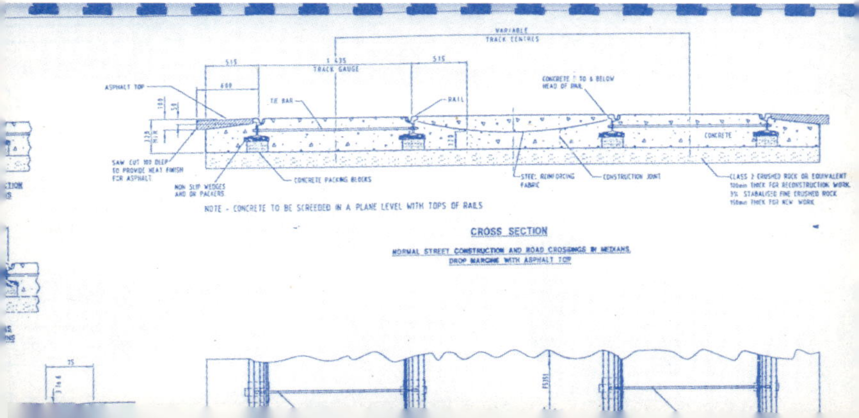

# Davies & Baird
*Founders & Engineers*

184-204 Newlands Road, Coburg
P.O. Box 343 Reservoir, Vic. 3073

Telephone: (03) 9350 4088
Facsimile: (03) 9350 2840
Email: db@db.tkl.com.au


The Calcutta Tramways Co.Ltd.
12,R.N.Mukherjee Road,
Calcutta-700 001

10/8/01

Attention: Mr. Sudhir K. De. Chairman-cum-Managing Director

Dear Mr. De.

Please find enclosed a budget price to replace the existing Wellington Junction with cast Manganese crossings switches, and mates supplied by Davies & Baird. The basis of the quote is C.T.C. drawing H.O. T-411/E/1 dated 1/4/82.

The price allows for four sets of switches and mates as well as three single crossings and two assembled crossings, which are highlighted on the drawing. The assembled crossings would be cast in seven pieces and four pieces respectively and then welded together to match the requirements of the drawing. Connecting rail between crossings and switches is not included in the quoted price.

Also enclosed are sketches of a switch and mate that are indicative of the type and design we would be supplying. A cross section of the crossings is also included once again as an indication. If by chance you have engineering drawings of any or all of the pieces we are quoting on, I would be more than happy to tailor the quote to match them.

1 Off Highlighted items on drawing H.O. T-411/E/1 @ A$ [redacted] total.

The finer points of the above price can be discussed on your upcoming visit to Melbourne. I am sure that your technical people will have their own requirements and ideas, which they may want incorporated into the design. These are things to be talked about in person when you arrive.

Yours faithfully.

M. McGufficke
Sales Manager

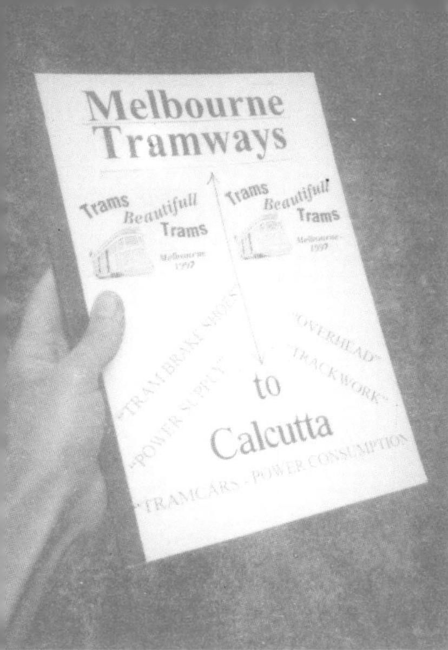
Melbourne
Tramways
Trams
Beautifull
Trams
Melbourne
1997
Trams
Beautifull
Trams
Melbourne
1997
"TRAM BRAKE SHOES"
"POWER SUPPLY"
"OVERHEAD"
"TRACKWORK"
to
Calcutta
"TRAMCARS - POWER CONSUMPTION"

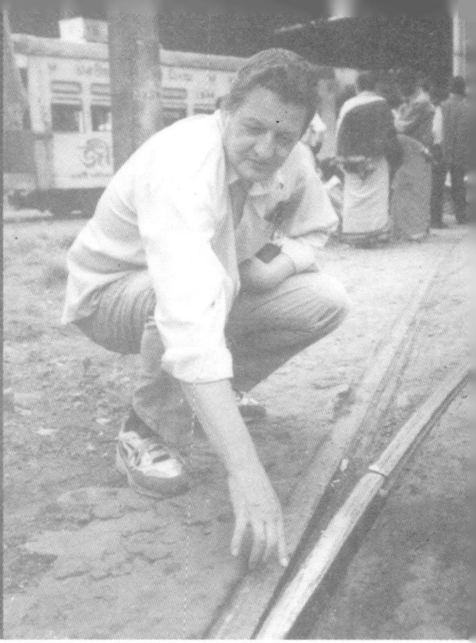

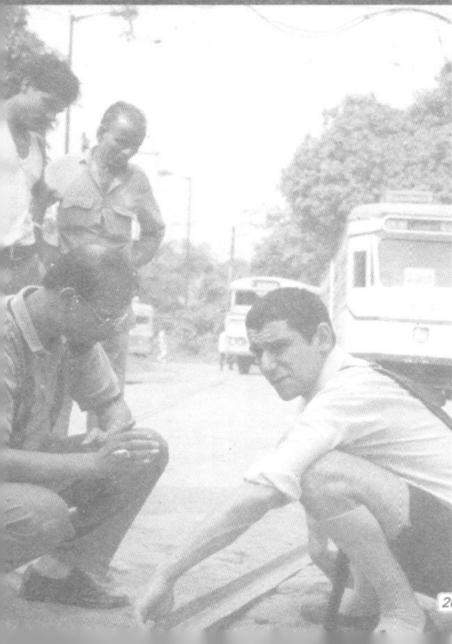

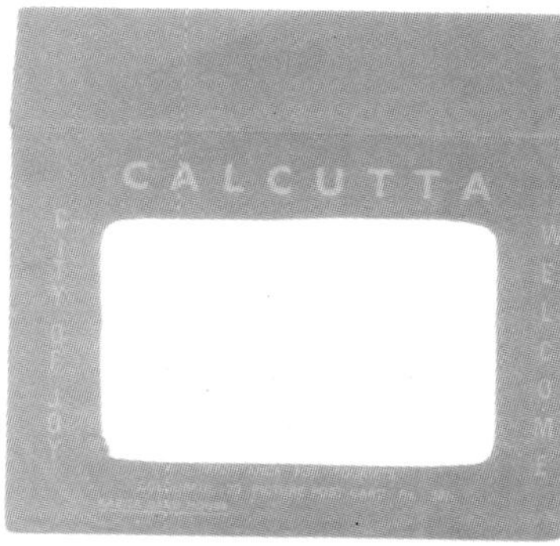
CALCUTTA
WELCOME

## Is the tram half empty or half full

Everyone gets up the same time
        they usually get up
have the same things for breakfast
        they usually have
take the same route to work
        they usually take
worry over the same set of problems
        they always worry over
        such as:
Is my tram off the road again

trams — the necessary element
of unpredictability
in everybody's life.

## ট্রামটি কি অর্ধ-শুন্য না অর্ধ-পূর্ণ ?

একই সময়ে ট্রামে ওঠে ওরা
        একই সময়ে-
একই প্রাতঃরাশে দিন শুরু করে ওরা
        একই প্রাতঃরাশে।
একই পথে কাজে যায় ওরা
        একই পথে।
একই চিন্তায় মন ভারাক্রান্ত ওদের
        একই চিন্তায়
        যেমন-
' ট্রাম আজ চল্‌ছে ত ?'

ট্রামযাত্রাই কি ওদের একঘেয়ে জীবনে
একমাত্র আবশ্যিক ব্যতিক্রম ?

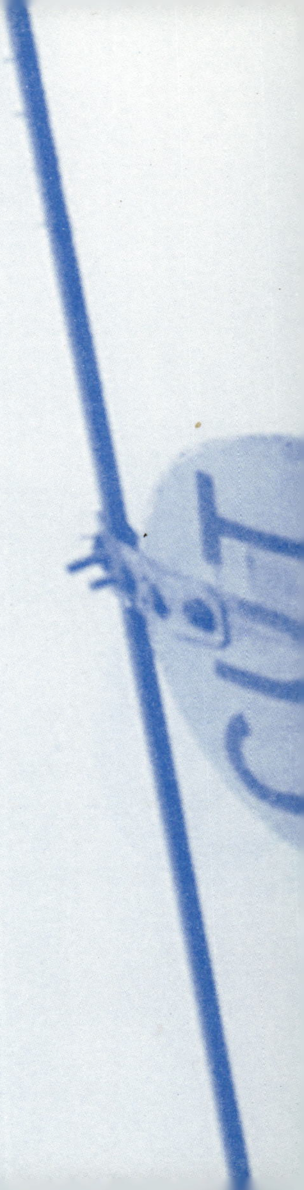

*poem by Malcolm Just*
*drawing with text by Mark Misic and Keith Butler*

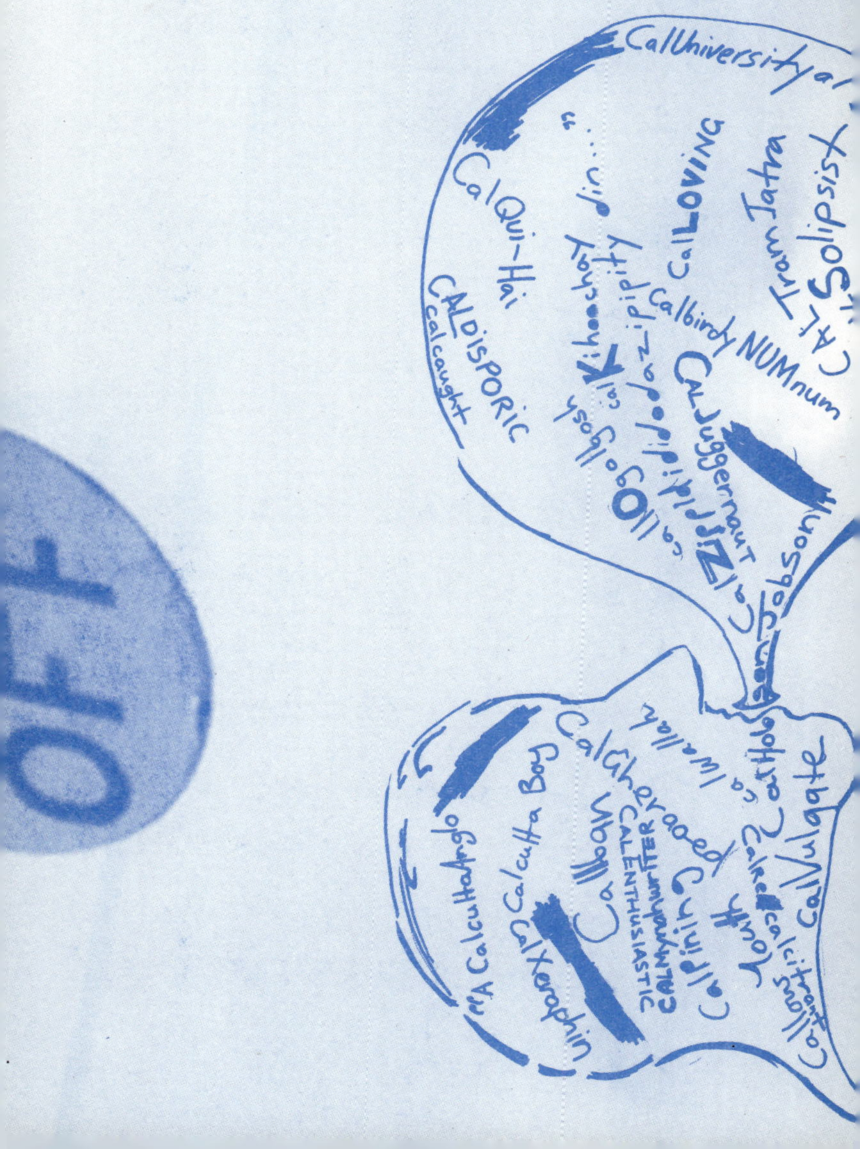

CalUniversity
CAL Solipsist
CAL Tram Jatra
NUMnum
Calbirdy
Cal LOVING
" ... din ... "
Cal Kihoochoy
CalQui-Hai
CALDISPORIC
calcaught
Calloogolloosh
Cal Zippididi-doodazipidity
CALJuggernaut
CalJobson
CalVulgate
Callous Calcitrant
Calre Calcitrant
Youth
Cal Wallah
Cal Pining
CALMynahwriter
CALENTHUSIASTIC
Calloon
CalCheraaed
Calcutta Boy
CalXeraphin
MA CalcuttaAnglo
OFF

**Some of the frames we installed inside the Kolkata tramjatra tram rattled loose from their fixings. A number of frames went missing. A week later I saw one of the frames on the wall inside the workers building at the CTC Esplanade tram terminus. The tramjatra content had been replaced by a photo portrait of Joti Basu, the former CPI(M) Chief Minister of West Bengal. And these workers dared me to remove the frame from there.**

*Jogi Panghaal, tramjatra critical passenger*

**Whoever does not get moving learns nothing,**
**Yes, depart, divide yourself into parts.**

*Michel Serres,* The Troubadour of Knowledge, *Ann Arbor: The University of Michigan Press, 1997, 7.*

**If the epistemological tends toward a 'representation' of its referent, prior to performativity, the enunciative attempts repeatedly to 'reinscribe' and relocate that claim to cultural and anthropological priority (High / Low; Ours / Theirs) in the act of revising and hybridising the settled, sententious hierarchies, the locale and locutions of the cultural. If the former is always locked into the hermeneutic circle, in the description of cultural elements as they tend towards a totality, the latter is a more dialogic process that attempts to track the processes of displacement and re-alignment that are already at work, constructing something different and hybrid from the encounter: a third space that does not simply revise or revert the dualities, but re-values the ideological bases of division and difference.**

*Homi K. Bhabha, 'Postcolonial authority and postmodern guilt', in L. Grossberg et al (ed's),* Cultural Studies, *New York: Routledge, 1992, 57.*

**...art is never an end in itself...It is only an instrument for tracing lines of life...What it lays out are paths - it is itself a voyage.**

*Gilles Deleuze, 'What children say', in* Essays Critical and Clinical, *translated by D.W. Smith and M.A. Greco, Minneapolis: University of Minnesota Press, 1997, 63, quoted in 'Passage' by Suzie Attiwill in this volume.*

No. 901

**BILL**

Date.............

# GARIAHAT ART FRAMING

**212, GARIAHAT MARKET COMPLEX**

**CALCUTTA-700 019**

**Room No. 167 ✪ BASEMENT ✪ BLOCK A & B**

Proprietor : GOPAL & DULAL

Name: Jogi for Tramjatra

Address: Gariahat Tram Depot, Ballygunj Phari

| Qnty. | PARTICULARS | Rate | Rs. | P. |
|---|---|---|---|---|
| | 24x242 25. P. 80= | | 2000 | |
| | 24x72 14 P. 160 | | 2240 | |
| | | | 4240 | |
| | [illegible] | | | |
| | | TOTAL | 4240 | 00 |
| | | Advance | 2000 | 00 |
| | *Thanking you !* | Balance | 2240 | 00 |

Date of Delivery: 20/2/2009

Signature

Time of Delivery : 5 P. M. to 8 P. M.

N. B.—We are not responsible for any Picture if delivery is not taken within 15 days from the Delivery Date.

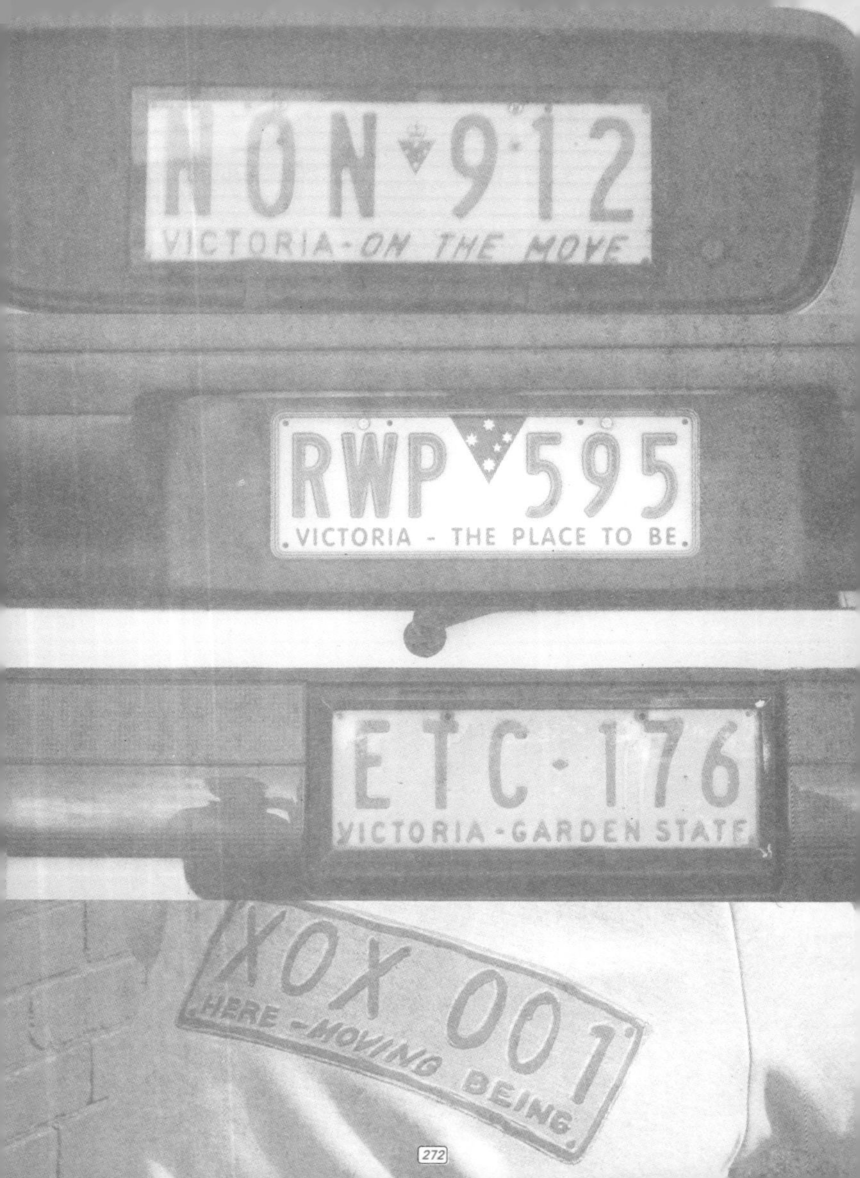
NON 912
VICTORIA - ON THE MOVE
RWP 595
VICTORIA - THE PLACE TO BE.
ETC 176
VICTORIA - GARDEN STATE
XOX 001
HERE - MOVING BEING

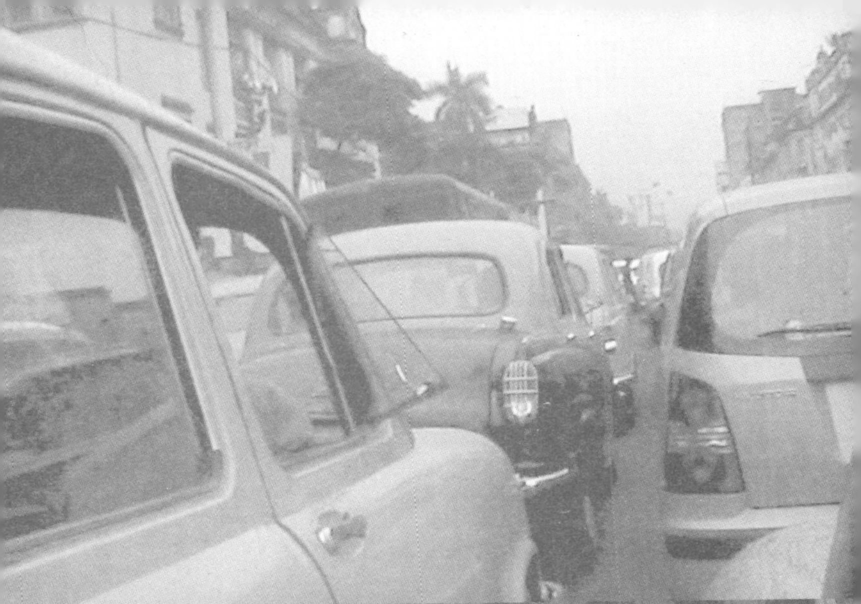

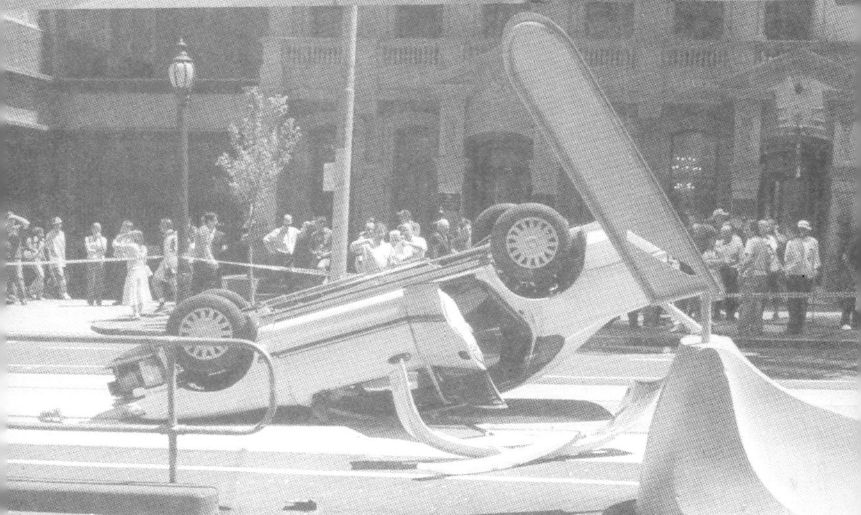

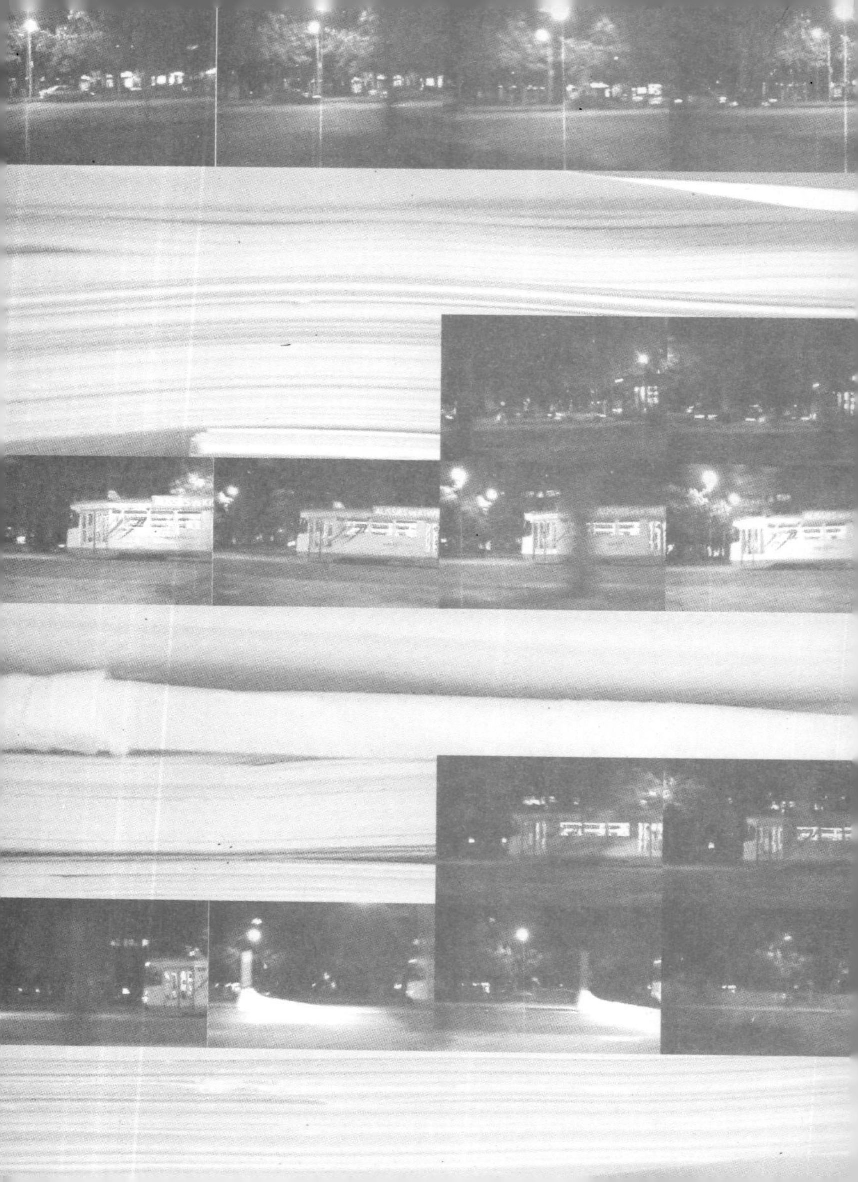

## image index

**Credit abbreviations**
**MD**: Mick Douglas, **SM**: Sanjay Mitra,
**RD**: Roberto D'Andrea, **JP**: Jogi Panghaal.

Front cover: untitled photo, JP 2001.

Inside cover image: detail views, *journey*, painting installation, Jayashree Chakravarty 2001.

Back cover and throughout: untitled painting (*tramjatra* lungs), MD, 2002.

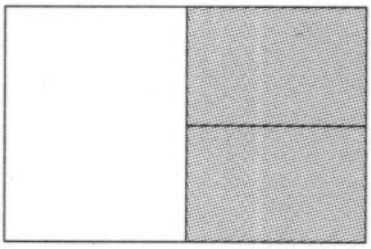

pp12-13: Top to bottom – (i) detail of *Melcutta*, tram installation, MD, Melbourne 1997; (ii) detail of *Calbourne*, tram installation, MD, Kolkata 1997. Photos MD.

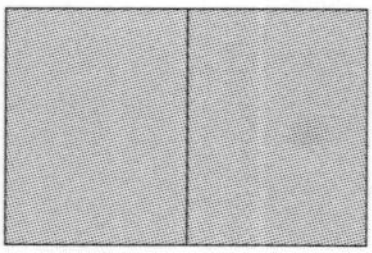

pp14-15: Left to right – (i) letter, Debasish Bhattacharyya, 1994; (ii) letter, MD and RD, 1996.

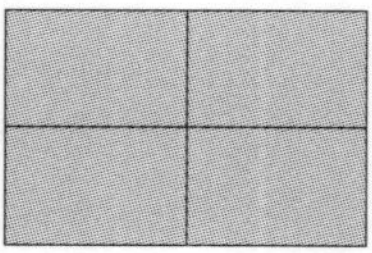

pp16-17: Clockwise from top left – (i) *Calbourne*, tram installation, MD, Kolkata 1997, photo MD; (ii) *adjusted prow*, drawing, MD, 2001; (iii) drawing of precast concrete prow for tram stop safety zones, dated 1976, © Victorian Government Department of Infrastructure and VicTrack; (iv) Calcutta Tramways Company Nonapakur paint shop workers, photo © David Whittle.

pp18-19: All – *tramjatra Kolkata tram*, Suzie Attiwill and Jogi Panghaal, 2001. Photos MD.

pp30-31: Left page clockwise from top left - (i) Debasish Bhattacharyya, photo RD; (ii) detail view *Melcutta*, tram installation, MD, Melbourne 1997, photo MD; (iii) photo Mark Misic; (iv) Mahadeb Shi, photo SM; (v) Prabir Kumar Goswami & Sanjay Mitra (ends) with Melbourne tramways workers, photo RD; (vi) passengers of *tramjatra Kolkata 2001*, photo RD; (vi) Rabindra Sarani tram stop, photo MD; (vii) CTC driver, photo MD; (viii) Melbourne City Ambassadors & RD, photo SM; (ix) Jayanta Basu, photo MD. Right page clockwise from top left - (i) detail view *Calbourne*, photo RD; (ii) MD, photo RD; (iii) detail interior view, *tramjatra Kolkata tram* 2001, photo JP; (iv) photo SM; (v) *tramjatra Melbourne 2001* participants, photo SM; (vi) photo RD; (vii) *the passenger* broadsheet on City Circle tram, *tramjatra Melbourne 2001*, photo MD; (viii) RD, Kolkata 1996, photo anon; (ix) detail view Citadis tram, Melbourne, photo MD; (x) detail interior view *Calbourne*, tram installation, MD, Calcutta 1997, from video MD; (xi) *cricket tram* and CTC staff Ujjal Dhar, *tramjatra Kolkata 2001*, photo RD.

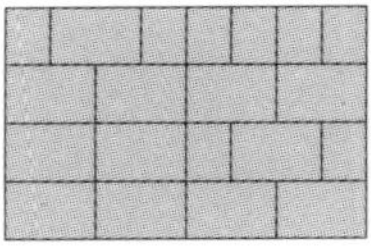

pp33-43: *tramjatra* curatorial tickets, MD, 2000.

pp44-45: Top to bottom – (i) detail of *Melcutta*, tram installation, MD, Melbourne 1997; (ii) detail of a Kolkata tram. Photos MD.

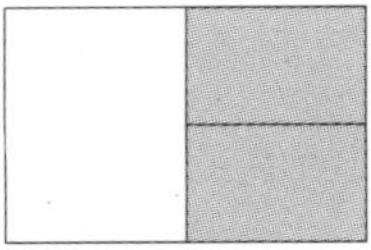

pp46-47: *9.27am Tuesday 19 October 2004*, photo collage, MD, 2005. Left to right – (i) Kolkata tram track, Esplanade tram terminus; (ii) Melbourne tram track, Nicholson Street. Photos MD.

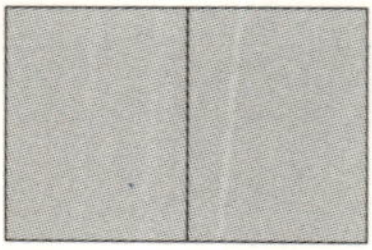

pp48-49: Left to right – (i) Prabir Kumar Goswami, from photo SM; (ii) Roberto D'Andrea, from photo SM.

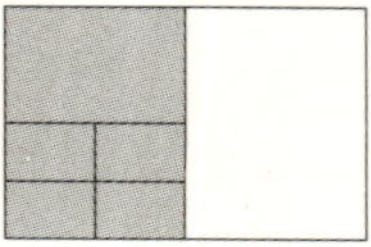

pp58-59: Clockwise from top left – (i, iii, v) RD and Prabir Kumar Goswami conducting *tramjatra Melbourne 2001*, photos SM; (ii) Melbourne tram conductor's leather bag, detail from RD in Kolkata 1997, photo MD; (iv) Kolkata tram conductor's leather bag, photo MD.

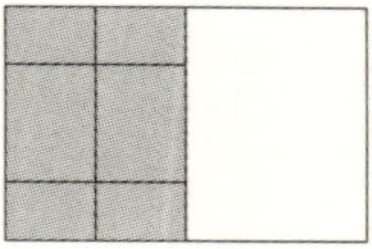

pp60-61: Clockwise from top left – (i-iv) Roberto D'Andrea and Prabir Kumar Goswami conducting *tramjatra Melbourne 2001*, photos SM; (v) RD, Kolkata 1996, photo anon.; (vi) Kolkata tram conductor, photo MD.

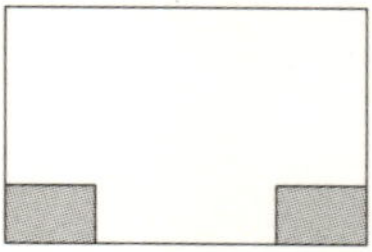

pp62-63: Left to right – *South Melbourne tram depot/Belgatchia tram depot friendship banner*, RD, MD, Andy Miller and South Melbourne trammies, (i) pictured with Belgatchia tramways workers 1996; (ii) pictured with South Melbourne tramways workers 1996. Photos anon.

pp64-65: English-made driver's controller in a Kolkata tram, as was used in Melbourne's W-class trams, photo MD.

pp68-71: Window views of *Calbourne*, tram installation, MD, Kolkata 1997, photos MD.

pp76-77: (i) *tramjatra Melbourne event ticket*, design Neal Haslem, 4000 distributed in Melbourne, November 2001; (ii) *tramjatra Kolkata event ticket*, design Lisa Young and Ranajay Gupta, 4000 distributed in Kolkata, February–March 2001.

pp78-79: Clockwise from top left spiralling inwards – (i-iii, x-xv) Roberto D'Andrea and Prabir Kumar Goswami conducting *tramjatra Melbourne 2001*, photos SM; (iv-ix) *tramjatra Kolkata* launch, Esplanade tram terminus, 21 February 2001, photos Mahadeb Shi.

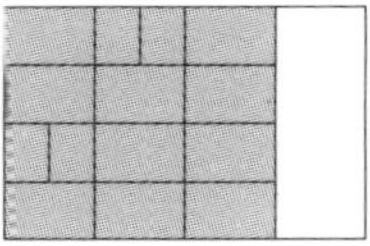

pp80-81: Left page – installation views of *tramjatra Melbourne exhibition: re-collecting imaginings by tramways*, RMIT First Site Gallery, 2001, photos SM. Right page – detail view *tramjatra Kolkata tram*, Suzie Attiwill and Jogi Panghaal, 2001, photo JP.

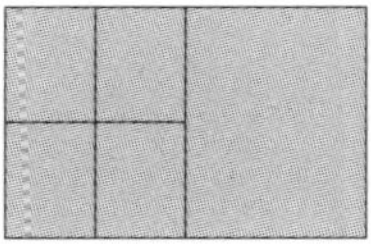

pp82-83: All – *diamond cutter*, Mark Misic and Kolkata tramways workers, *tramjatra Kolkata 2001*, photos Mark Misic.

pp84-85: Left page clockwise from top left – (i-vi) Calcutta Tramways Company workers, photos i, iii, iv, vi MD; photos ii, iv RD; (vi) Lisa Young installing *trambaby* posters, *tramjatra Kolkata 2001*, photo Mark Misic. Right page – *smart array*, Mark Misic, *tramjatra Melbourne 2001*, photos Mark Misic.

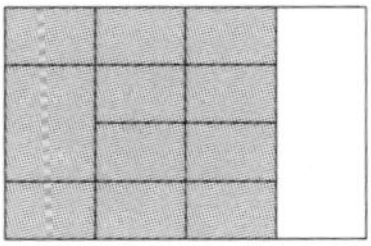

pp86-87: Clockwise from top left – (i, iv) *curious yellow*, Lisa Young, photos Paul Molyneux; (ii) *tramjatra Kolkata 2001*, Esplanade installation view, photo JP; (iii, v) *trambaby*, distributed card and poster, Lisa Young, *tramjatra Kolkata 2001*; (vi) passengers reading *The Passenger, tramjatra Melbourne 2001*, photo RD.

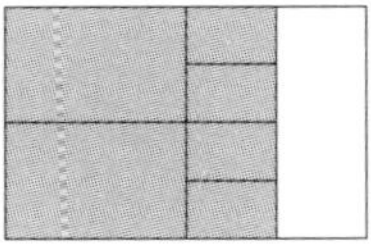

pp88-89: Left page, all – *pat*, Dukhushyam Chitrakar, *tramjatra Melbourne 2001*, photos SM. Right page – *tramjatra Kolkata 2001* (i) Dukhushyam performing, photo MD; (ii, iii) *jorano pat*, installation views of enlarged scroll painting, Dukhushyam Chitrakar, photos JP.

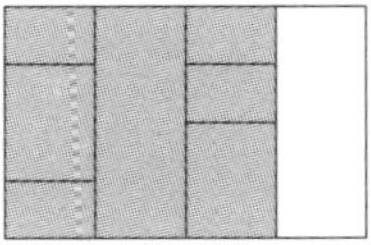

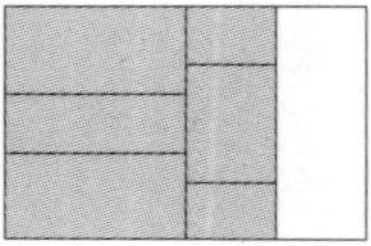

pp90-91: Left page top to bottom – (i) *tramjatra Kolkata 2001*, Esplanade installation view, photo JP; (ii) *ticket*, Jayashree Chakravarty, 2001; (iii) *maps*, installation view, Jayashree Chakravarty, *tramjatra Kolkata 2001*, photo JP. Right page top to bottom – (i) *journey*, installation view, Jayashree Chakravarty, *tramjatra Melbourne 2001*, photo Paul Molyneux; (ii) detail from *journey*, above; (iii) Jayashree painting at Esplanade, *tramjatra Kolkata 2001*, photo Suzie Attiwill.

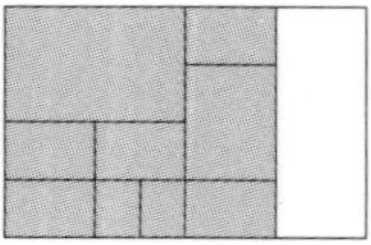

pp92-93: Left page clockwise from top left, all – *tramjatra Kolkata 2001*, photos RD – (i) Andy Miller with CTC workers; (ii) *'tram yatra' tram* initiated by Minister Chakrabarty and launched by Usha Uthup; (iii) *fruit fresh/healthy cities* tram, Andy Miller and CTC workers; (iv) dress-up connies on *tramjatra* poets journey; (v) Abbotsford Anglers Cricket Club vs CTC cricket match; (vi) *cricket tram*, Andy Miller and CTC workers. Right page, all – *together*, Sanjay Mitra encounters with people, *tramjatra Melbourne 2001*, photos RD.

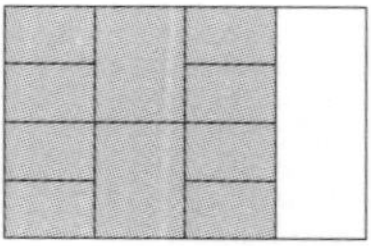

pp94-95: Left page clockwise from top left, all photos James Legge – (i) *Vault*, Ron Robertson-Swann's public sculpture in Melbourne; (ii-vi) *re: vault*, installation of a tram prow in the original city square location of *Vault*, James Legge, *tramjatra Melbourne 2001*. Inset – from *The Age* newspaper, Melbourne, 8 November 2001, © the author. Right page top to bottom – (i, iii, iv) *Melbourne's Vault*, installation view, James Legge with pandal makers, *tramjatra Kolkata 2001*, photos JP; (ii) pandal maker Goutam Dey with James Legge's model of *Vault*, photo James Legge.

pp96-97: Left page clockwise from top left, all photos JP and MD – (i-v) *lanterns and socks*, installation views, Amanda King, *tramjatra Kolkata 2001*; (vi) Greenwaves school children paintings developed with Amanda King, installed on *tramjatra Kolkata tram*, 2001. Right page, all – *moving message*, Amanda King, *tramjatra Melbourne 2001*, photos SM and RD.

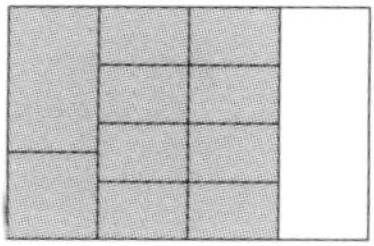

pp98-99: Left page – projection interaction with *Kather Baxo*, film by Mahadeb Shi, *tramjatra Melbourne 2001*. Right page – Mahadeb Shi and assistant filming, *tramjatra Kolkata 2001*. Photos Mark Misic.

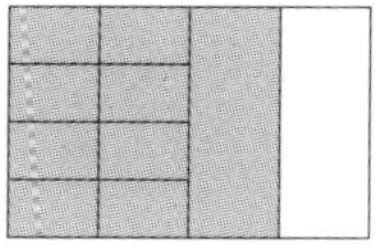

pp100-101: Left page clockwise from top left – (i) *jorano pat*, installation view of enlarged scroll painting, Sarna Chitrakar, *tramjatra Kolkata 2001*, photo JP; (ii) 'Rock-Bunny' performing pat song, *tramjatra Kolkata 2001*, photo MD; (iii) Moyna Chitrakar performing, *tramjatra Melbourne 2001*, photo MD. Right page – *pat*, panel views, Moyna Chitrakar, *tramjatra Melbourne 2001*, photo Neal Haslem.

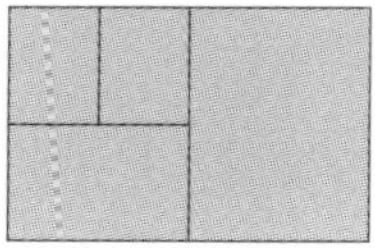

pp102-103: *tramjatra Melbourne 2001*. Left page – Prabir Kumar Goswami at *together*, tram prow performance, Sanjay Mitra. Right page – Prabir Kumar Goswami conducting (with twin trammie RD). Photos SM.

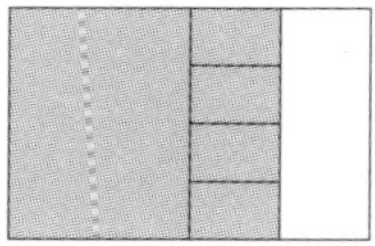

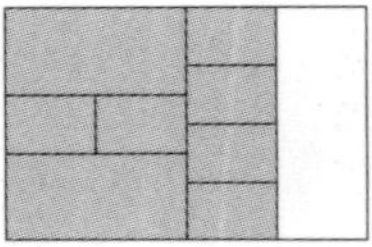

pp104-105: *tramjatra Melbourne 2001*. Left page clockwise from top left – (i, ii) *double prow*, intervention installation, Mick Douglas, photos MD except (ii) photo James Legge. Right page top to bottom – (i-ii) *prow*, intervention installation, Mick Douglas, photos MD; (iii-iv) *double prow*, intervention installation, photo iii MD; photo iv SM.

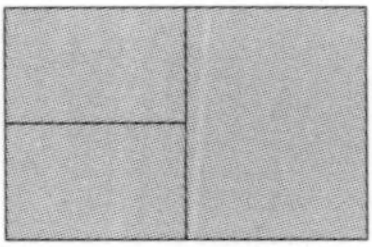

pp106-107: Left page – *Calbourne text installation*, MD (with signwriter Pobitar Gron Mona), Calcutta tram interior, 1997. Right page – *tramtactic shirt*, from *tramtactic collection*, MD, 2001.

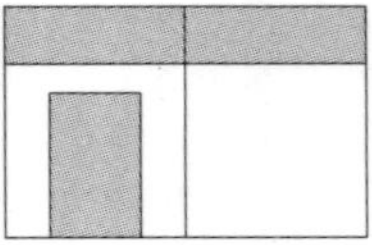

pp108-121: Sarna Chitrakar performing, photo MD. Tramjatra book *pat* (scroll) by Sarna Chitrakar, 2002. Pat *song* (text) by Sarna Chitrakar and Monoranjan Chitrakar, 2002. English translation of song by S.R. Rajen.

pp122-139: Untitled photos by Jogi Panghaal taken during *tramjatra Kolkata* and *Melbourne, 2001*. Arrangement MD.

p140: *lines of a poem*, Kolkata overhead tram wiring, photo © Anirbar Basu.

p145: *tramjatra Kolkata tram*, interior detail view, Suzie Attiwill and Jogi Panghaal, photo Suzie Attiwill.

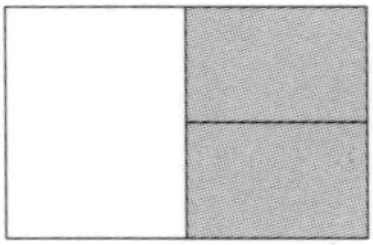

p153: Top to bottom – (i) Kolkata tram pole detail, photo MD; (ii) tramway overhead wiring drawing, MD, 2000.

pp154-155: (i) *tramjatra column* by Suzie Attiwill, appeared in *The Statesman* newspaper, Kolkata, over six weeks during tramjatra Kolkata 2001, photo MD; (ii) *The Passenger*, three editions of weekly broadsheet during *tramjatra Melbourne 2001*, edited by Suzie Attiwill and Jogi Panghaal, designed by Neal Haslem, photo MD.

pp158-159: (i) email correspondence from Ranajay Gupta, text content © *The Telegraph* Newspaper/ABP Pvt Ltd; (ii) personal correspondence to MD, © the author (name withheld).

p182: Kolkata tram, photo MD.

p184: Kolkata streets flooding, photos MD.

p187: Kolkata, photos MD.

p188: La Trobe Street tram stop, Melbourne, photo MD.

p192: *tramtactic bag*, from *tramtactic collection*, MD, photo Neal Haslem.

p202: *Calbourne*, tram installation side view, MD, Kolkata 1997, photo MD.

p204: Melbourne and Kolkata, photos MD.

p207: Video stills featuring *Calbourne*, tram installation, taken from *Tracking Between Melbourne and Calcutta*, 10 minute video, Mick Douglas, 1998.

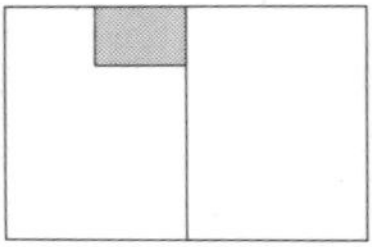

pp208-213: In approximate order of appearance - (i) Citadis tram, new to Melbourne since 2002, manufactured by Alstom, France, photo MD; (ii) Calcutta Tramways Company tram tickets, © CTC; (iii) *tramjatra* project tickets MD RD, artwork for ticket at top p212 by Hiron Mitra.

p215 (i) untitled drawing by MD; (ii) RD, photo SM.

p216: Cast track crossings, Melbourne, photo MD.

p219: Painting canvas on *tramjatra Kolkata tram*, 2001, photos JP.

p222: *diamond cutter*, Mark Misic performance installation, *tramjatra Kolkata 2001*, from video stills by Mahadeb Shi.

p227: *tramjatra Kolkata 2001* participants, photos MD.

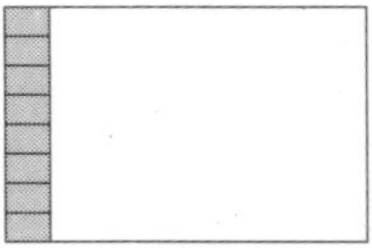

p230: Top to bottom – working with Naya village patuas, featuring (ii) S.R. Rajen, Sarna Chitrakar and family; (iii) Moyna Chitrakar; (vi, viii) Lena and Rachel Douglas, Aparna Das and MS. All photos MD except vii JP.

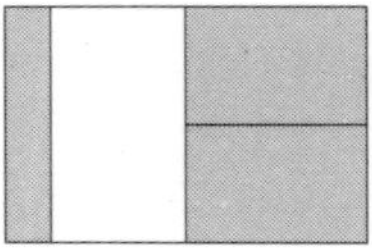

pp232-234: (i) Journal drawings by Andrea Mina from *tramjatra Kolkata 2001*; (ii) *tramjatra Kolkata tram*, photo JP.

pp234-235: Analysis and visual mapping of a tram route passage, top to bottom: (i), Chris Moore; (ii, vi) *Rory Fitzwilliams Hyde; (iii, viii) *Annette Warner; (iv) Andrea Mina; (v) *Lisa de Jong; (vii) Yuen Ping Tai. *Responses to 'volumes of direction' exercise by Suzie Attiwill.

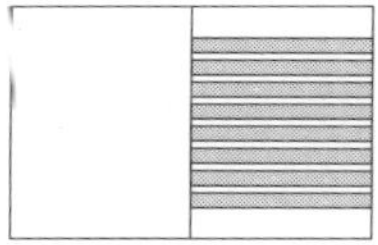

pp235-243: Works produced by undergraduate architecture and design students during the *tramjatra* Design Studio subject at RMIT University in 2001, led by Mick Douglas, Suzie Attiwill, Andrea Mina, Sand Helsel, Rene van der Velde and James Legge.

pp236-237: Text and images © Julian Canterbury.

pp238-239: Text and images © Rory Fitzwilliams Hyde.

pp240-241: Text MD. Images clockwise from top left – (i) Sophie Zelder; (ii, vi) Lisa de Jong; (iii) Yuen Ping Tai; (iv, v) Annette Warner.

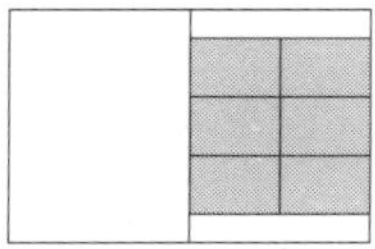

pp242-243: Text and images © Geoff Binder.

pp244-245: Text and photos MD.

pp246-247: Text/image, MD.

pp248-249: 'Rock-Bunny', photo Suzie Attiwill.

pp250-251: Video still from *tracking*, two-screen video installation, MD and Lawrence Wallen, 1995.

p253: Cardboard document file cover
© Calcutta Tramways Co. Ltd.

pp254-255: Melbourne Tram Network map
© Metlink Victoria Pty Ltd.

p256-257: Calcutta Tramways System maps
© Calcutta Tramways Co. Ltd.

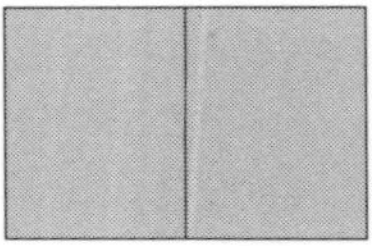

pp260-261: Left page – Calcutta tram, drawn 1956 © Calcutta Tramways Co. Ltd. Right page – Melbourne W class tram, drawn 1957 © Government of Victoria Department of Infrastructure and VicTrack.

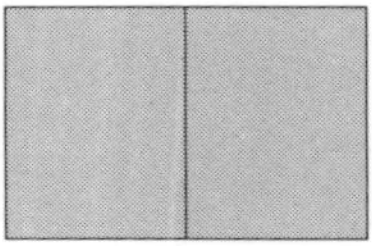

pp262-263: Left page – Calcutta tram, drawn 1978 © Calcutta Tramways Co. Ltd. Right page – Melbourne Z class tram, drawn 1976 © Government of Victoria Department of Infrastructure and VicTrack.

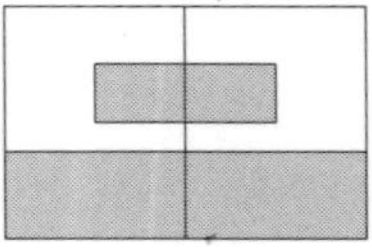

pp264-265: (i) #Detail view of 'Insulated crossings', Melbourne insulated trolley wire crossing drawing from 'tramway overhead appreciation' booklet, dated 16-02-95. (ii) Detail views of tram track laying drawings, left page – from Calcutta 'Typical Cross Section', marked T78139, undated, © Calcutta Tramways Co. Ltd.; and right page – from #'Track design concrete to surface grooved rail', drawing no. P.1401-A of the PTC Engineering Services Group, dated 12-12-1994. # © Government of Victoria Department of Infrastructure and VicTrack.

pp266-267: Left page – letter © Mike McGufficke of Flowserve, formerly Davies and Baird. Right page, clockwise from top left – (i) tramways technical booklet complied by Roberto D'Andrea 2000-2001, photo MD; (ii) Mike McGufficke, Kolkata 2001, photo RD; (iii) Calcutta postcard envelope; (iv) Roberto D'Andrea and CTC staff, Kolkata, photo anon.

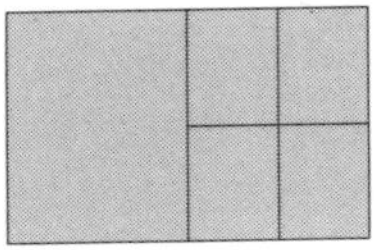

pp268-269: Left to right – (i) Melbourne overhead tramway wiring sign to tram drivers, photo MD; (ii) untitled drawing, Mark Misic, with text by Keith Butler, 2001.

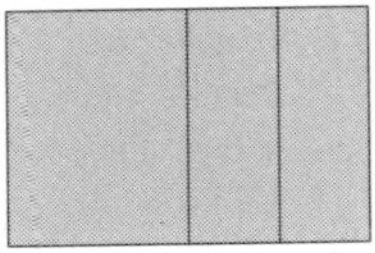

p271: transaction receipt from Gariahat Art Framing, 2001.

pp272-273: Left page top to bottom – (i, ii, iii) Victorian car number plate slogans, from (i) Liberal and (ii, iii) Labor governments; (iv) *moving being*, painted t-shirt, Mick Douglas, 2004. Photos MD. Right page – (i) Kolkata street scene, photo MD; (ii) Melbourne street scene after a car ran into a tram prow safety barrier, Collins Street, from photo anon, modified by Neal Haslem, 2005.

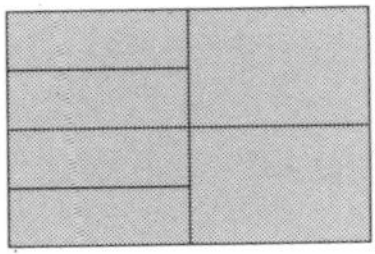

pp274-275: Untitled digital image, © Neal Haslem.

pp294-295: Left page – untitled collage image, Julian Canterbury, 2001. Right page – untitled *tramjatra* project t-shirts, from *tramtactic collection*, Mick Douglas, on an Australian 'Hills Hoist' washing line, photo MD, 2004.

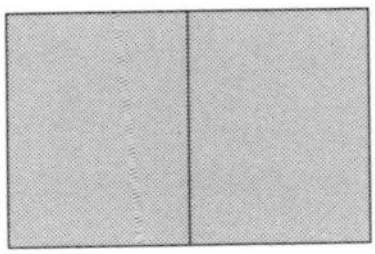

# contributors

**Suzie Attiwill** is a senior lecturer in Interior Design, School of Architecture and Design, at RMIT in Melbourne. Her independent practice involves the design of exhibitions, curatorial work, writing and working on a range of inter-disciplinary projects.

**Jayanta Basu** is a journalist on environmental issues and a zoologist based in Kolkata.

**Debasish Bhattacharyya** is a scientist at the Indian Institute of Chemical Biology in Kolkata and an environmental activist who has been campaigning for the improvement of Kolkata tramways.

**Dipesh Chakrabarty** is the Lawrence A. Kimpton Distinguished Service Professor in History, South Asian Languages and Civilizations at the University of Chicago.

**Jayashree Chakravarty** is a visual artist based in Kolkata.

**Gayatri Chakravorty Spivak** is Avalon Foundation Professor in the Humanities and Director of the Center for Comparative Literature and Society at Columbia University, New York.

**Sarna Chitrakar**, **Dukhushyam Chitrakar** and **Moyna Chitrakar** are patuas from Midnapore, West Bengal.

**Roberto D'Andrea** is a former Melbourne tram conductor who continues organising conductors today through his troupe 'The Connies' which theatrically distribute collectable tickets that yarn on themes of the environment and social history.

**Soumitra Das** is a journalist with the Kolkata newspaper *The Telegraph* who writes on the arts and issues of daily life and urban heritage. He is the author of a forthcoming book on Kolkata's streetscapes (Eminence 2005).

**Mick Douglas** is an artist and senior lecturer in the School of Architecture + Design at RMIT in Melbourne.

**Neal Haslem** is a visual communication designer based in Melbourne.

**Amanda King** specialises in making art for festivals and celebrations.

**Prabir Kumar Goswami** is a Kolkata tram and bus conductor and an assistant secretary of the Calcutta Tramways Workers & Employees Union.

**James Legge** is a director of Melbourne-based architectural practice Six Degrees.

**Andy Miller** is an arts administrator and artist in Melbourne.

**Mark Misic** is an artist and teacher who currently lives in Maningrida Community in the Northern Territory of Australia.

**Sanjay Mitra** is a social activist, development worker and photographer based in Kolkata.

**Catherine Murphy** is a public art and planning consultant who has curated and managed numerous public art projects including writing the recent public art strategy for the City of Melbourne.

**Jogi Panghaal** is a designer and director of Doors East. He has worked with the crafts sector in India for twenty-five years, and with women's groups evolving new media forms.

**Fazal Rizvi** is a Professor in Educational Policy Studies at the University of Illinois Urban-Champaign. Between 1999 and 2001 he was Pro Vice-Chancellor (International) at RMIT.

**Mahadeb Shi** is a filmmaker and social activist in Kolkata.

**Bruce C. Wearne** left lecturing in sociology at Monash University in 1998 to continue his vocation in social theory outside the academic context. He lives in Point Lonsdale and rides on Melbourne's trams every weekend.

**Lisa Young** is a visual artist based in Melbourne.

a

## ackowledgements


This book project has been assisted by:

Australian Government

Australia Council for the Arts

the Australian Government through the Australia Council, its arts funding and advisory body.

AIC AUSTRALIA-INDIA COUNCIL

city of Melbourne

RMIT UNIVERSITY School of Architecture + Design

***tramjatra 2001***

was kindly supported by Australia Council for the Arts, Victorian Minster for Transport, Arts Victoria, City of Melbourne, Australia India Council, RMIT School of Architecture + Design, West Bengal Minister for Transport & Sport, Calcutta Tramways Company and Accord Advertising.

**Artistic co-ordination and project management:** Mick Douglas

**Technical co-ordination:** Roberto D'Andrea

**Critical passengers:** Suzie Attiwill and Jogi Panghaal

**Participating artists:** Jayashree Chakravarty, Sarna Chitrakar, Dukhushyam Chitrakar, Moyna Chitrakar, Mick Douglas, Amanda King, James Legge, Andy Miller, Mark Misic, Hiran Mitra, Sanjay Mitra, Mahadeb Shi, Lisa Young

**Conducting:** Roberto D'Andrea, Prabir Kumar Goswami, Andy Miller and tram conductors of Kolkata and Melbourne

**RMIT School of Architecture + Design students participating:** Geoff Binder, Julian Canterbury, Yuen Ping Tai and Annette Warner in both Kolkata and Melbourne, and Lisa de Jong, Rory Fitzwilliams Hyde, Chris Moore and Sophie Zelder in Melbourne, along with Associate Professors Andrea Mina and Sand Helsel
**Melbourne forum and event participants:** Gaby Bila-Gunther, Keith Butler, Malcolm Just, Stuart Koop, Nikos Papastergiadis, Fazal Rizvi, Neil Thomas
**Kolkata forum and event participants:** Arunendu Banerjee, Manish Chakraborti, Greenwaves School of Art and Craft, Professor S.K. Rakshit and architecture students at Jadavpur University, S.V. Raman, V. Ramaswamy, Shyamal Sengupta
**Kolkata production management:** Pallavi Biswas
**Melbourne production management:** Philip Wadds
**Print design:** Neal Haslem in Melbourne and Lisa Young and Ranajay Gupta in Kolkata
**Tram track technical advisor:** Mike McGufficke
**Patua advisor and translator:** S.R. Rajen

#

Neal Haslem has worked with good humour, great generosity and sensitive aptitude to evolve a designed form and structure for this book with Mick Douglas. Suzie Attiwill gave astute advice on the book's development and Lizzy Newman always provided encouraging comments. Brenda Marshall and Parul Nayyar undertook editing and proofing. Thanks to Arpita and Parul at Yoda Press and Michael and Sarah at RMIT Press for making it a book. And many thanks to all the contributors, and those who have granted their permission for material to be reproduced in the book.

The journey that has preceded this book has involved the contributions of many people. It would not have gained momentum without the timely support of the Minister for Transport the Hon. Peter Bachelor, the Minister for Transport and Sport Shri Subhas Chakraborty and Calcutta Tramways Company staff Somesh K. Bhattacharya, Tarun K. Bhattacharya, Dilip Chakrabarty, M.K. Das, Sudhir De, Shri Rajdeo Goala, K.K. Gwin, S.K. Mitra and S.M. Pal. Thanks to Manosh Ghosh and John Thomas of *The Statesman* newspaper and Edmond Roy of ABC for being willing to join in the story-making of the project at the right moment. A special thanks for the warm friendship offered by all at CTC, especially Ujjal Bannerjee, Rama Pada Chatterjee, Ujjal Dhar, all those who helped paint trams, the tramways unions, the drivers and conductors of the CTC and the trammies of Balgatchia, Baghbazar, Esplanade, Gariahat, Kalighat, Kidderpore, Nonapuker workshops, Park Circus, Rajabazar, Shambazar, Tollygunge, the track and overhead electrical departments and the CTC head office staff and drawing department. 'Tram zindabad' indeed!

For their collaboration, advice and creative work in Kolkata, thanks to Phalguni Mukherjee and Sudeep Ganguly at Accord Advertising, Arunendu Banerjee, Alfred Edward Blazey, Manish Chakraborti, Goutam Dey, Pulak Ghosh and Tandra Chandra at Greenwaves, Pobitar Gron Mona, Professor S.K. Rakshit and architecture students at Jadavpur University, Rupesh (Pintu) Modi, S.V. Raman, V. Ramaswamy, Bitan Roy and Softline Advertising, Sunando Sarkar, Ronojoy Sen, Shyamal Sengupta and the staff of the Touring Guesthouse.

The sharing of ideas, meals and warm friendship with Mahadeb Shi and Aparna Das, Debasish and Nibedita Bhattacharyya and family, Jayanta and Sujata Basu, Pallavi Biswas, Jayashree

Chakravarty, Soumitra Das, Sanjay Mitra, S.R. Rajen, Ranajay Gupta, Jalladhar Mullick and the Naya community of patuas has been a delight.

In Melbourne the project has been kindly supported by MLA Robyn Cooper, Lou Di Gregorio and the Tram Division, Rail, Tram and Bus Union (Vic), Vic Foudoulis, Paul Mathews, Massoud Majidi and Tony Sabatino. Thanks to the Melbourne tramways world for your support, particularly to Bernard Commandeur, Norm Cross, Hugh Waldron, the Darjeeling Himalayan Railway Society, Preston Workshops staff, the trammies of the old South Melbourne and the Malvern depot and the drivers, former conductors and current trammies of the Melbourne tram depots. Special thanks for technical support from Ray Marsh, Barry Neilson, Ray Roberts, John Stewart, Richard Youl, and video support from Mike Costello.

For your support, thanks to the Abbotsford Anglers Cricket Club, Alison Carroll, Jane Crawley, Alison Fraser, Bernice Gerard and the CCD crew at OzCo, Dr Martand Joshi, Bimal Maity, David William Martin, Paul Mees, Candy Mitchell, Nicola Morelli, Mike McGufficke, Dan Mitchell, Kevin Murray, Scott O'Hara, Patrick O'Neal, Public Transport Users Association, Mantej Singh, Raj at the Indian Voice, Nicole Ryan, Julian Silverman, Judy Spokes, Neil Thomas, Traveland Clayton; and Peter Downton, Leon van Schaik, Sand Helsel, Andrea Mina, Bill Cartwright, Graeme Turnbull and Francis McGinley at RMIT. Friends, trammies and collaborators who are unintentionally omitted credit here are asked to forgive any oversight.

The experience of journeying is well known for producing special bonds of friendship. What is presented here owes particular credit to the friendships between Mick Douglas, Roberto D'Andrea, Mahadeb Shi, Debasish Bhattacharyya, Jayanta Basu, Suzie Attiwill, Jogi Panghaal and Neal Haslem.

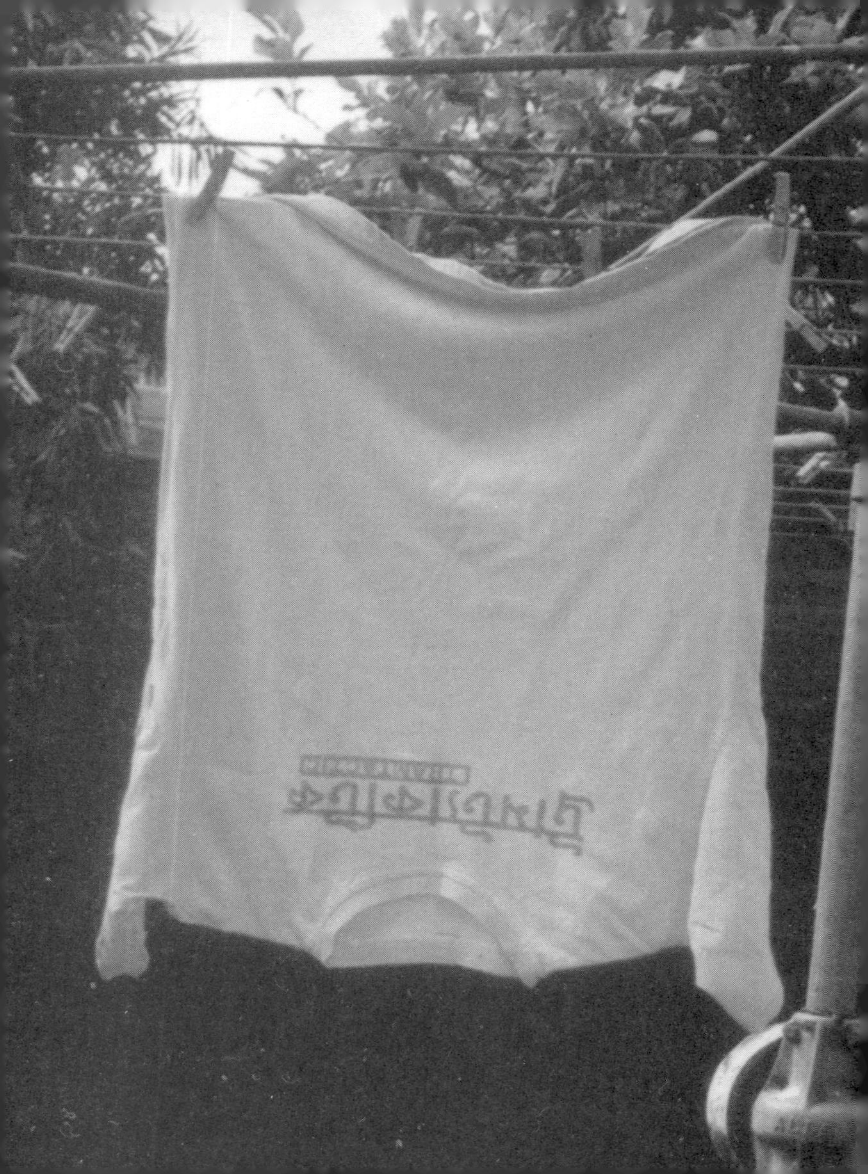

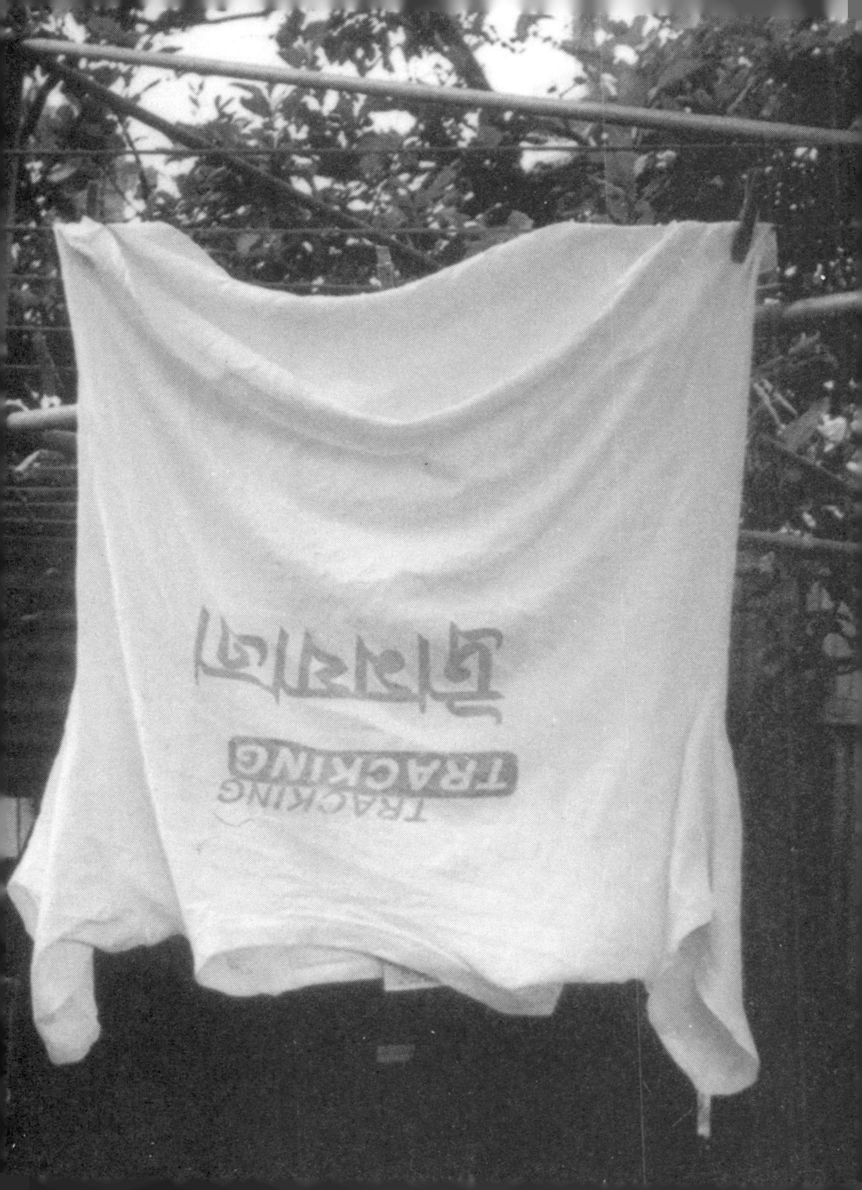

ট্রামট্যাকটিক

# TRAMTACTIC

**TRAMTACTIC makes art projects in public space to transport people.**

## TRAMTACTICS DEPART FROM THE POETIC POTENTIAL OF TRAMWAYS

TRAMTACTIC art projects draw from the practical characteristics of tramways to create poetic encounters with public transport that resonate with collective memory and imagination.

## TRAMTACTICS MOBILISE THE ART OF PUBLIC LIFE

Tramtactics celebrate the uniquely human attributes in ways of doing things in everyday public life. The art of addressing and engaging the lives of urban people is mobilised by the street-wise agility of tramtactics.

## TRAMTACTICS MANOEUVRE BACK AND FORTH TOWARD SUSTAINABILITY

Tramtactics follow the uniquely non-linear operating logic of tramways, moving back and forth, day in and day out, to explore how enriched encounters with tram travel can foster increased public transport patronage. Now undergoing an international revival a century after invention, tramways and light rail transport systems are becoming better understood for their practical and poetic contribution to more sustainable urban transport choices.

## TRAMTACTICS NEGOTIATE STREET SITUATIONS WITH TACT

Tramtactics demonstrate how the complexities of urban living may be negotiated with care and tact, responding to tricky circumstances in flexible ways. Tramtactics are constructed through collaborative working relationships of mutual advantage, creating a collective of people moved by a city's tramways in different ways.

**TRAMTACTICS MOBILISE EFFECTS TO GET PEOPLE MOVING**
Tramtactics build on people's shared experience of being transported by trams in ways that enable us to momentarily repose and feel emotionally moved in the circle of life. Tramtactics explore the relationship between the practical movement afforded by tramways and the contemporary social, political, economic and creative forces of movement brought to tramways.

**TRAMTACTICS ARE TACTILE**
Tramtactics celebrate the irreducible capacity of people to feel and make themselves felt, to move, and be moved. Tramtactics brush up against the textures of urban life to provoke us into encountering others and recognising that things could be otherwise.

**TRAMTACTICS NETWORK**
Tramtactics operate simultaneously at local and global levels, maximising the echo effect that a tactic here can have elsewhere. In the context of increased global forces, tramtactics lay the tracks for a different network of globalisation from below.

**TRAMTACTICS NEGOTIATE TRAMWAYS CONDUCT**
Tramtactics explore the conduct of users and organisers of tramways systems. Tramtactics contribute toward debates about the desirable attributes and competencies that will determine the sought after tram and light rail services of the future.

**TRAMTACTICS ARE FANTASTIC**
Tramtactics stimulate the urban imagination by heightening awareness of the fantastic dimensions of tramways life. Tramtactics come and go, appearing and disappearing so as to challenge popular certainty and point toward the extraordinary qualities of ordinary passages in life.

**www.tramtactic.net**

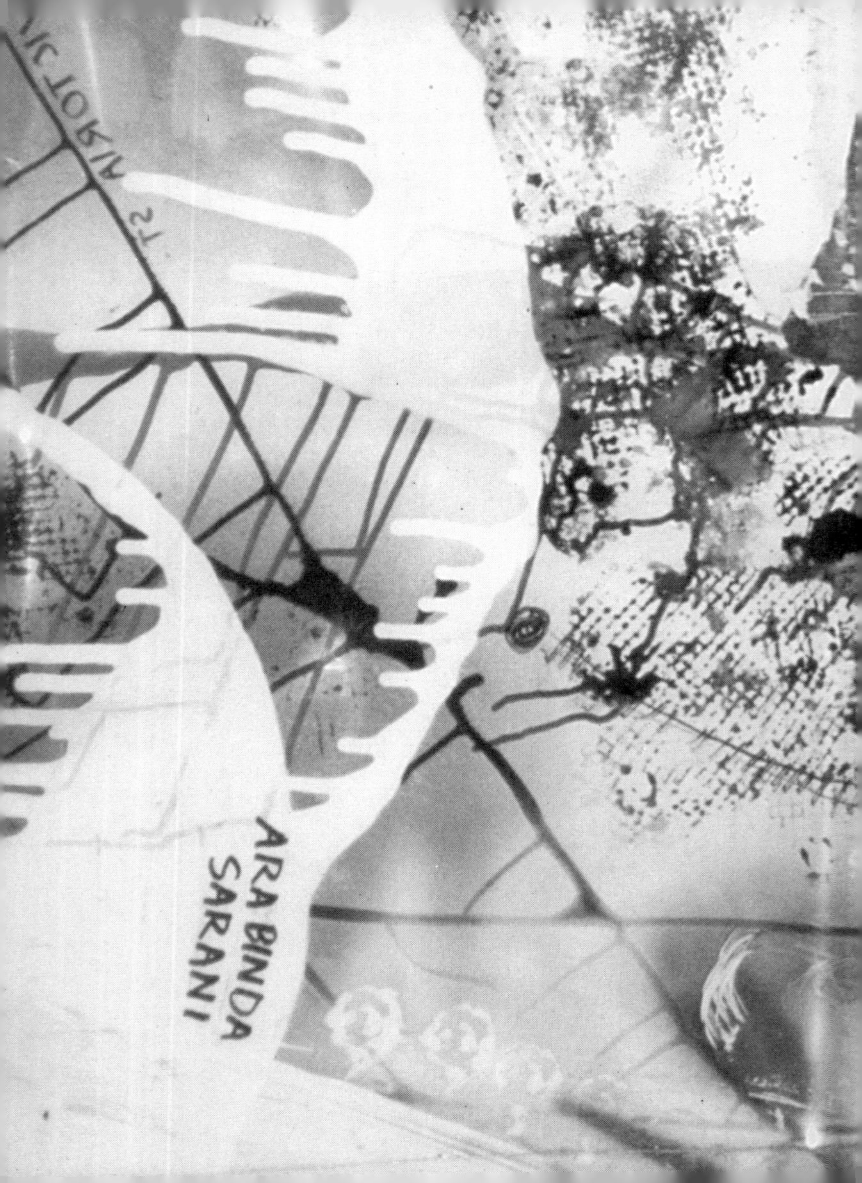
ARA BINDA
SARANI